TENDERFOOT

"All I'm out for is a good time -
all the rest is propaganda."

TENDERFOOT

"All I'm out for is a good time -
all the rest is propaganda."

Howard Jacks

FIRST EDITION
Book design by Howard Jacks

978-1-80541-377-6 (paperback)
978-1-80541-378-3 (ebook)
978-1-80541-379-0 (hardcover)

www.facebook.com/VinyljacksDJ

Dedicated to Diana Barber,
Morris Thorpe, and Billie The Cat!

CONTENTS

1

Tenderfoot

1950 to 1961

I saw my first film in 1950 aged four. It was *Samson and Delilah* at the Mechanics Cinema on Mansfield Road, Nottingham. I think that Dad must have been the one to choose which film we saw at that time, because there was often a strong element of raunch in them, including *Quo Vadis* in 1951 from MGM, and the first Cinemascope film, *The Robe*, in 1953 by 20th Century Fox, who created that wide screen technology and owned the rights. I was happy to be in the cinema for the two or three hours of entertainment, sitting on the tipped-up seat so I could see over the person in front of me. When I started at the Infants school, on Calverton Road in Arnold, I was already a member of the ABC Minors Saturday Film Club at the Metropole Cinema in Sherwood, a suburb of Nottingham.

The ABC Minors Anthem

♪♪ We are the boys and girls well known as ♪♪
The Minors of the ABC
And every Saturday we line up
To see the films we like and shout aloud with glee
We like to laugh and have our sing song
Such a happy crowd are wee – ee
We're all pals together
♪♪ We are The Minors of the ABC ♪♪

The ABC Minors Club was held from 9am until 12 noon every Saturday. As we went in, the manager and staff gave us cigarette cards with pictures of whatever serial we were about to watch, followed by cartoons and adventure films from the Children's Film Foundation. For the first year, like many others, my mum would accompany me there, but by age six I went on my own by bus. If the weather was good I could walk home and spend the bus fare on sweets, chewing wood (which was horrible), black jacks, and midget gems, Horlicks Tablets, sherbet dabs, and of course flying saucers that exploded in your mouth. Sometimes I would go back to the cinema that evening with my parents, where the manager greeted us, this time in a dinner suit and bow tie. The three of us usually visited the cinema during the week. There were two major cinema chains during the 40s, 50s and 60s: the English owned Rank Organisation and ABC (American Broadcasting Corporation) owned by Warner Brothers. Dad worked at the Raleigh Cycle Factory and his shift from 7.30am until 3.30pm meant we could go to the cinema at about 5pm, watch the last half of the main film, then the support all the way through and then leave after the first half of the main film so that all of us could get a good night's sleep. The well-used expression "This is where we came in!" came from this. Dad had to be up at 6.00am! At weekends my parents took themselves off to the Robin Hood and Little John pub

Howard with Mum 1950

2

or the Working Men's Club and The Cherry Club, both five minutes' walk away.

When not in the cinema, I had plans to be a missionary. At the Cross Street Baptist Sunday School, I had been given *David Livingstone. A Biography for Children* as a prize for good attendance and I thought that such a life would be full of adventure. There were many chapels in Arnold, of all denominations. They put on several events each year, including the Whit Sunday Walkabout, with brass bands and decorated carts and drays parading through the streets, culminating in a service on the Recreation Ground, then the whole thing would be reversed as we paraded back, dropping people off at their chapel or church. Our Cross Street Baptist Church provided a feast at the end, where we had sandwiches of potted meat and salmon paste, and jelly, plus stewed tea from an urn. Then there was The Anniversary each February, celebrating the Cross Street Baptist Church being built in 1909. A tall platform was set up on the main floor near the organ for songs and recital, held three times during the course of the day. My first attempt as a performer was there, in 1952, aged six. When I arrived at the chapel gate, ready to deliver a poem called *A Special Gift*, Old Wilf was there. In the films, he would be played by Moore Marriot as Harbottle in *Oh Mr Porter*. He directed me up the entrance steps where, inside, a lady I didn't know ushered me upstairs. This confused me because the platform was on the ground floor next to the pulpit opposite those stairs, but I dutifully went up eager to please. At the top of the stairs, I found myself in the congregation, and was directed by another stranger to the very back row. Eventually the preacher announced my recital, "And now we have Howard Wheatley who will recite to us that delightful poem called *The Special Gift*. Here's Howard!"

I was hemmed in by the congregation. It would have brought the house down had I shouted out, "I'm up here, sir!"

Being so far from the staging area, I could see no way to get through and retreated into myself, in the hope that no one would notice me.

"Oh well, Howard doesn't appear to be here today. Let us move on to our hymn, *Jesus Wants Me For A Sunbeam*."

The service seemed to go on for hours after that. As soon as it finished, I sneaked out as quickly as possible before any of the congregation that I knew could see me, and cried like a baby all the way home. I made it for the next two performances though! It was a long day, but I soon forgot about it, playing cowboys and Indians next day with friends in the overgrown orchards belonging to the Arnold House doctor's practice at the back. From the 30s to the 50s 2,000 B westerns were usually made by the Republic studios. Lots of action and shoot outs, and in the chase sequences the horses seemed to be galloping at 60 miles an hour. There were very few native Americans in the storylines. The only time they came in was as a crowd of whooping extras on horses and that was expensive. Nor were there many parts for women. Kissing and cuddling slowed down the action. The character I liked the most was Hopalong Cassidy, who always dressed in black and had a white horse called Topper. I couldn't stand those singing cowboys like Gene Autrey or Roy Rogers with their fancy, frilly duds. Thank goodness for *Saturday Morning*

ABC Minors Cinema, for along with the serials it was the inspiration for many of our games out and about in the countryside. I had a little canvas tent, in which I would camp out on a summer's night, feeding off the large, tough pears from the orchard. Those pears were the only ones I have ever enjoyed. In early summer, the trees were a mass of white blossom.

In September 1950 I started at Infant school, in a high ceilinged, cold Victorian building five minutes' walk up the road, very convenient. En-route there was a bakers where I would often pick up a hot mini-Hovis loaf. In spring we would rehearse our May Day performance in Arnold Park, dancing round the maypole quite easily in the large classrooms separated by high sturdy partitions. Gym lessons were conducted in the playground by a busty young woman who always smelt of BO. In 1951, Mum and Dad took me to see a brilliant film version of *Tom Brown's Schooldays* which starred a 12-year-old John Howard Davies. A really good, gritty film which exposed the cruel regime at Rugby public school. A few years later, at age 12, I saw it again. This second viewing had more of an impact on me, partly because I felt like I looked similar to John Howard Davies, and partly because Redhill Secondary Modern had a similarly strict regime, although there were no mortar boards or gowns, and certainly no learning attached. Later on in 1951 my parents took me to see *Scrooge* starring Alistair Sim. This just has to be the best of the many versions of *A Christmas Carol.* I was totally hooked on this fascinating classic and went to see it again on my own. Luckily, we had grandma's old Edwardian copy of the book with a faded colour cover of Ebenezer sitting in front of the fire. For the next five Decembers I used to read it as a lead in up to Christmas just to get into 'the spirit' of things. After that we had television which put paid to my reading novels. I was bowled over when I opened a large box for my sixth birthday present. It was a Hopalong Cassidy Stetson with a leather belt and 12 silver bullets which fitted neatly into the two silver metal six guns which shot caps as well. It was so real, and I was proud to be Hopalong in our games, as let's face it I had the togs!

On 15th February 1952, we took time out from lessons for an hour or so to listen to the funeral procession of King George the Sixth. It was a very rare event to listen to the radio at school. Infant school finished in 1953, memorable only for being given the New Testament, a mug with a picture of the Queen on it and a commemorative tin full of little squares of Cadbury's Dairy Milk chocolates to celebrate the Coronation on 2nd June. Much more interesting were the adult westerns I saw at the cinema with my parents, which were usually in technicolour. However, *High Noon* with Gary Cooper was in black and white, and I found it fascinating, so different to the other western films we had watched. By the final, bitter scene, when Gary Cooper as Marshall Will Kane throws his badge onto the floor in disgust at the townspeople, leaving him to face a criminal gang alone, I was enthralled by the idea of a hero that no one will help. John Wayne considers this an anti-American act. I think my dad saw himself in the film too, as he bought the theme tune *Do Not Forsake Me Oh My Darling* by Tex Ritter on a 78 rpm record and played it to my mum when they got home from the pub.

1953 was also the age of 3-D, a new idea that came out of the US to get people back into the cinema, where TV was starting to be a serious threat. We knew very few people who had a TV, only Clarice Nix our landlady who, occasionally invited us kids around to watch *Children's Hour.* (In the films she would be played by Hermione Baddeley.) Clarice lived across the road in The Manor, a large, gloomy five bedroomed house tucked away at the top of a drive surrounded by trees. We used to run all the way down the drive 'cos it was so scary. Once a week I would go over to purchase half a dozen freshly laid eggs. Her family of builders owned many other blocks of terraced houses in streets throughout Arnold. Her brother Horace lived in a small house further down the street. A bachelor in his sixties, he could frequently be seen, whenever he forgot to close the curtains, enjoying himself dancing tipsily around the living room dressed up in women's clothes.

Warner Brothers had five directors who had lost an eye: Raoul Walsh who directed *White Heat*, Fritz Lang, *Cloak And Dagger,* John Ford of *The Searchers,* Tex Avery who directed *Looney Toons* and Andre de Toth who ironically directed the classic 3D *House Of Wax.* My parents must have sneaked me into the latter, it being X-rated, although I don't remember it being all that gruesome. 3-D films were very expensive to produce, on top of which we threw away the 3-D glasses they gave us for every film, which must have been expensive for the industry. The films didn't survive for long: around eighteen months, although I believe that they lasted a little longer in the US.

In that year of 1953, aged seven, I started at the British Junior School in an old Victorian building along Arnold

Front Street, a 15-minute walk from home. It had an open fire in every classroom during winter when the caretaker would come into class to give us more coal. Unlike the Infant school, which was mixed, this was an all-boys school, although the teachers were both women and men. It was the first time I had experienced male teachers. The headmaster was Mr Rose, who had taught my dad 26 years before. As new boys, we each had an interview with Mr Rose in the first week.

I asked him, "Do you remember my dad, George Wheatley, Mr Rose?"

He raised his eyebrows, far above me. "Yes, I do recall him, good at maths, and a keen footballer before the war, wasn't he? I remember him being chosen for the Nottingham Forest B Team."

I was proud that my dad was remembered in this way.

You had to watch your belongings at the Junior school, especially if they were good quality. That December, I was due to meet my parents for a treat in town – a visit with Santa then a film at the Odeon Cinema. The school cloakroom was dark, and it was only when I was on the bus that I realised my brand-new wool overcoat had been switched for a much shabbier one, which I then had to wear to greet them. Mum spotted it straight away. I never met Santa that year. I was instructed to enquire at school where my new coat might have been. I had to go to the front of the school and ask if anyone had, perhaps, taken my coat accidentally, holding up the shabby replacement. But all eyes were turned away and it never reappeared. Mum was normally exceedingly kind to me but the loss of good money on a new coat was not appreciated. She helped me out with school dinners however, which I hated. I can still taste those mashed potatoes now; served from metal containers, they were horrible slimy things which made me feel ill. I reported this to Mum who gave me a key so I could walk home at lunchtime. Mum did a lot of cake baking with cut out biscuits in the form of rabbits, dogs and cats, and made me special Mum's coffee: this was milk flavoured with Camp Coffee liquid that was mostly chicory. Although she was out working at Mr Baileys, the greengrocers, every day a sandwich would be left on the table, carefully made with thick ham, dripping or egg and tomato. In the face of this care and attention, I described myself as a latchkey kid who had no mother at home during the day. Nonetheless, she continued 'packing my snap' all the way through to my early 20s.

At the end of the first year of Junior school I had another chance at performance. We were all given a part in a play celebrating the Commonwealth's contribution to The Coronation, coming on one by one as famous characters to say a few words. I came on at the end as Sir Edmund Hilary, wearing an old gas mask left over from World War II, to indicate that I was at high altitude. Wearing the gas mask meant I had no words to say, but I was elated to find that I was the final performer on stage and took all the cheers and clapping as my own.

The following year meant being in 'Pop' Marshall's class. We learned about using pen and ink which we filled from an inkwell (no, we didn't use quills!). I liked Mr Marshall a lot. In the films he would be played by Robert Donat in *Goodbye Mr Chips*. Mr Marshall gave us most of the lessons, except for football and gym once a week with a sports teacher. In

English and history, he would often mention a play or film he had seen. I felt sorry for him because no-one else seemed to be that interested. Between lessons, he read us stories and played the piano, mainly classical pieces, although one morning before the lesson he gave us *Stranger in Paradise* from the film *Kismet,* directed by Vincente Minnelli, father of Liza. I had told him I had seen this at the cinema the night before. He seemed quite impressed. Then he was off sick, for four months, and was replaced by a formidable Scottish woman called Mrs Lucas. (In the films, she would be played by Hilary Mason from *Don't Look Now.*) She too would read stories at the end of the day. They were gripping adventure tales, such as the story of tiny people who lived beneath the floorboards and were chased by cats. She used a stick to walk with. As I recall, it was never used to thwack any of us, so it must have been the force of her personality that kept us under control.

I can't remember an assembly service at Infant school, but for the last lesson on Friday afternoons the whole school would gather to sing folk songs and sea shanties, with Miss Dove on the piano.

♫ I love to go a wandering along the mountain track, ♫
And as I go I love to sing,
My knapsack on my back
♫ Val-de-ri – Val-de-ra ♫

We thought Miss Dove was having an affair with Mr Marshall. They worked very well together, although she was a well set up lady of about 40 while he was a slim, austere-looking man of at least 50 years. My Dad was a big fan of pneumatic blonde ladies, especially Jayne Mansfield in her tight-fitting, low-cut dresses, so we saw her in *The Seven Year Itch* and Marilyn Monroe in *Gentlemen Prefer Blondes,* plus *The River of No Return,* starring Robert Mitcham, and Tommy Rettig, who two years later would be my role model in the TV series *Lassie.* One film we watched which was very different from the swords and sandals, swashbucklers and westerns was *Moulin Rouge,* directed by John Huston and starring Jose Ferrar. It was an amazing film and quite alternatively arty too! This was an English film made by Romulus and it gained six Oscars and ten nominations. Seeing the trailer the week before, perhaps Dad thought there was more raunch in it than there actually was! However, he did get the Can-Can dancers and busty blonde Zsa *Zsa* Gabor wisecracking to the camera, so that was alright. Ten years later I read books about Lautrec. He had a congenital illness that weakened his bones. He loved horse riding and had two serious falls which affected his height. He stayed at 5ft tall with the upper body of a man and the legs of a child. He was more outgoing and gregarious than in the film, but I suppose that the insular and lonely character portrayed in the film made it more dramatic. That year, 1955, we also saw the *Dam Busters,* after which my parents gave me a 78 rpm record of the theme tune *The Dam Busters March,* written by Eric Coates from Hucknall near Nottingham. The film was made by the British arm of Warner Brothers – the start of a beautiful friendship, in my mind at least and with Jack L Warner. What a character he was! He sent this memo to the set of *The Big Sleep* 1946: "Word has got to me that you are all having fun on the set. This has got to stop!"

Then, when a radio reporter asked which films had been the best for the studio he simply went "Woof woof!" He meant the *Rin Tin Tin* films!

Jack L Warner also managed to attract equally zany, eccentric people onto his payroll. In *Charge of the Light Brigade*, David Niven and Errol Flynn were in hysterics over Michael Curtiz' instruction to "Bring on the empty horses."

He shouted back at them, "You lousy bums and your English language. You people think I know nothing. I tell you now I know f**k all!"

More chuckles from Flynn and Niven.

In 1956, we all saw the box office smash hit *Rock Around The Clock*. It was our first exposure to rock and roll and we wanted more. My dad went out and bought the 78 rpm record and he and I had a wiggle round the living room. Oh, if only we'd looked after this record. It's worth a small fortune today, as I believe it was the first rock and roll musical film. It is also one of three films where the same track is used in the opening credits, *The Blackboard Jungle*, 1955, *Rock Around The Clock*, 1956, and *American Graffiti*, 1973. Tom and I went to see Bill Hayley and the Comets in person singing *Rock Around The Clock* at the Odeon Cinema, the first time I ever saw audiences dancing in the aisles. Tom was two years older than me, and he was a great pal to have, re-enacting the action scenes from westerns and swashbucklers with me in the woods and fields that surrounded us. He also introduced me to train spotting and we often went to Nottingham Victoria Station to watch trains from all over coming through, or Grantham, where the express trains came hurtling past. Very noisy and dramatic it was. It took me back to the time my mum took me to Daybrook Square aged four, on a hot summer's day in 1950, where we looked up as a passenger train whizzed by on the bridge, followed by a long freight train, great heavy waggons thundering along. As it appeared, my mum shook my hand and said, "Wave now, wave now!" As the end of the train came into view, my Uncle Len could be seen standing on the platform of the brake van at the back, waving and smiling at me, in a magical, *Railway Children* type moment. He was a British Railways guard and had married my mum's sister Jennie.

Our family's big annual holiday was the fortnight when the Raleigh factory shut down. Most Nottingham families went to Skegness on the coast of Lincolnshire for their annual holidays. My dad was the only one in the family who worked there; his brother was a cobbler and later became a big man in the Boots trade union, his sisters worked in hosiery in Nottingham factories. My mum worked in the Meridian Hosiery factory, but she quickly moved into shop work as being more respectable. There was a lot of mining work in the area, which was hard and dangerous but well paid. Each house had running water to scrub up in; none of that metal tub in front of the fire you see in the films.

Mum, Auntie Tilly and Uncle Arthur,
1950 on Deal Promenade

For other holidays, the three of us usually took the train to Deal on the East coast of Kent, to stay with Auntie Tilly, my mum's sister who had married Arthur Barratt, a Derbyshire miner from Clay Cross who had moved to the Kent coalfields. (In the films they would be played by Joyce Grenfell and Jeremy Kemp.) The journey there was half the fun. We would get the Great Central train from Nottingham Victoria to Marylebone London, then take the Underground to London Victoria for another train, this time to the coast. On each train we would unpack the sandwiches, flasks, and fruit squash that Mum had made, cheaper than the refreshment rooms at each station and our treat for making it that far. The luggage went on the train the day before and would be waiting for us when we arrived at Uncle Arthur's. From Victoria we would go to Dover and then to Walmer, where it was just a 15-minute walk, with nothing but our little bags and sandwich wrappings to carry, until we arrived at Uncle Arthur's on the top of Mill Hill in Deal.

Arthur's brother Sam chose Calverton Pit near Arnold, while Arthur moved to work in the mines at Betteshanger Colliery. Many Northern families moved to Kent to find work, and for a bit of excitement. The holidays in Deal were perfect because we had the seaside to play in, but the atmosphere was a lot more relaxed than Skegness. It was in Deal that they took me to see *The Fabulous Dorseys* at the cinema in 1950. I was just four years old. A real-life pair of brothers, the story was about how they argued and split into two separate orchestras. It was a good film, and I was halfway there anyway, having been listening to Dad's Joe Loss, Benny Goodman and Glenn Miller records. Then there were day trips out by bus. Sitting upstairs on the long bench seat that ran the length of the bus, we could watch the coastal towns of Ramsgate, Margate and Sandwich go by.

We all enjoyed Margate for the Pleasureland fun fair, where we would play the machines in the amusement arcade, flicking balls around into sockets to win tickets for prizes, more likely money, or a free go. One paid out when the hands of the clock came together as it rolled around. We spent a lot of time on that one because it paid out better. Another had flashing lights on film stars and pop stars, one of which you would pick, then if the light stopped flashing on your chosen character, you won. We would put a penny in several machines side by side, getting, so we thought, more chance for it to pay out. On other occasions, we went to Dover and Folkstone, one a port and the other a lively harbour town. Of these towns, I liked Folkstone the best, because it had a sandy beach on one side of the harbour and a pebble beach on the other, much easier to play on than sand and without the itchy mess that would be uncomfortable in my knitted swimming shorts.

There was always a funfair at Folkstone, where I first went on the dodgems with a central reservation, much more civilised than the Goose Fair at Nottingham where it was everyone for himself in an open expanse of cars and great big clonking bumps from the side. On that last holiday at Folkstone in 1957, my school pal Alan Jones came along, and we found that we could whiz about without the bigger boys bumping us, as long as we were quick and dodged 'em. I also learned to roller skate there.

Sandwich was an unusual beach to visit in the fifties, because it was out of town, with no shops or houses around the beach area in those days. But for many years there was a reconstructed Viking Longship at nearby Pegwell Bay. It was at Sandwich, picnicking by the sea, that my dad tried to get me to learn to swim. His theory was that because the beach was sandy it should be a flat base under the water, without the dips a pebble seabed would have, so he could hold me up as we went along, and anyway in theory, I should float naturally in salt water. Off we went, with him holding me up, but every time he let me go, I sank quickly to the bottom and came up full of English Channel. He urged me on but after a few more attempts I said firmly I didn't want to do this anymore and waded back to the beach. Dad was grumpy about that for some time. However, holiday chums Alan and my cousin David could swim, so when they came along, he took pleasure in romping about in the waves with them. Aggressive teaching at school also put me off learning to swim, and it wasn't until I was 18 that I took lessons and nailed it.

In August 1955, the Raleigh factory had few orders coming in so my dad and many others were on short time. We had to miss out on a long stay in Deal, but Mum and Dad managed to get us a week in Great Yarmouth. I went to bed early as we had to get the 5.00am train from Victoria Station. When we walked across the footbridge and looked down, the platform was absolutely rammed with about 250 people. This was the annual holiday time for all the major factories in Nottingham: Boots, Raleigh, John Players and many others. We weren't used to this as most holidaymakers went to the East Coast or up North; very few went South, so we usually had a leisurely journey down to Kent. But it made a change and was great fun rattling through the

English countryside as dawn came up. For me this was the best part of the holiday, it was all downhill from then on. We were in a caravan, and it was like an oven in that tin can from late morning to early evening. The holiday seemed to comprise of being on the beach and walking up and down the lengthy promenade. There were none of the bus trips that we usually had, but I did enjoy the trip around the area in a biplane. I wasn't allowed to go into the pub with the adults, so it was standing outside with a bag of crisps and a bottle of flat lemonade for three hours. I'd rather have stayed in the caravan and read a book. Perhaps Mum and Dad felt guilty about leaving me on my own.

We had six members from either side of the family join us and I was the only one who was sunburnt. I could feel it searing through my T shirt. Why only me and no one else? I was cajoled into taking part in the beach games or being taught to swim by various members of the family, but without success. All I wanted to do was stay in the shade. I became really sore, and Mum did her best by applying liberal amounts of camomile lotion, but it was too late. Inevitably, this was followed by a lot of itching. I hardly slept all week in that caravan oven. We usually went to the cinema but not on this holiday. However, we did pay a visit to The Windmill Variety Theatre featuring many artistes including The Morton Fraser Harmonica Group, whose act seemed to consist of a very small man trying to join in with the rest of the troupe but being cold shouldered and excluded. I knew how he felt.

Among the films we saw during this period was *The Glenn Miller Story* with James Stewart, which all three of us loved and Dad bought his *String Of Pearls* on a 78 record. I just loved this gutsy big band number and played it endlessly at home. Then we saw the Warner Brothers' *Young At Heart* with Doris Day and Frank Sinatra. What a brilliant piece of casting this was, talk about opposites attract. The bar scene is a classic. *One For My Baby* and *Someone To Watch Over Me*, Frank is singing and playing the piano with his hat tilted back, fag in the corner of his mouth. Warners only occasionally dipped into the musical genre, and me too. But this one had some great songs, and even at ten years old I loved them. Frank played his character like Humphrey Bogart.

Mum and Dad kindly treated me again to the 78 single, as they also did with *Memories Of You* from the biopic of *The Benny Goodman Story* about the clarinet playing band leader. Ahh, now this was more workable, unlike Glenn Miller's trombone. "That's what I'll do," I decided, "I'll learn the clarinet." Mum and Dad treated me to a second-hand one after being pestered relentlessly by yours truly! I read the How To Play help guide booklet which gave some easy tunes to start with and guess what? There was *Drink To Me Only With Thine Eyes* which the whole school did on the Friday sing along! A few weeks went by until I mastered it and then asked Mr Marshall if I could accompany the sing along. He auditioned me and gave the go ahead to perform it the following Friday in front of the whole school. It went down well, and I did it again two weeks later with the whole school singing along. My first proper performance as a budding Benny Goodman. I got a real buzz from performing.

In 1956 I think Dad must have still been on short time, as we had a single week at Blackpool, which was packed with Northerners all having their 'Gala Fortnight' from their own factories. On the dreaded beach, mine was the only one out of eight donkeys that didn't have a saddle firmly attached, so I sat tilted sideways as the donkey trotted on, to hilarity and laughter among my companions. Evenings were spent at the Blackpool Tower Ballroom where the customers could dance between stage acts, which, to my great pleasure and surprise, included Jack Parnell with his orchestra. When he started a five-minute drum solo I was so excited that I ran around the back of the tables that clustered around the dance floor to get closer to the stage. Jack was the nephew of Val Parnell, theatrical impresario and part of the Grade empire that later became my employer when I was at ATV. However, at this point, I just wanted to be a drummer and pestered like a spoilt brat for a drum kit which, much to my delight, was presented to me six months later as a Christmas present. When we returned from Blackpool, my parents bought their first TV set at last. There was not one but two channels! If you only had the BBC, the roof aerial was either an H or an X. You could always tell the families that had ITV because their aerial had a horizontal zig zag attached. We watched the *Robin Hood* series starring Richard Green, which ran for four years and greatly improved my choreography of the fight scenes with Dick and Alan in the orchard at the back. ATV also put out a variety show every Saturday night with Jack Parnell and his Orchestra who was eventually the musical director at ATV. This was great for a budding drummer like me! They later did the orchestration and backing for the Muppets, so I will forever align Jack Parnell in my mind with Animal, *The Muppets* drummer. When my parents were out at the Cherry House Club, or the Working

Men's Club CIU Affiliated, I would set up my drum kit in the living room, so I could accompany Jack while he did his weekly drum solo. The Cherry House Club was only five minutes' walk from the back of our house and run by one Ben Cartwright. It was a large Edwardian house with square bay windows which stood on its own and had a manicured lawn at the side about half the size of a tennis court. For knowledgeable Baby Boomers we even had a Florrie Lindley on our street!

In 1957 we resumed our holidays at Uncle Arthur's in Deal. It had a pebble beach and on a clear day you could see France. For a few days during summer, you could also see the shipwrecks exposed on the Goodwin Sands. Over 2,000 ships floundered on The Goodwins over the past three centuries. Evenings were spent at the pub, either The Yew Tree, on the top of Mill Hill in Deal, or a half hour walk took us to The Five Bells at Ringwould village. Uncle Arthur never bothered going into The Miners Welfare just down the road.

"There's more coal dug in there than the colliery!" growled Arthur.

We had my best friend Alan Jones with us and when we visited the Folkestone Fun Fair, we could bump the hell out of each other on those dodgems with a central reservation. Alan was great to be on holiday with and with his help I managed to learn how to roller skate which pleasantly surprised my mum and dad. One day at Deal we were in a neighbours' big Buick car that pulled into a filling station when Uncle Arthur tapped me on the shoulder and pointed across the road.

"Howard, see that house over there. That's where Norman Wisdom used to live." Wow!

I later found out that Norman was born in London and was often beaten by his father and ended up in a children's home in Deal. He ran away when he was eleven but went back to Deal and by thirteen had a job as an errand boy in a grocer's shop. At some point he returned to the family home, but his father threw him out, so he walked to Cardiff and became a cabin boy in the merchant navy at fifteen. No wonder he had such a keen insight into characters at the sharp end of life! There'll be a little bit more about Mr Wisdom later.

Even though Auntie Tilly was now using a wheelchair, we managed very well on a narrow tarmac road through the fields. Pubs were chosen on a sing-along basis: if we knew they had a piano, and Dad could get his spoons out to play along, Uncle Arthur would accompany them with his harmonica. In most place, I had to stand outside the pub with the other kids, but in Deal I always seemed to be allowed in. I preferred being inside, where you had the luxury of being able to sit down and could hang out with the adults.

A few months after that holiday Uncle Arthur wrote to Mum saying that Auntie Tilly was unwell. As a young woman, she had fallen down the cast iron steps at the Nottingham Victoria train station and damaged her back, which is why for many years she stumbled around with a walking stick and eventually had to be in a wheelchair. Auntie Tilly passed away in the spring of 1958, a much loved and lovely lady. We went down for a week to attend the funeral, although after that we did not take holidays as a family with Arthur. During that week, whilst the family were out, I went out with the next-door neighbour's daughter Janet and fell in love immediately! She was quite a looker and at 14 nearly two years older than me. (In the films she would be played by Susan Oliver.) The two of us imitated the passionate beach scene in *From Here To Eternity* on Deal beach. I paid for my sins though, as when Janet looked in horror at my best raincoat we were laying on she saw it was smothered in tar. I spent the rest of the week hiding it from Mum, but she saw it on the last day which didn't go down very well. Another slippering from Dad when we arrived home. With hindsight I suspect Janet was a bit more experienced than me but was too shy to take things further.

I missed the 11 plus, because I developed a lump on the back of my knee and had to go into hospital to have it removed. Not that I would have passed it anyway. Mum and Dad were only allowed to visit every two days and I discovered I missed them hugely. I was in hospital for three weeks and then had to stay home for another two weeks to recover. I didn't want any further visits to hospital so I would push the lump back just before going in to see the doctor for a check-up. Eventually, despite this it re-emerged, and I had to go back into hospital in the autumn for another three weeks. My heart sank. Teatime on the ward was bread and butter on a tin plate – plastic wasn't quite so popular in those days – and the only drink on offer was hot milk. Oh, how I missed Mums' milky coffee! Our 'treat' was morning sweets doled out from a National Health Powdered Egg tin by matron. We called her The Dragon because she was so strict. Aged eleven and missing home, I was in no mood for her patronising tone and often missed out on the sweets because I was not pleased or grateful enough.

Returning to school, I was in Mr Wing's class for history, geography, English and mathematics. In the latter, he was fierce and easily irritated. On one occasion I got the slipper for getting equations wrong. At the front of the class, he asked me to explain my reasoning and after I stammered for a while, he went bright red and grabbed a slipper from his desk roaring "Right Wheatley, bend over!" At the front of the class, he slippered me on the bottom a few times and sent me back to my desk. I switched off and didn't bother with maths after that. He was alright in English though, almost Jekyll and Hyde, explaining words we didn't understand and reading us stories.

Looking for a book on the classroom shelves for the reading hour one afternoon, I thought I saw a book about the battle of Hastings, called *William The Conqueror*. On taking it down, I discovered it was about an 11-year-old boy who got up to all kinds of mischief. I had seen the excellent film *Just William's Luck* in 1952, directed by Val Guest, not realising the character was based on the books. I read ten *Just William* books from the autumn to the end of summer term, one after another. They were fascinating and I was totally hooked, another escape into a different world. By 1961 I had read all of them up to that year, but leaving school put an end to this very enjoyable pastime. Richmal Crompton who wrote the books had suffered from polio and breast cancer, but she maintained a remarkable work rate, writing 39 *Just William* books and 54 others.

When she passed away in 1969, she had sold over 12 million books in the UK alone and her books had been translated into nine languages. If you looked at the flyleaf you could see the year the books were published. It was interesting to note how her artist, Thomas Henry changed and adapted his style from 1919 to 1962. I looked around for more and saw that Thomas Henry also did a *Just William* cartoon strip in Women's Own magazine, which Mum bought every week. I cut these out and stuck them into a scrapbook, so that I could copy them myself. I tried for years to draw like Thomas Henry. Luckily for me *Just William* came out as a series on Children's ITV. I started to emulate William's lifestyle as best I could, encouraging my friends to become his gang The Outlaws, and going out for walks in the country 'looking for adventure'. One Saturday I had a perfect 'William Day' with my mate Chris Bowle, who was identical to Thomas Henry's drawings of William. Unlike my narrow features, Chris had the roundish face and snub nose, with an overhanging lock of hair. We went scrumping in a farmer's orchard, until we were chased off, then walked up to Bestwood Lodge, which was having an Open Day. Built in 1863, Bestwood Lodge was built as a royal hunting lodge set in acres of woods, used by the 49th Infantry Polar Bear Brigade as their headquarters. We had a great time there, wandering in and out of the rooms, telling the impressive-looking officers that our parents were just around the corner. There were other children there, but we were the only ones on the loose, helping ourselves to the free drinks and snacks. In the afternoon, fired up by our success, we went to Arnold St. Marys Church Garden

Tea Party, just up the road from my house. Adjacent to St Marys was the deserted and rundown Old Parsonage, where we played hide and seek, and Tommies versus Nazis. It was our captured chateau, until we were rumbled and had to go back to the tea party, where we looked in at the stalls and exhibits, and bought jelly, cakes, and orange squash for a penny each. It was a busy day and my parents thought I must be ill, not wanting any tea! I slept like a log that night! Perfection.

At the recreation ground, I would sometimes see a dog called Nip, who lived up the road from school. He was a short haired dog like a large fox terrier. He became my Jumble, like William's dog. I would walk past his house and shout his name. Out he would come, jump over the fence and off we would go into the countryside for a few hours. I never asked the couple that lived there if I could borrow their dog and they never said a thing to me. Like Jumble, Nip was a very well-behaved dog. He followed me through the fields to the brick works a mile or so away without a lead. The brick works were in a circular dip about the size of a football stadium, with a clay canyon in one corner, a pond in another, undergrowth and the actual works in the fourth corner. At weekends it was deserted, and the gate was always open. If Nip didn't come out, I would call three friends to make up Just William's gang. If we were going on to the wooded hills around Bestwood Lodge I would leave Nip at home, because it was over a main road. At the other end of the woods, a railway spur ran into the woods from Bestwood Colliery, where tubs on cables ran overhead. These were used to shift the slag out of the mine and onto the nearby heaps. Some dare devils used to hang onto the tubs and go from one summit to the other, a distance of about 70 yards. Very risky because sometimes they would stop the machinery over a drop of three storeys.

For my tenth birthday, on a hot sunny day in May 1957, Mum and Dad organised a picnic for me and some pals, after which we all went to see *The Girl Can't Help It* at the ABC Elite cinema on Parliament Street. Hailed the "most potent film ever on rock and roll," it featured many acts playing live in the film: Little Richard, Julie London, Gene Vincent, Eddie Cochran, Fats Domino, The Platters and Jayne Mansfield. On TV, I became hooked on the George Reeves *Superman* series, which was on ITV for two years up to 1958. He was so believable and even now he would be my first choice as an actor to play him. Looking back, I wish they had spent a bit more on the production values and made the storylines heavier. The episodes really caught my imagination and I bought many of the *Superman* and *Superboy* comics, at that time in black and white. There had been a pilot cinema film in 1949 called *Superman And The Mole Men,* which I didn't see until the 90s. It stood up well, showing Reeves as Superman, challenging prejudice and helping the Mole Men escape back to their underground world. With the success of the *Robin Hood* series on ITV, Sir Lew branched out into producing more half-hour historical dramas based on films from Hollywood. He released *The Buccaneers* ('Robin Hood At Sea!') using old stock footage of galleons from previous films. This was helped along by a gutsy performance from Robert Shaw as Captain Dan Tempest. Then Sir Lew brought out *The Adventures of Sir Lancelot* starring William Russell.

Meanwhile, from the US we had *Rin Tin*, about the adventures of a small boy, adopted by the commander of the cavalry post, with his dog Rin Tin. Then there was *Fury*, a boy and his horse, where the boy had also been adopted, by Jim, and Pete the ranch hand, and in which the horse would look sideways away from the camera when galloping across the titles. At the same time, you could watch *Champion The Wonder Horse*, about a boy who lives out in the old west with his uncle, a German shepherd dog, and the horse. In another US TV series, *Circus Boy*, the main character was adopted by the circus owners when his parents died in a trapeze accident. The lad was played by Micky Dolenz, who went on to be part of *The Monkees* band in the 60s. For me, *Lassie* was the one I liked the most. It was about an 11-year-old boy called Jeff, played by Tommy Rettig, whose father had died while on active service, so he lived with his mother and 'Gramps', who inherited Lassie one day from a neighbour, and the dog becomes the most valuable member of the family, foiling villainous plots, saving Jeff from a lion, and sorting out feuds. Every time they sat down at the table it was a gingham tablecloth, with milk and cookies. *Lassie* was the series where I started to really identify with a character, for the simple reason that he had blonde hair and looked a bit like me. I started to wear white shirts as he did and eventually I managed to learn to ride a bike, not without scrapes. Nip transformed from Jumble into Lassie. Now it was just me out there looking for adventures, with Nip running behind my bike on the roads leading up to Arnold's farms and quarries. Throughout that marvellous hot summer of 1959, Nip and I sped through the hot, dusty streets of California, although looking at *Lassie* episodes recently, there wasn't a great deal of location work so I guess a lot of it must have been my imagination!

In June 1959, Mum and Dad were on holiday from work and we went to the Roxy Cinema in Daybrook to see *The Big Country,* an epic western starring Gregory Peck and Charlton Heston. Normally, a program would start at 1.00pm and most film programmes ran for about three and a half hours. With the news, adverts and trailers added on we would get home comfortably around 5.00pm, in plenty of time to catch *Lassie* at 5.30pm. All went well, until I realised there was an interval and that the film was going to be a lot more than two hours long. At 5.00pm, about three quarters through the film, I vacated my seat, giving my apologies to Mum and Dad. "It's a great film, thanks, but I think I'll get home now, Lassie's on in half an hour!" This didn't go down well with them at all, but I rushed off. Then, when I arrived home, I realised I didn't have my key! I ran up to my mate John's house to watch *Lassie* there. Mum and Dad told me off for not staying with them, but I think by then they had resigned themselves to having a weird offspring. I was thirteen after all and starting to get big enough to look after myself. I saw *The Big Country* on TV a few years later and loved it. It's one of my favourite Westerns and in my top twenty films, but, you know, a boy and his dog always come first.

The UK showing of *Lassie* helped me get through the next four years until I left school in 1961. When George Chandler who played Gramps died in 1957, a married couple appeared who had a little boy that didn't look like me at all and was a bit of a cry-baby. Jeff and his mother moved away and left Lassie with them. Time to move on.

The *Robin Hood* TV series lasted from 1955 to 1959. In that time, they had two different Maid Marians and two different Little Johns, the original being injured during filming. They also had two different Sheriffs of Nottingham, but that was part of the plot. After three series, the actor that played the Sheriff of Nottingham was Alan Wheatley and his lieutenant, usually played by Paul Eddington, was called Howard. My full name is Alan Howard Wheatley and how weird was that! My bond with Lew Grade grew stronger as I watched the villains scheme to do away with Robin Hood. In 1957, *Ivanhoe* made by Columbia/Screen Gems was competition with Robin Hood. It was made in England initially, and then because of bad weather they filmed the rest of it in Hollywood. *Ivanhoe* starred Roger Moore. As soon as I saw him, I thought I liked him immensely. Fighting for his life, sword in hand, and the extra bit of polish and gloss to the series. It only lasted one year, but they shot more on location than they had in *Robin Hood*. By then, I knew when something was being filmed in a studio and when on location, usually down to the limitations of the camerawork and lighting. It seemed to be lit darker when in the studio. Because it was not filmed in forests, *Ivanhoe* could use more horses and have varied storylines. You could tell they had more horses and action in chase sequences, and more elaborate set ups for the fight scenes. Instinct told me that this bloke had got it. Something about Roger Moore had grabbed me and sure enough, two years later Jack L Warner put him under contract. I can distinctly remember one magazine saying, "Roger Moore is the new Errol Flynn," because he used to laugh a lot when fighting with a sword, ha! ha! ha! My other favourites were *Hawkeye* and *The Last of the Mohicans*, which was made by the Canadian Broadcasting Company but financed by Lew Grade's ITC. Running with Nip and my school mates through the woods behind Bestwood Lodge on a winter afternoon was just like when the last of the Mohicans chased through the snowy hills of Canada. *Cannonball,* a US series about a truck driver, his mate and their adventures on the highway was also an ATV/ITC financed series. Quite remarkable really.

Around this time, on British TV, there was also *The Range Rider*, a tougher version of the *Lone Ranger*. Both Jock Mahoney as the Range Rider and Dick Jones as his side kick were stunt men and did their own stunts on the series, giving it a much rougher edge which I found more believable than the fancy pants Lone Ranger, who never got hit and seemed to be wearing a one-piece jump suit, not to mention that ridiculous mask which hid nothing of his features. *The Range Rider* was produced by Gene Autry, a rodeo performer and singing cowboy, who set up his own production company in the late forties that also produced *Champion The Wonder Horse, Annie Oakley,* and *Buffalo Bill Jnr,* among others. Gene Autry also owned Challenge Records, which had their biggest hit with *Tequila* by The Champs in 1958 and help start the rock and roll craze, which went down well with me as a DJ on many a dance floor in the millennium years. Jock Mahoney went on to play my favourite Tarzan ever in *Tarzan Goes to India,* 1962, and *Tarzan's Three Challenges,* 1963, where again he did his own stunts, as did Woody Strode, who played the baddie in the latter film.

The autumn TV schedule for 1957 had brought about the first hour long Westerns showed in this country: Universals' *Wagon Train* with Ward Bond, and Robert Horton, who was marvellous playing the scout Flint McCullough. He had a huge fan following from 1958 to 1960. Even now, when I dip into *Wagon Train* on You Tube it's always the Robert Horton episodes that I look for. *Cheyenne* also came out in the UK at this time, having been released two years earlier in the US by Warner Brothers, but it was *Wagon Train* that was always Number One in the ratings. My viewing position was sitting with a cushion on the floor, where I stayed for the next ten years. *Maverick* was different. It was the first time a gambler had been the star of a TV series. With laidback humour, it became so popular they had to create another actor to ease the workload. After about eight episodes, James Garner's Bret Maverick was joined by Bart Maverick played by Jack Kelly. Easy going and always one to avoid conflict, Bret was my first exposure to an anti-hero.

My mother's family were too respectable to gamble, but a lot of my dad's friends played cards for money, sometimes for a laugh, sometimes not, and some men like my uncle Albert, Dad's brother-in-law, were known to have gone to the bad, taking the holiday money and losing it. In our chats during her later years, Mum told me that she enjoyed the lighter atmosphere and general naughtiness of my father's family. It a gave her a chance to be posh by comparison, a role she enjoyed very much. "I like you, Auntie Edna, cos you're posh," said one of my cousins. There was a farcical episode called *Pappy* in the third series of *Maverick*, when James Garner played his own dad. The Maverick brothers drawled out catchphrases about their father, played by

James Garner in a split screen, "Well, as my old pappy used to say...." Jack Kelly played their uncle. As well as himself, Bart Maverick, twinkling away at the camera on primetime television. It's a cliché now but then it was like a live action cartoon, which I found very funny, as did Mum. My dad gave it the accolade of being "Too bloody daft to laugh at!"

School photograph 1958

Back at school, 1957 was my first year at Redhill Secondary Modern School and this was a delight. We had girls in the class, the first time since primary school. It seemed the girls had not had the best education; we spent many lessons waiting for them to catch up and as a result I didn't have to work awfully hard. Except in maths of course, but even here my lack of skills was not so noticeable, because the girls didn't seem to have had any maths tutoring at all. There was an opportunity to escape Redhill if I took an exam for the art school in 1958. Unfortunately, maths let me down and I didn't get through, but my best mates Richard and Alan passed which meant

I would lose them at the end of the year. However, we saw each other off in style on the sports day. Alan came first in the relay race and, "The winners of the three-legged race are Richard Wheat and Howard Wheatley."

We three were very close and I was going to miss them a lot. Adios amigos. The second year, the girls had caught up and then steamed past me and most of the other boys. I was in the B stream all the time. On top of that, this was the year of Mr Rutt as our new maths teacher for the next two years. He made my life hell, and not just me. On one occasion he said to one of the girls, "I've told you before about biting your nails."

He went out of the room and came back with a bowl and said, "You can spend the rest of the lesson with your fingers in this bowl of salt water. I'll teach you!"

The girl was crying because she was embarrassed, and the salt stung, but he ignored her. Generally, though he was softer on the girls because they would cry easily and then he would stop, but for the boys, shouting, slaps across the head and thwacks on the wrist with a ruler were common. He also liked to open his desk and take out a slipper with much relish, before using it on you. He made the boys cry too eventually, but never, ever me. I just started to get angrier and angrier switching off totally with Rutt and his maths. I told my mum and dad I was falling behind in maths, "because of Mr Rutt." My dad then decided I should ask him for homework to help me catch up. Usually we were not given homework, probably because we were not expected to do it after school. Regardless, I was on a mission. I was not going to be scared by this man. Consequently, at the next lesson, while everyone else was scribbling calculations down, I went up to his desk and said, as quietly as I could, "Excuse me, Sir, as I don't seem to be doing so well at maths, can you give me some homework so I can catch up?"

He walked to my desk picked my exercise book up and looked at it.

Then he slung my exercise book face down on the floor and ground it under his heel, with the whole class staring at me. I looked down at his foot squashing my book on the floor, then up at him thinking what I would do when I had left school and could go back to sort him out. After that, the more he shouted and wacked at us, the more I switched off.

Eventually, he gave up on me and simply gave me the lowest mark of E on a regular basis. I was going to go back and get my revenge, but he died of a perforated ulcer after I finished. I was left with a huge chip on my shoulder about being taught in a negative and aggressive way.

After school was much more fun though. John Emberton and I clubbed together and bought a projector. You turned the handle, and a light projected a cartoon strip onto the wall. We had about ten comic strips to use, Dan Dare, Billy Bunter, Larry The Lamb, Archie Andrews and the cowboy Jeff Arnold, projecting them onto a white wall in my bedroom, or we showed them to the rest of our gang in their shed. We found that we could obtain a brighter picture by running it through John's electric train transformer which worked well for a while, until it eventually melted. That lurched me into the TV *Popeye* craze of the late 50s when they used to show three episodes every Monday teatime. I wanted to learn to draw. The body of Popeye was reasonably easy, but the face took me hours, starting with the nose and the eyes and building it up, doing it over and over again and getting the proportions right. I became obsessed, buying Popeye cigarettes and jigsaw puzzles, and then luckily the comics were published so I could copy from them. I also drafted up a cartoon called *The Four Just Jokers,* lifting the title from *The Four Just Men* which was a TV series made in England by ATV/ITC. *The Jokers* were Charlie Drake, Tony Hancock, Jimmy Edwards and Terry Thomas, all half hour comedy shows on the BBC. I copied the faces from my *Knockout* and *TV Fun* comics. Long-suffering John Emberton accompanied me to the ABC Metropole in Sherwood to see the new Warner Brothers films featuring these fine comedy actors: *Whacko, Sands of the Desert, The Rebel* and *School for Scoundrels.*

I lobbied hard to Mum and Dad for one of the new 'Flo-Master' pens and Christmas 1960 I was lucky enough to get one. Like the fountain pens used at school, you had to fill it with ink, but it had a felt tip nib that gave a broader line and had a screw cap lid. I spent an inspired Boxing Day, drawing upstairs in my room, full of creative ideas. But then I couldn't find the screw cap lid. I searched everywhere, rushed through teatime, and searched again but it was nowhere to be found. Knowing how my dad would react, I had a sleepless night. The shops were shut next day and meanwhile my Flo-Master nib had dried up. Later on that day I found the screw cap stuck in the turn-up of my trousers, would you believe. How? Why? What sort of lunacy is this I asked myself? You couldn't make it up. The Flo-Master was dead to the world and my creativity dried up too!

Other matters were also preoccupying me in late 1958. ATV released *The Invisible Man*, with innovative special effects and lots of location work, plus ethereal music from Edwin Astley, who wrote and arranged the music for 14 TV series and scored 24 major films in his career. His daughter married Pete Townshend of The Who.

Around this time, I went on a school trip to Paris, and I arranged for Uncle Arthur and Janet to see me at Dover Harbour Station. I had been writing to her, and now I asked if she could be there to wave me off. She turned up alright but had a sailor on her arm. A full-grown young man with a Royal Navy uniform on. I was heartbroken, the love of my life was now with another, although a week in Paris helped. Upon my return, I lost my enthusiasm for becoming a missionary and started to bunk off Sunday School, walking along the back streets to Woodthorpe Park in Sherwood to hang out, so I could then arrive home at the usual time. Actually, my parents were quite relieved when they found out I had stopped going to Sunday School. I had stiffly advised my mum that their nights out at the Cherry Club were a sinful, wicked activity. She came with me to one of the Christian Endeavour meetings once, but she still went on to meet my dad at the Working Men's Club afterwards.

For my 13th birthday, Mum and Dad presented me with a bike. I'd never ridden one before. It was second-hand but that was fine. What I worried about was Dad's tutoring and that he would expect me to be zipping about on it right away. I wobbled around precariously on it for ages while his impatience started to become more and more heated. Stubbornly, I left it unused on our back yard. Each time he said, "When you going to learn to ride that bike then?" I would shrug my shoulders and walk away. The bike seemed to need repairs all the time. That would require me to push it to the bike repair shop and back, because I couldn't ride, which he knew very well, so he could say when I returned home "Why didn't you ride it then?" One Saturday evening at sunset, when they were at the Working Men's Club, I wheeled the bike up to the top of the recreation ground, propped it up against a wall and wobbled off down precariously, riding it around until I got the hang of it. The grass was a soft landing. Soon after he said, as I knew he would,

"When are you going to learn to ride that bike then?"

"Maybe," I said, "I'll get round to it."

"Yes, well get round to it now," he said.

That was my cue. I hopped on the bike and rode it off down the road. He never said a word and, just to be awkward, if ever Dad needed his bike repairing, I used to walk with it!

Unfortunately, I then had to go into hospital again with housemaid's knee. Recovering at home a week before my birthday, it was so hot that I spent time in my canvas tent. Lying there reading comics, I finally learnt how to draw Popeye properly, having seen him on the TV.

In 1959, for our holiday we went to Ingoldmells on the Lincolnshire coast, which had none of the charm of Deal and the sea always seemed to be out. However, it was the start of the Western boom on TV, with at least one series on every night. My favourite was *Sugarfoot*, 1957 to 1961. Its main character, Tom Brewster was a very different type of cowboy, who didn't come on macho at all. And unlike most of the others he was fair haired like me. In the Wild West, he was deemed as being a wimp for studying his law books and never drinking alcohol, or carrying a gun, drinking only Sarsaparilla with a dash of cherry, derided for it every time by the rest of the saloon.

Will Hutchins (Sugarfoot), Jack Warner and Clint Walker (Cheyenne) take a break on the Warner Bros. backlot 1959

Meanwhile, I had the hots for a girl called Julie Wood who I met on the recreation ground just up the road, where we all used to meet at weekends. To impress her, I had spent an afternoon with her younger brother clearing out their old air raid shelter. I can still remember watching her walking across the rec. From the back, she had a sashay I found appealing. I was thirteen and still had no idea of how to go on. She was a year older and eventually I lost her to a guy her age who could presumably show her a better time than I! Tom Brewster had the same problem with a girl, who he mournfully lost to a well-spoken newspaper man. Once again art imitated life. Or life imitated art. I could hardly tell the difference.

In the first episode of *Sugarfoot, Brannigan's Boots*, Tom was in the town horse race with a girl. She had bet the farm on her winning; the lease was up. It was a draw, so they had a shooting match, aiming at a can thrown up between them. Everyone had been laughing at his 'tenderfoot' ways, but he knew why it would have to be her that won. I noticed they used footage from the original version, *The Boy from Oklahoma*, in which Tom had been played by a different actor. Tom put his loop on the gun so he couldn't draw it out of the holster in time. She went first and got it square on. When he tried, he was tugging at his holster and everyone laughed, but he knew he was doing the right thing, which made him my hero. As Mr Caine said about Harry Palmer and himself, it's better to be "a winner who comes on like a loser."

After my knee recovered, I rode my bike up and down the country lanes with Nipper running alongside, dust rolling out from my wheels just like Lassie and Jeff in the sub-bleached back roads of California. The Brickyard pond dried up totally, and Bestwood became Nevada, with the slag heaps nearby like mini mountains. Cycling everywhere now, I came across a bypass concrete surface half a mile long, between Calverton and Oxton. It was sandy coloured concrete like the roads featured in the TV series *Cannonball*, also leading me to cycle around the backroads because they were identical to the ones featured on *Lassie*.

The new school term started in September 1959, and we weren't given a choice of subjects which made it a waste of time as far as I was concerned. *Wagon Train* was back with a new season. Top position in the TV ratings war was contested on a Monday night at 8pm with *Wagon Train* up against BBC's *Quatermass*. In that autumn, we had another US TV series from Warner Brothers 77 *Sunset Strip*. It ran until 1964. It was an hour-long private eye detective series with a snazzy jazz theme tune. There were two unusual episodes connected to the writers' strike in Hollywood. One was the *Silent Caper*, a prolonged chase sequence with no dialogue whatsoever, and the other *Reserved For Mr Bailey* featuring only Efrem Zimbalist the lead actor with minimum dialogue, being hunted in a ghost town. Warner Brothers had opted out of the strike by recycling old scripts and listing them as being written by 'W Hermanos', that is, 'Warner Brothers' in Spanish! Western scripts were transferred to detective scripts, change the horse to a car and vice versa.

77 Sunset Strip was so successful that it created a cult following, with smooth-talking car hop and trainee detective, Kookie. He dominated the front covers of all the American fan magazines for 18 months and was certainly on a parallel with Elvis during that time. He even had a global hit pop song, *Kookie, Kookie (Lend me Your Comb!)* by Edward Byrnes and Connie Stevens from the series *Hawaiian Eye*, charting in both the US and the UK in 1959. In reality, the *77 Sunset Strip* offices didn't exist. All the buildings in that area had four digits in their address. However, Dean Martin's night club Dino's Lodge certainly did exist and was featured in numerous episodes. *77*

Sunset Strip spawned three similar series. *Hawaiian Eye* (1959 to 1963), *Surfside Six,* (1959 to 1960) and *Bourbon Street Beat* (1959 to 1960). They were all set in exotic locations but were in fact rarely shot away from the Warner Brothers backlot. I watched that many Warner Brothers films and TV series I could easily identify their product by that backlot and their use of the same recorded door clicks and gunshot sounds over a ten-year period!

I liked Jack L Warner a lot. If ever you see pictures of the top seven Hollywood moguls, Jack is usually the only one laughing. Of course, you could say it was all the way to the bank! Also, the only mogul who took the mickey – sorry Bunny – out of his studio and himself in the Merrie Melodies cartoons.

Starting about a month before Bonfire Night on 5th November, my friends and I would build up a whole mess of tree branches, waste and old furniture, going round to people's houses asking if there was any rubbish they wanted taking away. We stored them scattered around the bushes at the waste ground back of our house, keeping a low profile because other lads were also building up a bonfire horde, and would be looking to steal our firewood. When the time came, we would drag it all together to impress the family with a big blaze at least 25 feet high. In November 1959, *Sugarfoot* fell on the night we had the bonfire planned, but I figured I could make an appearance around the bonfire then sneak off inside to watch the TV. On the night, eager to get things going, I set off a Catherine Wheel on the wall to start proceedings. I hadn't noticed that my cousin David's firework collection was close by. I set the whole lot off in the first quarter of an hour. David and my dad's brother Uncle Lol were not best pleased. Dad sent me to the shops to get some more, so I missed *Sugarfoot* anyway. The next day it was drizzling with rain. I decided to keep the bonfire going for as long as possible. Before I went to school, I added some firewood to the bonfire and covered it over with the wheelbarrow. I had forgotten it was made of wood. When I got home from school all that was left was a set of wheels. That didn't go down well at home either!

The TV series *William Tell,* produced by ATV/ITC, was heavier than Robin Hood and the fight scenes were better; although restricted a lot to the studio, North Wales stood in for Switzerland. The location shooting was filmed without sound, which would be dubbed in later as it saved money, and only the faces of the main actors were filmed. The supporting ones were shot from the back and replaced by the actor's full face in the studio. William Tell had a good villain, Willoughby Goddard, who played Landburgher Gessler, fat and always eating chicken legs. For the first time, I saw the political side of film making. It was not just the good guys against the bad guys. I found out that a lot of the crew and the production staff were exiles from McCarthyism in the US. They had worked in Hollywood on films about the 'underdogs' winning through, and that brought them trouble. They were simply named by others in desperation, or maybe they were communists attempting to overthrow America, I don't know, but they couldn't get any work in the US, so they came over here. In December 1959, Hollywood came nine miles north of Nottingham to Eastwood. Amazingly, 20th Century Fox were filming D H Lawrence's *Sons And Lovers*, and it was shot in the unchanged pit villages of Brinsley, Eastwood and Underwood. Up until Nationalisation there were 49 pits in Nottinghamshire. I wish I'd realised at the time they were filming because I would definitely have cycled over there to watch. Although Dean Stockwell did a reasonable acting job as the aspiring artist Paul Morel, he was American and a star, under contract to 20th Century Fox. But it's a brilliant film with lots of location shots round the area. Trevor Howard nailed it as Paul's father, a miner. It went on to achieve seven Academy Awards gaining the Oscar for best cinematography. I just loved it when Hollywood came to England from the forties through to seventies. They simply said, "Here's the money, do your best and get on with it!"

Autumn 1960 brought about the half hour *Danger Man TV* series. This was another notch up the ladder of success for ATV/ ITC. A marvellous thriller series extremely well produced using top directors, quality acting and cleverly staged fight scenes, all with jazzy background music from Edwin Astley. A global smash which made a star out of Patrick McGoohan. I am convinced that the success of the series inspired Harry Saltzman to go into making the Bond films. All Harry had to do was finish producing *Saturday Night And Sunday Morning* in Nottingham, contact Cubby Broccoli, then they could start work on producing Dr No. What a contrast eh? Three years later, due to the success of *Dr No, Danger Man* returned, in an hour-long format for a further three years. What goes around comes around! We were starting to beat the Americans at their own game. *Coronation Street* was first aired in December 1960 and this soap would continue to smash the ratings war by being at

No 1 most of the time, further contributing to the northern kitchen sink saga that would continue with *Saturday Night And Sunday Morning, A Taste Of Honey* and *A Kind Of Loving*, etc.

Redhill Secondary Modern put girls into cookery and domestic science and boys into woodwork and metalwork. I would rather have been in with the girls, a lot more fun and learning to cook at the same time so I could look after myself. I didn't understand what difference woodwork and metalwork would make to me and after a year had made nothing at all. My mate Morris Thorpe was at the same school thirteen years later, facing some of the same vicious teachers. The metal work teacher The Colonel, liked to remind you he had a military background by intimidating you as loudly as possible in front of the class. (In the films he would be played by Kynaston Reeves as Quelch the Form Master in the *Billy Bunter of Greyfriars School* TV series.) I took violin lessons as they coincided with metalwork but dropped them the following year when the timetable was altered! I wouldn't have minded the discipline if the education had been good, but we were factory and pit fodder. Technical drawing was for working out how to make squares and circle, presumably so that we could cut out of steel for coal mining, or panelling. One day in technical drawing I did a lovely round circle freehand but ended being shown up and humiliated in front of the class. Defeated the object I suppose.

American comics were released into this country in 1959 and I cheered up no end. It was mid-year, around about my birthday when I went into the newsagents and saw a big pile of comics in the corner. I opened the top one up to find it was in colour throughout, not just the cover. British comics had a colour cover, but inside it was black-and-white and seemed to be printed on Izal toilet paper. I soon went back for more of these new comics every time I had some cash. There was a fresh batch every fortnight. We had Superman, Superboy and Jimmy Olsen, Batman, Walt Disney comics, Bugs Bunny comics, Sergeant Bilko, Kid Colt and The Rawhide Kid. On top of all this glorious material there were 'The Movie Magazines', imported film magazines and loads of 'em too, with everything I needed to know about Hollywood films and TV series. I became very knowledgeable about show biz especially the stars of TV series. I don't know how I found the time to attend school! But back to English comics, where one I still enjoyed was the Fleetway Classics Picture Library, black-and-white graphic novels in the small booklet format. One particular thriller adventure I liked was *The Picture Of Dorian* Gray by Oscar Wilde. I decided to purchase the book version and found it was a fascinating read. I was about halfway through and looking for the book when Dad pounced. "I wouldn't bother looking for that book of yours if I was you, I've thrown it away. Ruddy filth!"

"But why, Dad, there's nothing in it. Look, it was a comic originally!"

"Don't argue!"

End of story. Even now I can't see anything that salacious in it, but those were the times.

For our summer holiday in 1960, we went to Rhyl in North Wales for a change, but when we arrived the advance weather forecast wasn't very good so Dad had the brilliant idea of purchasing a Railway Runabout ticket which meant you could travel all over North Wales at a minimum cost and it was quite extensive too. What an amazing week this turned out to be. No more sun burning and soreness on the beach. We went everywhere, stopping off at various stations for lunch or tea and then hopping back on to continue our voyage of discovery. Coming down from the slate mines the driver even let me sit with him in the cab! You could travel all over North Wales in those pre-Beeching Axe days.

Howard, Dad and Mum, Rhyl Prom, 1960

All three of us were into it big time and it was an excellent finish to what would be our last holiday together.

In 1960, the *Lady Chatterley's Lover* Old Bailey court case came about where the jury found in favour of Penguin Books and brought about more liberalisation of publishing to which some saw as the beginning of 'The Permissive Society'. I reckon it must have simply been the name Oscar Wilde my dad objected to. Makes you wonder how he knew about him in the first place doesn't it? It would hardly be essential reading during his school days! Our rift continued. Meanwhile, John and I managed a few adventures together. In our last year at school, we went to Ada Sulleys off-licence and bought a bottle of cider and some cigarettes. We bunked off school on a cold and snowy Friday in February 1961 to sit in the derelict stables in the grounds of the local doctor's posh house. It was so cold that we built a small fire to keep warm. Unfortunately, the lady of the house caught us and demanded we followed her back to the house where she took our names and addresses. Why the heck we didn't simply run off or lie I'll never know!

That weekend, it was snowing, so we asked our mate Jeff Gilbert if he could swop his dad's ladder with our sledge for the day. On the Sunday, we snuck the ladder into my house through the front door and up the stairs to the attic. My dad was always at the Working Men's Club on Sunday lunchtime and my mum was in the back, in the kitchen preparing the lunch that we would devour on his return. No one ever used the attic in our house. It was huge, stretching across all three of the terraced houses in our block. Up there, we smoked Senior Service – we had expensive taste – drank cider and talked rubbish, in whispers. However we weren't as quiet as we should have been.

I heard our extremely eccentric, generously bosomed neighbour's daughter Rita exclaim, "Mam, I'm sure I can hear somebody at the top of our stairs!" Unfortunately, behind us further along the attic, another hatch opened. Hurriedly we stubbed the fags out on the rafters and switched off our torches, terrified of Phyllis next door, as she was a big woman, with muscular arms and a very quick temper.

A head moved about but it was completely dark up there and she didn't appear to have seen us. That hatch closed and we slid out down the ladder, then hoisted it out the front door and into the back garden. Full of triumph, I went in the back door for my Sunday lunch, and John went home. Come teatime, an angry Mrs Gilbert was there, demanding to know why I had stolen their ladder. Jeff had obviously not told her he had agreed to swap it for the sledge, and she didn't believe me, but my dad was dozing on the settee by that point and just shrugged his shoulders.

On the Monday after school, John and I walked back home planning our next jaunt. That evening, there was a loud knock at the door and there stood a burly police officer. The doctor's wife had complained to the police that we were trespassing and trying to burn down her stables. My dad's face got more and more red as the policeman told him all of this. However, I was relieved to hear that I was just getting a telling off and that John had already been told the same.

"Now be a good lad, don't do it again, eh, or if there is a next time, I will have to take more serious action, alright?"

I nodded frantically too scared to say anything.

"Goodnight then sir," he said to my dad and off he went.

My dad closed the door and turned on me. "Now have I got this right, tell me if I'm missing anything. You played truant from school, wrote each other's sick notes, to smoke fags and make a fire round at the doctor's? You could have set fire to the place. You stole Mrs Gilbert's ladder and I've had a complaint from mad woman Phyllis next door that you were up in the loft smoking cigarettes."

Oops. I had hoped that Phyllis hadn't seen us.

"Don't you bloody well realise that you could have set fire to the place?"

No, I hadn't realised that. I started to apologise but it didn't help matters. He produced his slipper, gave me a good belting, and told me to go to bed straightaway. This was *Just William* territory gone mad all right. I had to stay home in the evenings all week. John only had a telling off! It put him off from doing any more truanting though!

The next time I fancied playing hooky I did it alone. One Friday in June of that year, I set off at 8.50am and turned right towards the recreation grounds instead of carrying straight on to school. There was a narrow pathway that ran alongside the rec. ground that I walked along, head down to avoid catching anyone's eye. Only to walk almost headlong into a police constable. What the heck was he doing walking along the rec at that time on a Friday morning? Looking for truants like me perhaps? I put on a limp. Really, I did, so that I could say I was taking my constitution after coming out of hospital. Why not? I'd had housemaid's knee. It was bound to work. To my surprise, he carried on walking without questioning me, but just to be on the safe side I carried on limping until he was out of sight. It was a beautiful, blue-sky morning. I headed up the pathway and then onto the Calverton Road. I was half-way down the very steep George's Hill into Calverton when who should be coming up the opposite way but another constable, wheeling a bike up the hill. Now what the hell was he doing early in the morning, halfway between Arnold and Calverton? I resumed the limp, but luckily, he didn't even look at me and passed by. I reached the road that led to the woods near Calverton Pit when, honestly, coming the other way was yet another policeman. I continued the limp and he carried on. You couldn't make it up!

By this time, it would be about 10.30am. I entered the woods and headed inwards. It was a nice dry heat morning as I lay down on a grassy incline amid the smell of pine trees and reflected on my lot in life. In barely three weeks I would be free of Redhill Secondary Modern. All I had to do was get through the forthcoming job interviews. Tom Brewster had to study but all I had to do was present my drawings. After about fifteen minutes, I started to drop off, so I thought I had better get on the move back to Arnold. I walked through the woods and went round onto the Ollerton Road. By this time, it was almost 11.30am. I had timed it well. With Dad being on the 2.00pm day shift at Raleigh and Mum working at Fords, the Drapers, I would have the house to myself in the afternoon. It was a good day to play hooky because Fridays were my worst subjects, woodwork, metalwork and gym!

I did a test and interviewed to find out if I was eligible to get into the advertising and printing trade, and it seemed to go well. I was taken round Staffords of Netherfield, who were known around the world for producing colour cinema posters, using a process called Lithography, on stone with grease repelling water. Their output was incredible. That was it for Redhill as far as I was concerned, the rest was just biding my time until departure. On my last day, the headmaster Mr Weddel called our class into his office to give us a pep-talk for the future and presented us with a scroll each. When it came to my turn, for some reason I had switched off and started to drift towards the door.

"Wheatley!" Roared Mr Weddel. "Where are you going lad? You're walking out without your scroll."

"Oh, sorry sir," I replied. "I nearly forgot."

"You'll have to buck up your ideas lad, you'll never get on in life that like that."

Said with a smile of course, but that was it. End of, closing credits, curtain down!

2

"All I'm out for is a good time – all the rest is propaganda"

1961 to 1965

In the summer of 1961, I dutifully went for a couple of interviews at the Raleigh bike factory. This is the factory where Arthur Seaton worked in *Saturday Night and Sunday Morning* and for Redhill School lads like me it was either that, Boots, Players, or down the mines. Raleigh said they would be able to set me on in two weeks' time, and Mum and Dad went on holiday, happily assuming that I was taken care of. But I wanted to be drawing for a living. While they were away, I had an interview to enter the printing trade at the Nottingham branch of its governing body, Thomas Formans on Hucknall Road. Sitting in the waiting room with other candidates was a bit off-putting because some of them knew each other and were showing round their artwork. They were quite something, very stylish with some brilliant pen and ink sketches of galleons and castles. They must have come from the art school. When I went into the large, dark, smoke-filled meeting room, there were four middle-aged men sitting at the interview table, a bit like four town councillors, portly and each wearing a three-piece suit. Pipes and cigars were smoked. I was directed to a single chair facing them with a wave of a hand and asked me a few questions about myself.

"What have you got to show us then, lad?"

They shared out my work and were leafing through them without comment. The silence grew as they looked stern-faced at my colour cartoons of cowboys, *Popeye* and *Just William.*

"Ah, this one you've done promoting the cowboy series, *Have Gun Will Travel,* which was on the television last night, wasn't it?"

"Yes, that's right sir, one of my favourite Westerns. I really want to go into advertising."

"Hmmm, not bad lad. Anyway, thanks for calling in and we'll let you know."

Short as that.

At this time, I was taken by a new half-hourly TV series called *The Pursuers* on ABC Television. It was set in London and featured Detective Inspector John Bollinger and his german shepherd dog called London. There were excellent chase sequences with the dog charging after the villains, all on location, with tracking shots, and the use of handheld cameras. I can still remember the thrill of watching a chase around the fun fair that used to be held on Battersea Park. I have tried to get hold of the series again but so far it is unavailable.

I also watched *Ghost Squad,* the first whole hour-long TV series in the UK, a joint production between ITC and The Rank Organisation. It was another crime series, although it lacked the excitement and pace of *The Pursuers.* I also noticed that after the first series it lost something on screen and the sound was flattened. By now, I knew enough to point out to my mum and dad that this was because it was now mainly studio bound and shot on the cheaper video. They said they couldn't tell the difference, which is ironic considering all the years they spent in the cinema, but that said, without them I would never have had that cinema experience until much later in life. By 1962, I also had ATV's *Man of the World* to watch, about an international photographer who gets caught up in many dramas, with hour-long episodes purportedly set in a variety of locations. In fact, the first two episodes were shot in Gibraltar and Spain, but the rest were all shot in England, dressed up with palm trees.

In 1962, a new series produced by ATV was announced, *The Saint*, about 'a modern-day buccaneer' to be played by Roger Moore, already a well-known figure from *Ivanhoe*, *The Alaskans* and *Maverick*. It started in the autumn. At first, Roger's accent started off as mid-Atlantic and over time settled down into Received Pronunciation, or 'posh' English. Palm trees were placed in front of the camera to give the impression of exotic foreign locations, but if you looked at the background you could see there were no leaves on the trees. The best episodes were those set in England, such as my favourites, *The Talented Husband*, the first one, and *The Well-Meaning Mayor*, about a corrupt public official 'Up North'.

Fortunately, I had passed the interview for the printing trade and in late October 1961, I started work at 'The Ashfield Photo Litho', with fellow apprentice Tony Martin. In the studio there were twelve 6 foot high x 15 foot wide wooden partitions where we each had a bench, a drawing board and a shiner, which was a glass table lit from underneath. Four colour screen separation printing in those days was a laborious process. A drawing or a photograph, would be set up vertically in a frame, then photographed with a checkerboard of dots called a 'half tone screen' over the camera lens. This came out as a negative image made of dots – what would now be pixels I believe, but back then you could see the dots that made up the image with a linen tester or small magnifying glass.

A positive was made from the negative. I had to lay it on the shiner light and use a magnifying glass to go over it, applying ferro-cyanide with a tiny brush to remove individual dots where the image had come out too dark, followed by hypo to keep the dots intact! It was processed again by the technicians using a chemically sensitized thin metal plate. If it was a colour product it was Gerhardt the printer who would first put the yellow ink into the printing press and print it off in yellow, then blue, then red and finally black, each on top of the other lined up with a cross on the width and length. In the films, he would be played by Gert Frobe in *Goldfinger*. He was nicknamed 'Gert' of course. The completed product would be assessed by the boss, Arthur Walters.

We called it 'the dot game'. By 1965, the first computer versions had come in. One was called a Klischograph, ironically German too! It scanned the images onto plastic orange foils, which was a huge saving in time and effort. We did a lot of cartoons, children's book covers and annuals, mainly for Collins Children's Books and Fontana paperbacks. I loved working on Supercar and Fireball XL5.

As an example of how it worked, one of my early attempts was that I had to reproduce a photograph of a young woman smiling for a diary cover. I had completed the yellow and blue, and when it came to the red, I thought I would take out the single dots on her teeth to give her a whiter smile. When it was printed, those teeth! Yellow and blue make green, so she ended up with spinach teeth! After six months' probation we were signed up as indentured apprentices for five years and expected to go to college in the autumn.

Around that time, I joined 'The English Westerners Society', a group who were obsessed with all things to do with the Old Wild West. The Nottingham branch consisted of four blokes in their fifties who met quarterly in The Cross Keys pub in town. Attending a pub in Nottingham by myself with four middle-aged blokes was a big deal for me. As I sat with them, it dawned on me that I knew very little about the real Wild West. I couldn't contribute very much at all. I also blotted my copybook later on in the evening when the house lights flashed for time.

"Hey, the fuses have gone!" I said.

"Not really Howard, it's last orders, gerrum in lad!"

I stayed with The Westerners for about a year, with lots of material coming through the post. After that I realised my interest really lay in The West as portrayed in films and TV series.

At work, after two years, we started our day-release and two evenings a week at Nottingham Technical College. We really should have gone the year before but for some unknown reason they held back the application. Right away, it seemed as if we were given even more labouring jobs to do at work. For example, we had to make certain they were stocked up with chemicals the day before we went to college.

We couldn't have 'The Journeymen', as they were called, having to mix up their own chemicals! In fact, labouring jobs made up two-thirds of our work for most of the apprenticeship. We talked to other students at college, who told us what kind of training they were getting. It was then that we found out that labouring jobs, errands plus fetching and carrying, were only meant to be a small part of the training. Arthur Walters and his co-manager Alan Fraser and the staff were always grumpy on the day after we had been to college. It became clear that they would have preferred to train us up on-site. I ignored them. For me college meant new people and took me out of myself.

In the September of 1963 I signed up to some rock-climbing night classes run by Doug Scott the mountaineer, at Cottesmore School. Doug was one of those university types, but he was amiable and keen for us to learn. A few years later, he became world famous for his many exploits on rock faces, and in September 1975 he made the first ascent on the Southwest face of Mount Everest. You could tell that he was passionate about his subject and wanted to share the joy of it.

The classes were held in the gym. My first location climb was in the spring of 1964, when the nights were lighter and the whole class went out in a minibus one evening and did the Black Rocks at Cromford. It was the perfect place to start and had been Doug Scott's first climb too, which was probably no coincidence. I was not a particularly good climber but enjoyed the whole experience immensely, plus it toughened me up. I knew I had to get fitter and hardier, and did my best to throw myself about, but I was cautious in the main. Once we had to start from the vaulting horse and hoist ourselves up the gym ropes with carabiners and slings round our thighs, attached to a main rope held by Doug. Prussiking, they call it. I managed to get myself into a stable position, albeit at an angle, and hung on manfully, looking down for Doug's approval. As I did, he knocked my vaulting horse away and left me stranded in mid-air waving about on a loose rope, about ten feet up at a 45-degree angle.

"What are you going to do now then, Howard?" said Doug, with his usual humour.

I managed to struggle into an upright position and hook myself down. But it livened me up and despite my legs being like jelly I was able to stagger to the door afterwards. When Doug said "Well done, lad," I was a happy bunny.

On the music front, The Shadows and Cliff Richard were regularly at the top of the UK pop charts. Cliff tried hard to be a bad boy just like Elvis Presley, sneering at the camera, but his heart wasn't in it and by 1961 he had become the boy next door in *The Young Ones*, followed by *Summer Holiday* in 1962, *Wonderful Life* in 1963 and *Finders Keepers* in 1966 and others. Such was his popularity that the mass of fans for the premiere of *Summer Holiday* at the Warner Cinema, Leicester Square, meant that Cliff was unable to get out of the car, so he had to go back to his hotel and watch it on TV, missing out being presented to the Queen.

The radio station I listened to was the BBC *Light Programme*. In the early morning getting ready for work it was Mantovani, The Northern Dance Orchestra or The Big Ben Banjo Band, very few vocalists. Then, in September 1962, The Beatles released their first single *Love Me Do*, the same day as the first James Bond film *Dr No* was released and things started to change.

I first saw The Beatles on ABC TV's *Thank Your Lucky Stars*, but the real excitement came with *Ready Steady Go*, which launched in the autumn of 1963, every Friday night at 6pm – "The Weekend Starts Here!" with a big, beautiful bite of pop music. *Top of the Pops* came in January 1964 although, unlike *Ready Steady Go*, it wasn't aimed at the Mods and played mainly Top 20 material, and there was more miming going on from the artists. These two shows were still quite formally presented though, university and bank manager types trying to look cool!

And then, and then ... there was Pirate Radio! On Good Friday, Easter 1964, Radio Caroline made their first broadcast. I didn't try to hear it because I assumed it was beamed to the south of England, with a weak signal at points north. It was irreverent, totally focused on the music and had masses of airtime with tunes we had never heard before. By 1966, ten pirate radio stations were broadcasting to an estimated audience of 10 to 15 million, which is when the Swinging Sixties really started to kick off. Pop music was never the same again!

In early 1963 I started going back to the cinema regularly. I went to a matinee showing at The Gaumont Cinema in Nottingham of Hitchcock's *Psycho*, two and a half years after its initial release. Better late than never. It was a dark gloomy afternoon and there were only about twenty people in there, so I sat on the front row of the circle upstairs to get the best view. I knew of Janet Leigh from her starring roles in Universal films so was not expecting her to meet her maker a third of the way through the film. It scared the hell out of me. I had never experienced anything like it. There are only three major shocks in Psycho. Shower, staircase and cellar. However, the sheer sense of evil and suspense Hitchcock created was phenomenal. All done on the back lot at Universal, with the crew from his TV show. It's in my top ten of films ever.

Alma Revill, Alfred Hitchcock's wife, came from St Ann's in Nottingham. The family moved down to London when she was quite young. Her father worked at Twickenham Film Studios and Alma eventually obtained work as a film editor, script writer and director's assistant. When the studios closed in 1919, she gained a position at Paramount Pictures UK where she met and married Hitchcock, working alongside him as screenwriter, editor, and production assistant throughout his career. There is a Blue Plaque in her honour outside The St Ann's Valley Public Library in Nottingham. 1963 was also the start of the boom for UK based horror films. With productions from Hammer, Amicus, Anglo-Amalgamated, Tigon, and Tempean, I was now back as a regular visitor to the cinema. There were lots of double bills, especially from Hammer.

Late again, I was a year behind watching the first Bond film *Dr No* in the summer of 1963. In the autumn I saw *From Russia With Love*, which clinched it for me. It was like watching a very expensive episode of *Danger Man*. *From Russia With Love* really grabbed me and I must have watched it thirty times over the years. For the first time, we were giving Hollywood a run for their money. Thank goodness United Artists had the faith and good sense to finance it with Broccoli and Saltzman's know how. I had seen *Dr No* twice already by 1964 and went for a third session one Wednesday evening at the Elite Cinema on Parliament Street. Halfway through, I had to find the manager and tell him that the film had jumped a reel and missed out some scenes, noticeably the spider in the bed sequence. To his credit, the projectionist wound the film back to include the missing fifteen minutes so we could watch the film in its entirety. I missed the last bus because of this and had to get the late service full of the bus crews.

In September 1963, *The Fugitive* TV series was premiered on ITV. During the next four years, until August 1967, I managed to watch every one of the 120 episodes through to the nail-biting finale. This was ground-breaking stuff. Quinn Martin, who produced the show, didn't hang about. Every episode was out there at many varied locations. The timing for me couldn't have been better. It didn't deal with clear cut issues; shades of grey came through, much like life. When I started hitchhiking a year later, it was a case of life imitating art again, hitchhiking from town to town just like Richard Kimble. Nobody told me it was a classic series, my desire to watch quality was purely instinctive. The series was nominated for five Emmy Awards and won for Outstanding Dramatic Series in 1966. In 2002, it was rated No 36 in the 'TV Guides Greatest Show of All Time'. The finale came in two parts which were aired globally. Part two, *The Judgement*, in August 1967, was the most watched TV episode ever up to that time.

In April 1964, I bought a return ticket on the Great Central Line from Nottingham to Elstree. Knowing that ATV, MGM, and Warner Brothers (Associated British) had their UK bases at Elstree and Boreham Wood, I wanted to see something being filmed. My first port of call was the security gate at Associated British, just off the main shopping street in Elstree. Seeing me walking up and down outside the gate, looking for a front office in the white Art Deco building, the security guy came out of his booth to me,

"Of course, we get 'em all 'ere y'know," he said, "Cliff Richard's musicals, The Saint and The Avengers."

"Could you direct me to the front office to get in?" I asked.

"Sorry pal, can't let you in 'ere without a pass or prior appointment."

"Can I get one? Just to watch?"

"It's not up to me to arrange anything like that pal, you'll have to write in."

As I walked away, he said, "Tell you what, they're filming an episode of *The Saint* round one of the estates nearby. Why don't you go over and see if you can spot 'em?"

Of course, I never thought to ask him exactly where.

Maybe he was joking but I thanked him and set off. I walked all over the nearby estates for an hour and a half and finished fed up.

Next, I went up to try MGM, on Shenley Road. This was laid out in a huge park, although the frontage was not as impressive as Associated British. It was the same story. I walked back down the road to the station deflated. I never did write in.

On holiday in Spain, Mum and Dad met two young women from Dewsbury, near Manchester, and invited them to stay over in Nottingham. They came down in 1964 for the Nottingham Goose Fair, which is held on the first weekend in October. I was eighteen. They were a couple of years older: Kath and Sharon. I had nothing in the house to play apart from Dad's collection of 78's, so I bought the *Beatles For Sale* LP that had just come out and we danced along to some of the tracks. We took them out to the Elmhurst Working Men's Club, meeting up with family and friends there, which luckily meant that my cousin David was on hand to make it a foursome. By 9pm we were blasted. David called a taxi to take us to the Goose Fair. I had just been to see *Saturday Night and Sunday Morning,* three years after its release, about a young man working in a factory and how he was determined to have good time; 'All the rest is propaganda'. This was running through my head as, like Arthur Seaton, David and I took them on the rides. We went whizzing round on the dodgems, screaming to the top of the big wheel. I got a lot of hand holding and waist clinching in that night. We finished at midnight and were still drunk, so we walked into town and went ten-pin bowling at the Excel Bowl until two in the morning. It had 12 lanes downstairs for the general public and 12 upstairs for members only. Bright lights, loud music, and a lot of giggling while we tried to bowl and listened to the tunes being played. I remember *Ragdoll*, by the Four Seasons and *Move Over Darling* by Doris Day and *We're Through* by The Hollies. We walked the four miles home, which David and I claimed was for a laugh although in fact we had run out of money. It took an hour and a half along frosty Mansfield Road at 4am, arm in arm with a bit of canoodling. My first proper date. Back home, I waved the girls off to bed in the spare room. I totally lacked confidence for anything else, but I had a great time anyway. The next day, Mum, Dad and I took them out for a meal at the Moulin Rouge Restaurant in Trinity Square and had a walk around the Nottingham Arboretum, putting them on the bus at Huntingdon Street for home to Dewsbury about teatime. Kath and I kept in touch for a while, but never managed to meet up again.

At the climbing classes, I struck up a friendship with two blokes: Bob Wark, who was 16, and Bill Ingham, in his 40s and like me in the printing trade but working at Multigraph Office Printing. Bill ran the youth club at the Methodist church on Parliament Street. In the early summer of 1964, we joined up with the youth club and did an overnight walk from the top of Winnats Pass in Derbyshire all the way down into the valley. It was great seeing the sun come up like this, something I'd never really seen. We would each put in a bit of overtime on Saturday morning and then meet up to go climbing in Derbyshire. Then in September, Bob contacted me to ask if I wanted to go climbing at weekends. He acted a lot older than 16 and we worked well together on the climbs. From September 1964 to March 1965, we hitchhiked and climbed all over Derbyshire. The plan was to hitchhike from Derby Road Island, near the University entrance, into Derbyshire on the Saturday, sleepover and climb all day Sunday. At first Bob brought his tent, so we put that up. I had a Primus stove and we cooked up the bacon we had brought for breakfast. It was great. Another trip we did was in thick fog. We found a local pub in Dovedale and had a couple of pints before dossing down in the tent, so we slept well. Next morning, we woke up as the fog cleared and looked out to see our tent resided in the middle of the well-kept lawn of the Izaak Walton Hotel, a large, 17th century country house on a hill. We sorted ourselves out and cooked our breakfast on the lawn. None of the cleaners bothered us and that set the precedent for the rest of the weekends over that period, sleeping in weird places sometimes in public view but always looked upon kindly. After our first trip out, Bob left the tent at home, and we roughed it in sleeping bags. I found that as long as you have a roof over your head you can sleep anywhere, which we did. In a kiln, a water mill, on the roadside, inside the deserted station at Tissington in December 1964, where it was so cold that we broke up chairs and lit the old stove in the waiting room. Bob was quite stocky, looking a bit like Eric Burdon from the Animals. Early one Sunday morning, Bob rolled out of his sleeping bag. 'Fancy a shower, youth?' Curious, I followed him out into the bitter cold. He pulled off his top, stripped down to his underwear and went over to the water tank for filling up the steam trains and pulled a lever. Out came a jet of freezing cold water which he splashed about in for a bit. Did I follow him? Did I hell!

Another weekend we were at the large Ambergate Station, shaped like a triangle set between two lines. We were able to sleep in the waiting room. Steam trains seem to be running past all night, so it was quite dramatic, gushing steam and flashing lights. That day we went on to Matlock Bath, to climb up the limestone there. I did not face these weekends without trepidation. I could see us, stranded and starving, half-way up a hillside in the mist, or being murdered in the middle of nowhere, but it never happened and what's more many people stopped to give us a lift. Once we were outside a church near Leek and a London style taxicab driver picked us up *en-route* to a call, took us onto Hoxton where we wanted to climb next day, no charge. On another occasion, we hadn't made good time and were stranded late at night. A farmer was just pulling into his yard and asked where we were headed. He said it was late for getting a lift, but we could sleep in his hay barn if we liked. We certainly did, what a stroke of luck, as it was a bitterly cold night. Next morning, he shouted up did we want some bacon sandwiches and a mug of tea? Ahh, what amazing good luck this was, all my fears were unfounded! I wish I had him and his wife's address, I would have definitely sent him a Christmas card.

One late Saturday afternoon we met up and Bob said, "Let's go up to Newcastle just for the kicks!".

We hitched from the traffic island at Redhill and arrived there about 9pm, covering about 160 miles in four hours, not bad for two lads with rucksacks travelling just for the fun of it. We walked through Newcastle city centre around 10pm. It was lively, lots of girls around, almost as good as Nottingham and so we indulged ourselves in the nearest pub for a couple. We had to get back for Sunday evening so didn't stay too long. We slept in the bushes on a dual carriageway and then hitched back early next day. Other times we went a few miles up the road to my neck of the woods at Bestwood Country Park and slept in the woods there overnight, but it was just as much fun, arriving at Mum and Dad's just in time for breakfast! We went all over Derbyshire and slept once in the kiln for Friden Brickworks near Buxton, where it was so hot that we had to take our anoraks off – in January! In the moors bordering Derbyshire and Staffordshire, we found an old chapel called the Roaches Chapel because it was near a rock formation of the same name, which we climbed the next morning. We did the Matlock Bath Limestone Climb and another time the Black Rocks at Cromford. That was on a really cold mid-afternoon.

If you had a good sleeping bag you could sleep out anywhere. I had chosen one just for this reason, but it was so cold that we had a fire going in a rail storage shed on a hill near the railway line that hauled trucks up. It must have been seen across the valley. Three policemen appeared without warning; they parked the car down below and walked up, taking our names and addresses for trespassing on railway property. Again, I don't know why we didn't give false names and addresses. The police seemed quite bored by the whole thing. We hadn't done any damage, but I suppose someone got a thrill on a quiet Sunday afternoon in winter by reporting us. A couple of days later, an officer from the Arnold Police Station came round and issued a polite warning to Mum, Dad and yours truly about trespassing, but even he said it was a bit of fuss over nothing, "I'm just going through the motions." Fortunately, my dad felt the same. Apparently, setting things on fire is fine as long as you are roughing it in a manly way outdoors. Parallel story to the playing truant incident four years before!

No girls came climbing, which was a great shame in my eyes as it would have made a pleasant change. We were just two lads in their mid-teens stomping about the place. It might have been seen as a risky operation to go out just the two of us to deserted fields and sheds and let just anybody pick us up when hitchhiking, but I never had a moment's doubt. People were frequently generous with their time. Quite often I would be dropped off a few minutes' walk from my own house. One night, at Ambergate again, we were struggling to get a lift at the crossroads late one Saturday night.

"Howard, keep a look out and shout if anybody's coming."

Bob went over to the closed filling station and undid the long plastic Green Shield Stamp banner and proceeded to cut it in half. I could see another visit from the constabulary looming!

"What the hell are you doing, Bob?"

"This is perfect. There you go, two ground sheets for you and me pal!"

As part of my personal 'development', during January 1965, I decided at long last to learn to swim. One Friday teatime after work I cycled round to Noel Street Baths in Basford and booked six swimming sessions. When I first walked through those doors and smelt that chlorine it brought back all those grim memories of aggressive sessions from teachers and my dad from ten years before, and I very nearly did a U turn! My coach was an ex-policeman and he was very good, no holding back, really putting me through my paces. It was embarrassing at first being in the shallow end amongst young kids swimming away and sinking with inflatable arm bands on! It was a very cold January and February and sometimes I would cycle round from work to get some practice at lunchtimes. But I cracked it and was one of the best things I could have done, giving me that extra shot of confidence. It also helped greatly with my burgeoning social life.

Bob and I usually met up at Saturday teatime, but one afternoon he said, "We could do something different tomorrow if you're up for it". I found myself on the way to Matlock Bath where we met four others, sleeping in a cave overnight ready to go potholing next day. I had never been potholing before and didn't fancy it much, but I couldn't back out now, so I hooked up. We were going down 'Thermal One' with torches only, and not the proper headlamps and boots, or any wet gear. Outside it was pouring with rain. Inside, it was dark and slippery, the damp quickly seeping into our clothes. I thought this was a poor substitute for rock climbing in the fresh air, nonetheless we managed to get down the tunnels. At first, we could almost stand up but after about half an hour it began to narrow, and we couldn't see well at all. We only had three torches for the six of us, so we decided to turn back. As we clambered along, we had passed a hole about 20 feet in circumference and about three feet deep, and we had been able to walk along a narrow ledge around it. By the time we came back it had filled up to at least eight feet with water right over the edge of the ledge. We had to use climbing techniques to navigate round it, clambering round hooked up. I was the last to go round and I slipped in. This being a thermal pool it was warm, but deep, and as I couldn't get a grip on the clay-like surrounds, which were sticky and loose due to the warmth of the water, I flailed around, half swimming. The others pulled back, shouting to each other and hauled on the ropes. Thankfully, they managed to get me out, and we emerged near to the Derbyshire town of Matlock Bath, where we trundled off to recover in The Grand Pavilion café. This is an old Edwardian music hall that still puts on gigs, a favourite haunt of bikers. We stomped in, to a table near the fire surrounded by large men and women in worn leathers and boots. I was just a Sugarfoot, wet through and muddy, determined never to go potholing again. No one bothered with us though. Steaming by the fire to dry out, we fitted right in. Derbyshire certainly became our playground for six months.

Come Easter Monday 1965, everyone seemed to have something on except me. I went round to see Grandma Hilda, Dad's mum. She enjoyed a drink, a fag and a singsong, as did most of my dad's family, and upon seeing me suggested we went to the local working men's club called The Elmhurst. It was lunchtime. She was a regular there and knew just about everyone.

"Eh up Hilda, who's your boyfriend?"

"That's my George's lad, you know him, you cheeky bugger!"

Shades of *Saturday Night And Sunday Morning* here.

I knew a few people there, including Harry Leigh who ran the transport-type café on Nottingham Road in Basford that I used to call in as part of my errand boy duties as an apprentice. It was all very convivial. We had a drink and played the fruit machines together. The bells came up and we'd won two pounds! Roughly equivalent to £40 today. This was a considerable amount. We could have bought a week's shopping with it, or a good night out. We happily split it between us, had another couple of drinks, and I walked her the short journey home then hopped on my bike, wobbling home up Front Street in Arnold. Hilda could take her drink. I was absolutely plastered. Even now, drinking in the daytime is like drinking double at night for me, so I staggered off to bed for the afternoon. I had a few hours kip then tottered off to dancing lessons. Roy & Mary Knight's Dance Studios on Cranbrook Street in Nottingham held a weekly night of dancing lessons followed by a disco. With Tony and Derek, who I had met at college, and Derek's sister Pam, I was attending these regularly. We paid extra to go in early for the lessons in how to jive. By then, the jive was a bit old fashioned, but I could tell it was good experience for getting on the dance floor. I had even learnt cha-cha, waltz and quickstep at that point, tutored by Sid and Doreen Wildgust in the scout hut in Arnold, clutching various housewives around the waist to their great amusement, and I am proud to say I won bronze medals in all three in 1966. I never did learn to jive properly though.

The next day I was up early to go hitchhiking down to Uncle Arthur's. Easter Tuesday, it was pouring with rain as I set off at 5am. In April 1965, the M1 only went as far as Leicester. It was being extended to Nottingham at the time and reached there about November. At Redhill, not far from my house, I managed to get a lift to the Nottingham ring road near the University. They were still building the Clifton Bridge flyover, so I walked over the bridge to the Nottingham Knight traffic island, where I quickly got a lift to Leicester. I had never tried to hitch on my own, let alone down South, nor had I seen the motorway before. London was completely unknown to me and a bit daunting. I told the driver what I was planning as we sat having a cup of tea in a Leicester café, and he was kind enough to drop me off near to the first available junction of the motorway. After about 15 minutes walking, I arrived at the junction and was lucky again, getting a lift right away, this time to the outskirts of London on the North Circular. I was not that keen about travelling through the centre of London, which I imagined to be a huge and confusing set of roads in all directions. Eventually had another lift, this time all the way to Sussex. This driver bought me beans on toast in a transport café halfway. No funny business, he just wanted to treat me! Not dissimilar to *The Fugitive*.

"For Richard Kimble another journey begins."

But I looked more like Woody Allen, a skinny youth with geeky glasses. Michael Caine later made these kinds of glasses cool, but we hadn't arrived at that point yet. The driver dropped me off on Hastings' seafront just as I was coming out of my hangover. It was 9pm. I walked west to east along the seafront and found a community hall on the outskirts that had a well-covered porch, where I settled down. It had been good fun hitching with Bob, but I much preferred being on my own as I was getting lifts more frequently.

The next morning was one of those bright clear blue-sky days in early spring, with a slight frost still around. I had my primus stove with me and made a mug of tea. I was feeling very satisfied with myself as I walked the coast along the A259 at about 8am, and my luck held, as it was

73

not long before I had another lift, going to Dover. We went the scenic route round Romney Marsh and Dungeness. Along the way, the driver had the radio on. This was a year after the launch of Radio Caroline. I was aware that pirate radio was going on, but I hadn't thought we could get the signal in Nottingham because pirate radio at that time was all about down South. I sat looking at the pebble beaches going by and hearing tunes like *Wonderful World* by Herman's Hermits, *Nowhere to Run* by Martha and the Vandellas, *Little Things* by Dave Berry and *Stop In The Name Of Love* by The Supremes.

"This is an interesting station," I said. "What is it?"

"Ahh this is Radio London, a pirate radio ship. We have a couple of them down here."

It's hard to express how exciting pirate radio was to us then. Aside from Edmundo Ross, The Big Ben Banjo Band, Mantovani, Joe Loss and His Orchestra, you only had one pop tune every 15 minutes because the BBC had 'restricted needle time' to keep employment and fees paid to the Musician's Union. At first the pirate radio stations didn't pay needle time, and because they were exciting and new, both UK and US record companies sent over their latest releases.

The driver dropped me off in Dover about an hour later. I figured I had done enough in 24 hours, so I caught the bus to Deal. It was the first time in eight years that I had been to see Uncle Arthur, and the first time I had visited him after Auntie Tilly's death. Mum's other sisters included Aunt Jesse, who passed away with cancer in the early fifties and the formidable Auntie Gladys, who had apparently felt sorry for Arthur and invited him over to stay in the house she shared with her daughter Bonnie. Her husband had died not long before. Then Arthur invited Gladys to Deal and they "seemed to get on alright" so in their sensible, pragmatic way, a year later they were married.

I was not impressed by Auntie Gladys. My mother had very clear ideas about a woman's role, and it was to ensure the house, the man and the child were turned out immaculately, which she did while holding down a part-time job. In return, the man 'turned up his wages', keeping his pocket money for beer and oddments, the wife making nearly all of the household decisions including cleaning and organizing repair jobs when necessary. Arthur was a great believer in my mother's version of equality. He said to me once, "If I'm putting up the cash, Gladys can do everything around the house." However, Gladys thought the cash was for a little light housekeeping and the rest for her own pocket. Arthur stubbornly refused to tackle her about it or to do the work himself, after all he was working, and she was a lady of leisure. Between them they let the house run down and pile up dust. After a while, things just stopped working, the plumbing had something weird on the cistern and after the toilet was flushed you put a poker on the top to stop the water running continuously. The bathroom taps also ran water all the time. When I went back five years later it was still the same. Arthur worked hard for a living and was a kind and generous man. Gladys was big on church socials but short on charity. Talking with her was hard work – a strong case of verbal diarrhoea.

While the hill and surrounds where Arthur lived were filled with miners and ex-miners, the seashore at Deal had the fishermen and the Royal Marines Music academy near

Deal Castle. Arthur was unusual in that he preferred to go around the fishing pubs rather than the mining ones. He was made welcome there and I enjoyed every bit of it. Occasionally, at weekends, Arthur played the accordion or the mouth organ, joining up with other men who played the ukulele or tin whistles. We walked everywhere, meeting characters all around. One evening we went out to Betteshanger Social Club at the pithead. It was a Wednesday night and there weren't many customers around, about half a dozen or so. It had a bleak atmosphere and we only stayed for one. The Mill Hill Miners Welfare was a much livelier affair as were the pubs in Lower Deal, which I liked the best, as did Arthur.

Five days later, on the Sunday morning it was time to return home. I wanted to get an early start on the hitchhiking, but my heart sank when Arthur was very keen to walk the six miles with me to a main road suitable for hitchhiking. only because I knew that I wouldn't be able to get a lift until he'd started back. After about half an hour down a country lane, a man in a 1930's Austin 10 stopped and called out to Arthur. It turned out to be a man he had not seen for 20 years, who gave us a lift while they exchanged nostalgia. I felt as if we had gone back in time. Was he a ghost I wondered? He dropped us off at the main road, then Arthur shook my hand and set off briskly walking the six miles back. I admired Arthur, he was loyal and stuck to his guns, and conversation always flowed well with him. "Dog eat dog!" was one of his expressions when coming up against ego or arrogance.

Shortly after that, I had a lift to the North Circular. I didn't know London at that time and thought it would be tricky getting a lift right through it, so I walked around, luckily getting a lift north, then a man in a Ford Zephyr picked me up at the bottom of the M1 and dropped me off near Long Eaton, acquiring another lift into Nottingham city centre. By now it was about 9.00pm and it busy with lots of people out on pub crawls. That's the beauty of Nottingham city centre, it has lots of pubs and restaurants in a small area. I was too tired, so I caught the bus to Arnold.

This was the end of my first big hitchhiking alone. I had initially had some misgivings but thought, if you can get lifts with two, surely one can get a lift in half the time. I was proved right. But the first thing I did when I returned home was tune in to "Wonderful Radio London" and "Sounds Fine, It's Caroline."

This was the start of a beautiful friendship with Offshore Pirate Radio. Heady times!

3

"A little bit of me, a little bit of you"
1965 to 1968

Spring 1965 heralded the start of my personal 60s revolution. I realised that the skills I had been so keen to learn were on the way out. Photo-litho, photogravure and letterpress were soon to be replaced by technology made by Germany and Rank Xerox. Gloomily, I listened as Tony from college told me all about the new 'reprographics', and that he had a day off from his job at County Hall to go to a Trade Show at Earls Court. Finding that he planned to ride there on his scooter, I said I would go with him and share the petrol. I took a day's holiday and we set off on his Vespa GS to the outskirts of London, where he parked up at a filling station and we took the Tube to Earls Court. On the platform, I saw posters for the premier of *The Ipcress File* that week at Leicester Square. It was finally being released! Much encouraged, I spent a couple of hours at The Trade Show with Tony, and then we bunked off to go into Soho, where we visited a strip show for the rest of the afternoon. It was our first time. The club was a small place with about 30 men, much like the strip club in *Beat Girl 1960*. Several businessmen were actually doing paperwork, at least until a particular girl took an interest. I sat there in awe the whole time, as did Tony. We recovered with a few, much cheaper, drinks in the pub and returned to the filling station to pick up the Vespa. It had a flat tyre.

The filling station attendant rang a garage to pick us up. By that time, it was about 9pm as we sped along, crouched next to the Vespa on the open back of a pickup truck zooming round the flashing lights of the West End. The garage took no time at all to repair the tyre and we were off up the M1. Then we started to wobble and as Tony picked up speed, he had trouble keeping it on the road. He pulled off the road and we found that the power tool used to tighten the wheel nuts had shredded two of the six. We struggled to the next service station, which was at Watford Gap, but it was clear we were going no further. Neither of us knew what to do. We had spent most our money and were miles from home. In desperation, I asked some lorry drivers if they could give us a lift up to Nottingham complete with scooter. The first couple gave us the thumbs down but then a guy with a large 'Lyons Cake' lorry said he would do it. I can't remember whether we offered him any money, I doubt we had even enough for that, which we should have done because he did a lot for us. He said that if the scooter fell over it would spill out and stink out the interior, which could lose him his job, so he laid tarpaulin down and then proceeded to hitch the scooter up on ropes from the ribbing inside until it was held vertically. He was a great bloke and I wish I could thank him now. He stopped at Trent Bridge in Nottingham at about 1.00am and unhitched the scooter. We rolled it to an all-night garage just below The Ice Stadium. Then we walked along the deserted early morning roads to Arnold, and I went exhausted into work after only three hours' sleep.

Ever since I saw an article about it in the magazine for extras called *The Film Artistes Association*, I had been watching out for *The Ipcress File* posters. There were photographs of Michael Caine with the article and I said to myself, "Hang on a minute, heavy framed glasses, blonde hair, slim build and looks a bit like me!" The Westerns and other TV shows I had seen all had dark haired handsome chaps as the hero, muscular or rangy. The exception of course being *Sugarfoot*. With Mr Caine, I was off again, this time identifying as the anti-hero, the 'winner who comes on like a loser', as Mr Caine described both Harry Palmer as well as himself. The funny thing about it was that I already had the jacket, the knitted tie and the grey overcoat. My brown trousers were wrong, and my nose is always going to be the focus of any profile photograph, but you can't have everything!

In August, Tony, Graham and I decided to go off in the Dormobile together on another holiday: a week in Paignton, Devon. Tuned into Radio London, we rattled along, listening to The Yardbirds singing *Evil Hearted You* and The Who thumping out *Anyway Anyhow Anywhere*. We parked on the harbourside, where we saw an advertisement for a chance to learn how to waterski – two hours in the morning and two hours in the afternoon. It was quite cheap. I had only learnt to swim six months ago, but I really wanted to have a go at this. By the end of the morning session, Tony and Graham had got the hang of it, while every time I set off I went headfirst into the water. Basically, what happens is that you are sitting in three feet of water with the skis vertical and the boat goes out and pulls you into the standing position. Not me. Each time the boat went off I fell face forward and lost my grip on the handles. Tony and Graham didn't say anything. They were good lads.

I felt hot, geeky and a sweaty idiot. All through the morning I bounced in and out of the waves without picking it up at all. Then in the afternoon, for some reason, I lifted up onto my skis and mastered it, gliding around the bay as if to the manor born. That evening we sat with some beers in the Dormobile. Even now, every time I hear Tom Jones' record *With These Hands* and Billy Fury's *In Thoughts Of You* (both on Decca) my mind goes back to that glorious summer day in the water waiting to be picked up by the speedboat, knowing that I had cracked it. My rites of passage year.

In a newsagent on the Paignton harbour, I picked up a magazine about the filming of James Bond's *Thunderball*, due to be released later that year. In those days, magazines would come out about three months before the film itself. Amazingly, this one had full colour photos throughout, which I knew from the trade was laborious and expensive to make. I still have that coffee table book. *Thunderball* is my favourite Bond soundtrack, with the second *From Russia With Love*, all composed and orchestrated by John Barry. Walking past the harbour, we saw somebody with a yacht having trouble uncoupling the rope at the top of the mast. He was pulling on it and cursing. Graham was a plucky chap and said, "Oh I'll see to that." He shinned himself up right to the top of the mast and then freed the coupling. It was brave, although a bit foolhardy. The man shook his hand, and we slapped him about a bit.

Instead of burning in the sun, I was prepared with plenty of suntan lotion this time. I had the beginnings of a nice tan. On the day of departure, I thought I would put on some fake tan to enhance the effect and impress my work colleagues. There was only one kind in those days,

Kwik Tan which I bought from the chemist and smeared all over my face and arms. Within an hour I had turned orange and was being pointed at by children in cars as they passed the Dormobile on the journey home. The lads said nothing all the way through our four-hour journey. At work the next morning my colleagues were much amused by my appearance, and I went out on errands glowing like a *Ready Brek* advert.

I was starting to think that I wasn't going to settle down in the printing trade. We apprentices were used as labouring errand boys and not much else. Every morning at 8.30am I would go round 25 staff to get a list of what they wanted from the shops: newspapers, cigarettes and sandwiches, then I had to get everything and bring it back in time for the tea break at 9.45am. By 11.30am I would be getting orders, chips or whatever, for the lunchbreak at 12.30 until 1pm, then another afternoon shop about 3pm. In between my errand duties, we were still being given labouring work, such as mixing chemicals.

What made it worse was that a certain Johnny Hill finished his apprenticeship and came down from the Sutton-in-Ashfield branch to start with us as a fully-fledged journeyman. A Jack The Lad psychopath (in the films he would be played by Dennis Hopper as Frank Booth in *Blue Velvet* or Billy The Kid in *Sugarfoot's* Brannigans Boots). Right from the start, he threw his weight around with a constant barrage of sneering and barking at the apprentices. He threatened to "take me outside" and sort me out a couple of times but it luckily came to nothing because if it had, I would've been transferred. Hill had a radar for when to pick on the apprentices. Every day after we went to college there was always a bad atmosphere waiting for us, and whenever that happened you could be sure that Johnny Hill would be showing his aggression. We had a trade union representative on site. He saw it all happening, but we weren't important enough for him to do anything about it. After a while I strongly suspected that he was in cahoots with management who simply wanted to get me transferred to another firm if I had a go at John Hill. Or he was too scared. I finally started to switch off when I realised how much more training the other students were being given by their companies, compared to Tony and me. They put their studying into practice and really learned the trade.

Going into town for a Friday night out, I was on the same bus as two mates from Redhill School: John Emberton and Brian Marsh. We arranged to meet up the next night, and many nights thereafter that following year. At this time, I had the Harry Palmer specs and smoked Gauloises just like Harry Palmer. Brian and John smoked Park Drive and thought Gauloise weren't any good. I could only smoke them with a beer as they were really dry, and after a month decided they were in fact weird and went on to Embassy for the vouchers, or Players, because they were made locally. We would start the evening in the Lord Nelson pub in Hockley, just off Nottingham city centre. A bit of a clique gathered around us after a while and we were often able to get a lock-in after hours. (In those days, the pubs used to close at 10.30pm.) From there, John and Brian would take me to the Mecca Palais. Going around with those two was like going back to that pre-Beatle era of Elvis, Adam Faith, and Billy Fury. They were always smartly dressed but not quite the Mod style. However, they used to pull the girls regularly, while I, booted and suited in my Mod threads, was just an extra in their show. If I was not with John and Brian, I would be going on to the local Mod clubs, The Boat, Britannia and Union, tiny venues all in a row along the bank of the river Trent, where new groups like John Mayalls Bluesbreakers, The Alan Bown Set, Wayne Fontana, Led Zeppelin and Fleetwood Mac and many other soon-to-be-famous bands played.

The year of 1966 was a crucial one at college, because it was the summer of the City & Guilds Intermediate examinations, which would be a milestone in our apprenticeship. I decided to pass just to annoy the firm. I don't learn things easily so for six months, hour after hour, week in, week out, I memorised facts by repetition until it clicked. Two weeks after the exams, Arthur Walters, the boss, came up to me with my certificate. He slapped it on the desk in front of me and said, "You passed then, well done lad." Not much of a fanfare, but Johnny Hill was glowering at me in the corner, so that was alright. My mate Tony didn't pass unfortunately, but he said he didn't care. As it turned out, we then started to receive more production work. Better late than never.

I had a couple of other good memories from 1966. Ken Murray from school days and Alison, a mutual friend, came up with the idea of driving down to Italy in Ken's mini to meet up with their youth club on holiday at the seaside resort of Cattolica, in the northeast. We only had twelve days from 27th July to 7th August, so it meant travelling overnight, and poor Ken was the only driver. We arrived at Dover in the late afternoon and were driving along the prom alongside the harbour, when I saw my mum and dad! I couldn't believe it. I knew they were on holiday in Deal ten miles away, but I never expected to bump into them. We chatted briefly and then headed off for the ferry. It was a good omen. We arrived at Dunkirk after a very choppy crossing and hit the road. I tuned the radio to the very powerful Swinging Radio England. It was FAB. Very American in concept with all these marvellous tunes being pumped out, many that I'd not heard before. Plus, they made a point of showcasing tracks from the latest Beatles LP *Revolver* and The Beach Boys *Pet Sounds*. Even today 56 years later whenever I hear *Eleanor Rigby* and *God Only Knows* I'm transported back to that holiday. It certainly helped to keep Ken awake driving through the night. Going down through Belgium, into Germany we entered Austria where we stayed in a cute farmhouse in the mountains overnight. The farmer and his wife entertained us all evening and plied us with lots of the local beers. Somehow, we managed to get over the language barrier with gestures and drawings. The next day, entering Italy, we lost the signal for the radio. Not bad though, eh? By late afternoon we started to notice a lot of Italian cars giving us some rude gestures. I thought that as we looked so English with the number plates and right-hand drive, they'd taken against us for some reason. It was only when we called into a filling station that the man behind the counter beamed at us and shook my hand vigorously.

"Bravo, ben fatto. Inghilterra aveva battuto la Germania quattro gol a due, complimenti!"

Howard, Lake Como in July 1966

Customers came over to us and patted us on the back, full of smiles. Finally, we clicked. Those gestures were telling us the score. England had won the 1966 World Cup. Because of all that had been happening we had forgotten about it! This was my first visit to Italy, my first joining in with Ken's Sutton-In-Ashfield youth club, my first time going on a package holiday. It was OK, going up into the mountains with a chicken in a basket dinner and dance buffet musical extravaganza! I enjoyed meeting the Italians during the course of that week, they made us very welcome. There was some beach activity, but our hosts supplied us with a large umbrella, so no painful sun burn to deal with. As I wasn't a member of the youth club, I found it difficult to get to know people and join in the group activities, and there was a certain amount of relief when we set off back home through Europe. Anyway, I was really looking forward to travelling towards England to hear all that marvellous music from Swinging Radio England again. One of our stopping off points was a traditional guest house in the beautiful Black Forest. As we booked in, I noticed *The Fugitive* had just started in the lounge, albeit in German, but that didn't bother me. That was my next hour spoken for.

Back in Nottingham, on Wednesday day release to college, I got chatting to Sharon at the bus-stop and she invited me to lunch. She had a fistful of luncheon vouchers from her office job. Off we went to an up-market restaurant on Mansfield Road. It made a change from the El Toreador Café, opposite the college or the Trocadero on Trinity Square. She was brunette, quite tall, about 5 foot 11 inches and very leggy; she should have been a model. She was a real Mod and dressed well. Even now, I can remember the bright green mini skirt with matching jacket ensemble. Along with the policeman's helmet on the table in the hall at her home. Turns out her dad was also very tall, although much more burly, especially in his policeman's uniform. It didn't put me off, in fact it gave her a certain extra something, and we started to see each other regularly. That is, until she was given a ticking-off at work because of using so many luncheon vouchers. Luckily, she kept her job, but she didn't want to see me anymore. I never had the chance to reciprocate, which I wanted to – honest! I was rather hoping she might end up with her own police uniform.

Shortly after passing my City and Guilds Intermediate, I started knocking about with Paul Hughes, a chum from college who strongly resembled Dave Clark of The Five, and we started to go and see bands at various venues. The Small Faces, at The Beachcomber on 17th July. Dave, Dee,

Dozy, Beaky, Mitch and Titch on the 27th, The Hollies on 17th August, The Who on the 23rd August. I had a great buzz from seeing them smash up their instruments! In 1966, we also saw The Ivy League and The Fortunes at The Dancing Slipper in West Bridgford. So many gigs, I don't know how I managed to fit in the studying...

We were also hooked on Hammer and Universal horror films, which in the mid-sixties were constantly reissued. It would be the norm to meet up after work and go to a cinema, quite often in the sticks, and get the double bill 6pm performance, and if the film didn't show that much promise, leave and go to the pub. The late buses picked me up at midnight on Huntington Street or at 12.45am. I got to know the conductor Hedley quite well; he was a friend of Mum and Dad and used to ring the bell to slow down the bus so I could hop off outside my own house.

In February 1967, I asked the tutor if I could take a couple of hours off for my driving test. I didn't want my workmates at the Ashfield Litho to know I was taking it in case I failed and got more gloating from Psycho Hill. Ironically the test centre was round the corner only five minutes' walk away from my workplace! Luckily no workmates saw me. I managed to pass, and what a huge relief that was as it meant I was gaining even more independence.

March 1967 brought a reprise of my Elstree scenario. I had read that the third Harry Palmer thriller *Billion Dollar Brain* was being filmed at Pinewood. I took a day off work to see if I could watch the filming. I took the train down to St Pancras and then by underground to Iver, followed by a three mile walk down what was then a pleasant country road. However, the security man on the gate, while kind, said that without a prior arrangement with someone involved on the film he couldn't let me in. I hung around for ten minutes looking hopeful but to no avail. Funny the things you remember. The Monkees *A Little Bit Of Me, A Little Bit Of You* was playing on the security man's transistor radio. Whenever I hear that Monkees song, I think of Pinewood Studios.

For my 21st birthday in May 1967, workmates Dick, Pete and Tony bought me an expensive Mod narrow leather tie. It was a FAB tie and I wish I hadn't thrown it away when they became unfashionable in the 70s. My new leather tie proudly displayed, we went off to the Mecca Palais, then caught the 1.00am night bus back home, which saved paying out for a taxi.

About this time, I saw Antonioni's film *Blow Up* and it knocked me out. It really did manage to capture the spirit and excitement of 'Swinging London'. A very subtle and clever film with a largely jazz soundtrack, and *Stroll On,* the only rock tune from The Yardbirds. I wanted to be there and part of it, but unfortunately, I was in the wrong place at the wrong time.

The Summer of Love started with The Monterey Pop Festival on 16th-18th June 1967. It was organised by John Phillips of The Mamas And Papas and Lou Adler the well-known record producer. It attracted 80,000 people. Apart from Ravi Shankar, who I always thought was out of place, all the artists played for free with the profits going to charity. Out of it came the hits *If You're Going To San Francisco,* written by John Phillips and *Let's Go To San Francisco,* by The Flowerpot Men, which included session musicians John Carter and Ken Lewis from the UK, originally of the

Ivy League. I didn't see the full film until the early 80s, showing the most amiable, incredible rapport from the audience, good vibes and bonding from both artists and the crowd, unlike the long-drawn-out tracks and indulgent music of *Woodstock* two years later.

Tony and I finished our indentured apprenticeship in June 1967. It was traditional for every member of the 26-strong staff to bang on something loudly when this was announced. Total silence for us. I grinned at them all. I had plans.

At the end of June, I'd planned to hitchhike up to the Lake District for a week's holiday with Steve, John's brother and his school mate John Whalley. They were both sixteen and hadn't hitchhiked before. Steve's dad Fred said he'd take us to the M1 motorway to give us a start. When we got there, he said, "Tell you what lads, I've got nowt on today, I'll drop you off at the top end of the motorway for the Lake District." Fred was a star and no mistake. He was a miner at Calverton Colliery and was very much in the uncle Arthur down to earth mode – forgive the pun! This saved us a quite a few hours. When we got there, he said, "Well, I may as well finish the job off proper, I'll tek you to the camp site." Fred Emberton, Superstar! Hitching back a week later on my own was an unusual experience and no mistake. I arrived on the outskirts of Liverpool late on Friday night somewhere near the docks. I decided to sleep under a large bush and resume hitching by dawn's early light. After about two hours it started to rain, so I thought I may as well carry on hitching under the bridge nearby. After half an hour a big lorry stopped and said he could drop me off somewhere near Huddersfield at a steel foundry. That was a great help.

When we arrived as I was getting out of the cab. he said, "One of our lads will be at the yard taking a load down to Nottingham in about three hours' time. If you want to hang about in that timekeeper's shed over there, I'll get him to pick you up if you like?"

Would I like?

"Yes please, and thanks a lot. That's good of you both and I really appreciate it. Cheers."

It was all a bit surreal. This was a huge foundry with lots of lights, noise, steam and smoke.

I laid out my sleeping bag in the timekeeper's shed and set my alarm for two and a half hours. I didn't want to risk missing him. Sure enough, about half an hour after the alarm went off another large lorry turned up.

"Eyup youth, are yo Howard?"

"Certainly am sir, and very pleased to meet you."

Looking back, it was a bit risky for these two drivers wasn't it? Picking a strange youth in the dead of night. If anyone had seen this going on they may well have been in trouble. I'd been lucky on the road again, and arriving on the outskirts of Nottingham I went for a coffee and waited for the record shop to open so I could buy The Who's double A side single *The Last Time* and *Under My Thumb* as a tribute to the Rolling Stones drug bust. I still have it.

July 1967 brought about *All You Need Is Love* by The Beatles. The end result was phenomenal. You could say that this was a love anthem tribute to the hippy philosophy and, it was Britain's contribution to *Our World,* the first live global television link which the band performed at the EMI

Studios on 25th July via satellite, also featuring The Rolling Stones, The Who, and The Small Faces, Eric Clapton, Graham Nash, Marianne Faithfull and others. It was seen by an audience of 400 million in 25 countries following the release of the *Sgt. Pepper* LP. The single topped the charts in the UK, USA, and 14 other countries and many others in the top ten. Pirate Radio of course fully endorsed the single and *Sgt. Pepper*.

Also in July 1967 I handed in my month's notice. I'd finished my apprenticeship, so there was no question of having to pay back the indenture. So, on the day the pirates died I was still working at the printers. At its height, pirate radio had ten stations broadcasting round the British Isles. Tony Benn had decided that pirate radio was not suitable for Britain, and he therefore brought in the Marine Offences Act to close them down. Effective from 14th August 1967, broadcasting from a pirate radio station out on the ocean became illegal. Most of them were broadcasting from the North Sea. I chose Radio London's closedown, because it was the one I had listened to the most for two and a half years. Finishing at 3pm, it was a professional and moving farewell, with DJs and recording stars paying their last respects to Radio London – Big L. December 1964 to August 1967. The final record played over the airways was The Beatles *A Day In The Life* (which the BBC had banned for the scandalous line 'I'd love to turn you on'). I saw it on the news: thousands of fans greeted the DJs at Liverpool Street Station that evening, bringing it to a standstill.

Meanwhile, on TV, fifteen days later, after four years of The Fugitive, the final episode *The Judgement* brought the cult series to a close. William Conrad (Cannon) a Warner

Brothers contract player, spoke the last words: "Tuesday August 29th – the day the running stopped." Though for me, the running was about to start. Following up on an advert in the Evening Post, I had met up with two lads from Aspley near Nottingham who needed a third to help share petrol costs with their trip to Morocco so that was a great start. I had been buying *Showtime* and *ABC Film Review* magazines at the cinema for five years, along with *Photoplay*, and *Films and Filming* from my local newsagent. I asked Mr Swindell who ran it if he could save the latter for me while I was away. He was a great bloke; we had always got on well. He trusted me and didn't even ask for a deposit.

I had just one more thing to complete before setting off. I rang the SLADE Union branch secretary to tell him to cancel my membership.

"Are you sure Howard, we can always put you on an associate membership in case you should change your mind when you get back?"

"Well, I appreciate the offer, but I don't think I will be returning. Thanks anyway and goodbye."

Within a week of finishing at the Ashfield Photo Litho, on 5th September 1967, I was on my way down the M1 on the road to Morocco. The lads had a Ford Zephyr which we'd chipped in to get serviced, and off we went. At Dover, we discovered you had to have clip-on deflector lenses on the headlights, to make the beam suitable for continental driving. We slept in the car park at the AA offices until they opened so we could buy them. A fine start and I began to get a foreboding! We had each contributed £10 for a £30 service, roughly equivalent to £450 today, and that should have meant a damn good going over of the vehicle. However, just outside of Evreux, near Paris, the engine went 'clunk' and stopped. We all had a look but had no idea what was wrong. We were stranded in the middle of nowhere, on a very busy road in the midday sun with no air-con in the car. I volunteered to find help and walked along until I found a farmhouse a few miles away, where my pigeon-French met their smidgeon of English, and they rang for a pick-up truck. I *merci'd* my way out of the door, very grateful, and then had to walk back in the heat. Two hours later, the recovery truck arrived and took us to an AA registered garage at Evreux. We hauled out our belongings and set up a tent on a nearby camp site, then staggered round to the nearest bar for a few beers and some cracking mutton pieces char-grilled on a skewer. After two days waiting for the verdict, we were told the half-shaft had jammed up in the differential thus seizing up the back end. How the UK garage service had missed that, or if there had been a service at all, I don't know. It was too expensive to repair on the spot and they decided to have the AA tow it back to the UK.

On Sunday 10th September, we broke camp. We had decided to split up and finish it all by meeting up at Portbou just over the border in Northeast Spain, 50 miles from Gerona and 15 miles from the French border. The other two hitchhiked on together, which was a relief to me because I blamed them for the evident lack of service on the car. Looking back, I suppose what I should have done was call it a day with them and carried on through Spain alone, but I felt I needed a break for a few days while I made a decision whether to go back to England or carry on regardless. I walked to the main road and stood there for three hours waiting for a lift. I had my sleeping bag rolled up in a groundsheet and carried my suitcase with a duffel bag over the other shoulder with my cooking equipment, this was how I was to travel. While I was still thumbing, a wedding party turned up at the large house opposite. That could have been me and Sharon if I'd stayed in the safety and security of the printing and advertising trade. I confess I started to feel pangs of regret.

This was starting to play out like a real-life episode of *The Fugitive*. Then a lift turned up and I forgot all about the wedding. They took me about 80 miles to a small town in rural France, don't ask me where but there was a café, and I had my only food of the day.

Me, pointing, "Jambon?" (A ham baguette.)

"Oui. Café? Grand?"

"Oui. Merci."

I felt very continental and wholly pleased with myself. Afterwards, I found a derelict building where I dossed down in the sleeping bag. I was hoping to get to the border with Spain by the end of the next day, but the lifts were sluggish, and it took until late afternoon for a chap in a Citroen 2CV to pick me up. I was incredibly relieved that after a poor start the trip was taking off. After about an hour he put his hand on my knee and started rubbing upwards. I was a bit over the top in my language and made him pull over, nearly making a huge mistake by jumping out because my suitcase and bag were in the boot; he could have easily driven off and that would have put an end to my career as an adventurer. I whipped around the back, opened the boot myself and pulled them out.

As I watched him drive off, it started to pour with rain, and I realised I was in the middle of nowhere next to a forest. I decided that this was enough for one day and bedded down in the trees, but the rain was so bad I had to move. I could see the lights of another road through the trees and stumbled through the forest for what seemed like ages. My coat was drenched and hung against my skin giving me the shivers. Nothing to do with the darkened trees and noises off, or things moving about which I was not going to investigate. I came out of the forest to see that it was not a road but a small hamlet. I spread out my sleeping bag in somebody's porch and was out like a light. I had about five hours sleep, then dawn came up, so I thought I'd better move. I walked back through the woods onto the main road. This time I was luckier and within an hour I managed to get a lift in a van into the next town, with a chap who was taking his farm produce to market: carrots, lettuce and what smelt like onions and garlic. I found that people on the continent were very kind to me. Maybe the geeky glasses and innocent abroad look helped, even though I didn't actually feel I was either.

I discovered that there was always a café which opens at dawn, full of men taking a coffee and a glass of cognac. One appeared before me now. I had my jambon and large coffee again, which worked wonders on me, and tried to figure out where I was. My French was non-existent. I didn't know what town it was I breakfasted in. I knew I had to find a suitable area for a car to pull into, so I walked through the town until I found a lay-by on the road. After half an hour, a maroon Renault Dauphine picked me up. The driver spotted I was English and told me in my own language that he was a teacher on his way to start a new job. He quite happily chatted away, telling me we were on the road to Chartres, and treated me to yet another, very welcome, jambon. I had eaten so little in the past thirty-six hours I was getting a bit pessimistic again. However, it was very pleasant to chat with him about what he was doing and where I was going, as we passed plenty of cafés down long leafy roads and small towns. He dropped me off and I quickly picked up a lift with a woman and her ten-year old twins on their way to visit their father in hospital. They all spoke reasonable English and we did another 50 miles until she dropped me off in Chartres. From there, after only a 15-minute wait, I had a lift in a lorry to Limoges, about 150 miles away. This was good going, but I had nothing further to eat and was quite a skinny lad to start with, so it felt like my ribs were digging into me as I sat there. At Limoges, I found an empty barn on the outskirts of a farm and spent the night there.

Standing on the road the following day, I had a marvellous lift all the way to near the Spanish border at Perpignan in a cattle lorry. I was so hungry it was painful, but the driver was keen to try out his English, so it was only polite to chat, and it took my mind off the pain in my belly. From then on, to keep going, I had a Jambon and a large coffee at the end of every day when the light started to fade. In the café, I would keep a letter diary to Mum and Dad of the day's events and read for a short time before going out and looking for somewhere to sleep.

The next day, I had an excellent lift from three French lads who were absolutely FAB: very into pop music and film. They spoke a little English, but I only had to say "The

Who" and they were off, chatting all the way. It was a great lift, and they took me right to the border with Spain, at a seaside resort called Cebère, where they also treated me to a snack, and we wandered around the resort as if we were lads on holiday together. After the week I'd had, it really cheered me up and I was very sorry to be saying au revoir. I was also a bit concerned about customs at the French/Spanish border, because Spain was still under the dictatorship of General Franco then, but the customs officer stamped my passport with the same sullen manner as they did the French lads, so that was alright. The Spanish authorities never gave me any trouble and on the contrary were most helpful. I had another night sleeping in some woods, these ones near the sea where, it being calm and dry, I could hear the waves as I drifted off. It was the end of a great day.

Next day, I walked a couple of miles to Portbou, arriving at the small port and easily found my two travelling companions, but it was with mixed feelings. Looking at the map now, I can see we had only travelled 377 miles before that Ford Zephyr had broken down completely. A completely worthless AA service then, if in fact they had it done at all. After a few days, they said that they were going to go back to the UK. I had thought about returning home myself, and what my mates and my parents would say about that. I had my hitchhiking legs on now, although I would a need a job if I was going to stay on. I hit upon Gibraltar, an English outpost on the edge of Spain. In those days the UK military forces were still there, so it seemed like a good bet and I settled upon it. In March 1967 Gibraltar held a referendum on The Rock and voted unanimously in favour of staying British. 12,138 in favour, 144 against.

The boys and I decided to have a few days' holiday before going our separate ways. It was pleasant enough, the odd party and there were disco bars, but I began to think that I could easily have done all this in Nottingham!

Then, on the penultimate day, we took a trip to Rosas for a flamenco night, 26 miles away. On the bus, I met two English girls on holiday with their aunt and uncle. When I told them I was leaving, they said I could stay with them and catch the dawn bus to Figueras, then hitchhike to Gibraltar from there, thus saving me a lot of time. Warmed by their interest, I took on quite a lot of white wine and settled down to the flamenco show. It was put on for the tourists, but I was blown away. I had never seen it live, just that clever scene from *A Shot In The Dark* with Peter Sellers. The dancing area was in the round on a raised area the size of a boxing ring. For the next hour I watched the best dancing and footwork I had ever seen. A drum solo with feet if you like, and I was gone on drink, well and truly immersed, thinking also of the Jack Parnell drum solo I'd seen at the Blackpool Tower eleven years before that had the same vibe. Both the man and the woman sang, I had no idea what about, but I was totally absorbed. My love affair with Spain had begun.

The next evening I met the girls for a few jars at an outside disco and took myself off to their apartment. They had four bunk beds in their bedroom, so I took one. Neither of them showed any interest in me other than hearing about my adventures and I was just grateful for a good night's sleep. As I was getting up in the early hours, I slept in my clothes. We were all fast asleep, when their uncle popped in to see if they had got back safely. It was immediately apparent that he had not known of the girls' kind offer. It really hit the fan when he saw me lying in the bunk bed and he demanded loudly I leave the premises. I protested that my intentions were honourable, but he was having none of it. He loomed over me in the bunk telling me to get my bags and be off, which I did. I wandered down the harbour and luckily spotted a deserted fishing boat, so that was me sorted. As my Ol' Pappy used to say, "As long as you've a roof over your head, you can sleep anywhere."

The following day, I was up early and caught the first bus to Figueras, 21 miles away. As I looked over the other passengers, I was transfixed by a Spanish woman in her mid-twenties, who looked exactly like Lauren Bacall, as she was in *The Big Sleep* and *Key Largo*. I was too reserved to try out the few words I knew. However, 1 saw her presence as a good omen, a touch of class sent by the spirit of Jack L Warner. I felt as if a huge cloud had lifted. I planned to hitch from Figueras towards Gerona, then Barcelona, and then down the coastline to Gibraltar. I had a couple of good lifts from amiable Spanish blokes, and arrived at the Southern limits of Gerona. I spent the night sleeping in a large drainage pipe on a building site. I knew that an early start would get me more lifts, so I had an alarm clock with me, plus a Boots battery shaver for a smart appearance!

Next morning, I had a couple more lifts from taciturn Spanish men – "No habla Inglese" – who nonetheless set me down in good spots and I ended up on the outskirts of Barcelona. It was not the hive of activity it is now, and to me looked like a sombre place as I walked through town. Late afternoon, I came across the train station. It was sweltering and dusty from the grit that made up the pavements, so I chickened out and decided to get a train to Gibraltar. At the counter, I verbalised "Un billet a Gibraltar por favor," which they understood and gave me the right ticket from the morass of different choices of times and 'status'.

We set off through the countryside of Northeast Spain. Hot air came in through the windows and it was so warm that I drank straight from the tap in the toilets. Very risky. I was really tired and fell into a deep sleep. Each time I awoke, there was someone different sitting opposite me, similar to that sequence in Hitchcock's *The Lady Vanishes*. Suddenly I was woken by somebody touching my groin. When I looked up, it was an attractive Spanish woman, resting her foot on the seat between my legs for balance while she breastfed her baby, looking at me with a twinkle in her eye. "Viva Espana!"

At roughly 30 miles from La Linea, on the border with Gibraltar, we had to change trains, and to my delight this was a smaller, steam train. It had wooden seats and I'm sure a cow catcher at the front! But my memory could have been playing tricks on me and I was very tired. Being aware that the Dollar Films were being shot at that time in Spain, I thought wistfully that it may have been used in one of the westerns. For me, it was a real-life adventure and from that moment I seemed to enter another world. As the only fair-haired male, I thought I might be the only Northern European around these parts and was waiting for 'Hey Blondie, badges?!', but all the others on the train were quiet and not interested in me, seemingly exhausted by the effort of dragging themselves on board at the height of the day.

When it became dark the train stopped at every station, each one bathed in a soft orange glow which highlighted the flower boxes overflowing with enormous blooms and the overwhelming strong aroma of jasmine. The women seemed to outnumber the men four to one, odds I was used to in Nottingham due to the lace and hosiery industry there! Several of the women getting on threw me glances, which I hopefully thought was due to my charisma, but it was probably because they regularly travelled that way home from work, and I was the only stranger.

When the train arrived in La Linea at 10pm, a lad offered to take me to the border, carrying my luggage on a trolley. "50 pesetas," he kept saying, in English. Ha! Joke! I knew we were only five minutes' walk away. Nowadays, I would take him on just so we could have a chat, but I was feeling cynical after the Ford Zephyr experience. Ignoring him with a smile, I walked through the Spanish customs across the barren tarmac strip of no-man's land. So, this is Gibraltar, 3 miles long by 0.75 miles wide. I was the only one walking across, well it was a Sunday night.

I thought, I could be in *The Spy Who Came In From The Cold* or *Funeral In Berlin*. This occupied me for a few minutes walking and then I looked ahead to find a Spanish looking man in an English policeman's uniform complete with tall helmet, sullenly pointing me into a building. In fact, he must have been the first Gibraltarian I had ever met. Inside stood another Gibraltarian officer chatting in Spanish to a colleague at a counter.

"Good evening. What is the purpose of your visit?" he asked unsmilingly.

Like an idiot, I announced that I was there to see what kind of job prospects Gibraltar had to offer.

He looked me up and down and asked, "How much money do you have?"

I wondered if he was looking for a tip.

"Twenty pounds," I replied (which is about £300 in today's terms).

"Twenty pounds is not sufficient to enter this country" he sneered. "You must have at least thirty pounds."

I glared at him. "But I'm English," I protested in vain.

"That is irrelevant," he said, happily. "Without the requisite amount of funds at your disposal we cannot allow you to enter Gibraltar." He handed me back my passport.

I trudged back across the tarmac into Spain. On the other side the Spanish border control guards were sympathetic. Their pointing and shouting about the Gibraltarians were a balm to my wounded soul. That is just one of the reasons I support Spain when it comes to football! I love the choreography of the much-criticized Tiki-Taka style of play in recent years.

Back in La Linea, I now had to find somewhere to sleep as it was gone 11pm. Going round the back of some buildings I struck lucky at the rear of the Post Office. There were about six couples rolling around in the semi darkness. The sight of a man walking past, scruffy, with a suitcase in one hand and a sleeping bag over the shoulder, didn't put them off at all. I turned into the next corner, just a few yards from the electrified barbed wire fence with searchlights. There I unfurled my sleeping bag and went to sleep until dawn. If there were guards patrolling, they didn't notice me, or, more likely, couldn't be bothered.

The next day, Monday morning, was foggy in a way that sank into my bones. I stopped for a coffee and tostadas con tomate at the café. I had not eaten for a day and must have lost a few pounds around this time. The rest of the café were all men, each with a coffee, cognac and a Ducados cigarette or a cigarillo. The place was thick with smoke and banter. They kept your tally chalked on the bar. Men in suits mixed with guys in overalls and they chatted together. I was pondering what to do next when two English lads came in for their breakfast. I went over for a chat. They were Mark and Roy and in much the same situation, except they were waiting for the Post Office to open so that they could make a phone call to their parents asking for money to be sent out to them. No such luck in my case. Mum and Dad didn't have a phone until 1976. They invited me to crash at their hostel, so off we went, to the Post Office first of all. Inside, the first thing you saw was a gigantic picture of General Franciso Franco on the back wall. To the right and left were numbered telephone booths. Each available booth was announced by number over the tannoy. Mark was good at Spanish, so he went to the counter and sorted it out. When they came out of the booth we went to their hostel. Luckily, it was on the ground floor near the main door, so they could sneak me in to drop off my suitcase and bag. Then we wandered around La Linea for the rest of the day. It was great fun going into a record shop and getting the girls behind the counter to play us some tunes; they loved The Monkees and happily played my favourite: *I'm Not Your Stepping Stone.*

Mark and Roy told me they were from North London. I was hugely impressed when they told me they regularly went into The Elstree Way Hotel bar in Boreham Wood where all the actors went, and only two weeks before had a chat with Patrick McGoohan. I decided I needed to earn some money in order to extend my stay. Mark told me I would be paid £4.00, roughly £40.00 in today's value, for donating blood, but I had to go to Malaga to do it, some 80 miles up the coast. They gave me a doctor's name and address, so leaving my suitcase with them I hitchhiked up to Malaga along a convenient main road. There were plenty of lifts, but it took me about four hours. Once there I found 'El Medico' They did a preliminary test and told me to come back 24 hours later, mid-afternoon on the next day, without eating anything on the day of the bloodletting. Having had nothing to eat that day and was really starving, I had a cheese roll ('boca con queso') and a coffee ('grande' rather than 'grand' this time) in the nearest café.

It was a lovely warm afternoon walking around Malaga and through the Paseo Parque, it seemed as if everything was in technicolour. Sitting down on a park bench and drifting into a doze, I vaguely became aware of someone sitting at the other end of the bench and looked up. As Sean Connery said in *Goldfinger* – "I must be dreaming!" At the end of the bench was a young woman who was a vision of loveliness. She had long shiny black hair and wore a dark purple and green mini dress, revealing very long legs. She must be a model, I thought, but she was an everyday girl and she spoke to me! Mercedes and I got on very well, and luckily she spoke a little English, so with gestures and my AA Motorists Guide to Spanish we muddled through. I remember we talked about films and TV. I can clearly recall talking about James Bond, The Fugitive, The Saint, and miming the halo at the top of my head. "El Santo," I said, and she understood. We spent the next four hours together. It was a great afternoon.

Mercedes took me to Malaga's Cathedral, where I was in awe at the size of it, never having seen anything so huge and magnificent. She asked me to light a candle, and lit one herself, and told me it was to say a prayer. I followed her lead and crossed myself. As a good Baptist boy, I had never done this, but I was not about to rebel. She told me she had to get back to her village. I can't remember the name, but it was up in the hills, and she was catching the local train. Holding her hand walking along The Alameda Principal, Mercedes became increasingly nervous as we approached the station. She hung back and became distant. I guessed she didn't want to be seen with someone who didn't look like a local. In a village or small town in the 60s, the word would spread, and she might have been branded a harlot. Don't forget this was still Franco's Spain and the Guardia Civil were very powerful, challenging anyone they thought was out of line. Had an officer seen me with her the whole family could have been tainted. I know this now, but then, I was selfish. I had not only instantly fallen in love with Spain but with Mercedes as well. I was fantasising about settling down in a small Spanish town, perhaps teaching English. You could do that a lot easier in those days (six months later at a railway station in Paris, I was offered a teaching role in Holland). However, eventually her anxiety got through to me and I realised that we had to part. We shook hands and kissed politely on both cheeks, and she was gone. I immediately felt lost and alone. We had been together only four hours, but it meant a lot to me and still does.

It was early evening when I looked for somewhere to sleep. I was hungry but had to fast ready for the bloodletting the next day. I went around to the back of the train station, wandering around the goods yard, hoping for an out-building or goods wagon to shelter in. As I rounded the corner of some deserted sheds, I came face to face with an armed Guardia Civilia officer. He took hold of the rifle strapped round his shoulder and shouted at me. I promptly put my hands up. In a rush, I said, "Ingles. Auto-stop. Auto-stop!", gesturing with my thumb outstretched. He lowered his rifle and rolled his eyes. "Sal de aqui pronto!" he barked. I understood that alright and fled.

It wouldn't be the last time that looking harmless had got me out off a jam. He followed me out of the yard and watched as I walked smartly down the road back into town. The streets were thronging with mainly family and couples on a night out in the balmy air. I was starving, not at my best, and lurked around until I found a demolition site where some houses had been knocked down, probably a throw-back to the Civil War thirty years before. I unfurled my sleeping bag and was asleep in no time. I woke up with a jolt when something went over my leg. The lights from the shops nearby were still on and lit up the area nicely. To my horror, the place was a central meeting ground for hundreds of rats. It was a scene straight out of the sewer sequence in *From Russia With Love*. Gingerly, I got up, grabbed my sleeping bag and picked my way carefully through them until I got back onto the street. It was still busy, with courting couples walking hand in hand, and engaged in more amorous activity on benches, against walls, and in cafés.

I found myself at the excavations for the new canal flood basin. There was a nice spot at the contractors hut next to a wall, where I couldn't be seen but would see anyone, or anything four-legged, creeping up on me. I was exhausted and slept through until mid-morning. I walked back to the doctor's, where I donated a litre of blood. I'd not done it before, and I felt really weak when I walked out of there. No tea and biscuits either! I hit the first café I could find and had a large café con leche and a jamon bocadillo. This of course went down extremely well; it was all I'd had in nearly 24 hours. It made me feel a lot better. A service had started in a small church nearby, so I sat at the back and thanked the gods for my blessings. I figured that Mercedes had done alright by me; she had lit a candle for me at the Cathedral after all. After the service, I walked to the main road out intending to hitch to La Linea. I blacked out momentarily, so I lay down on a grass verge and dozed off. After that passed, it was two hours before a car picked me up and took me to the outskirts of Marbella bus terminus, by which time it was about 8pm. I noticed there was a bus that said 'La Linea' and thought I would see how much it was. It turned out to be very cheap, so I bought a ticket, took a seat and tried to doze off. After about three miles I suddenly came out of my stupor. Was it my imagination or was it going back the way I had come? Yes, we were, and I ended up back at the outskirts. All I wanted to do was get back to La Linea, those two lads, my luggage, and have a good night's sleep, but suddenly I was plunged into this farcical situation. I lumbered down to the driver and asked, "Vamos a La Linea, no?" He replied "Si, si," and waved a hand at me without much interest. So I stayed on the bus, and off we set again. When we reached the far side of Marbella, we started to go back to the outskirts again.

I nearly lost it. What kind of sadistic lunacy was this? I went up and asked him again, but this time said, "La Linea, Gibraltar, no?" Sudden understanding and interest came over his face. He spoke a lot of rapid Spanish that I missed most of, but with gestures made me understand that "La Linea" was the word for 'The Line' in Spanish. The central bus line that went from one end of Marbella to another, but not the 44 miles I needed to get to Gibraltar. So I got off. That was at least an hour of my time wasted. Back to hitching; at least you knew where you stood with that! I got a couple of lifts fairly quickly, arriving about 11pm. I was lucky, too, that the two lads were honest and reliable. They could easily have stolen my luggage but instead it was all there. I slept on the floor, but it didn't matter. I was out like the proverbial light.

Mark and Roy encouraged me to try Gibraltar again, this time by going round the bay to Algeciras and getting the ferry across. I dressed in my best gear as if I were a tourist. On the way across, I met two guys from the US. They were escaping the draft into the Vietnam War. We hatched a plan to put me in the middle as we went through customs, hoping I wouldn't catch the eye of the same customs officer should he be on duty. Off we went, chatting away intently. I never gave the customs officers a glance but kept eye contact with the lads, and that was it. I was through passport control without a word. I asked if I could stand them a drink and a bite to eat, but they were due to take a boat to Ceuta in Morocco that afternoon and couldn't wait. I shook hands with each of them and wished them all the best. I started humming the *Danger Man* theme from the jazzy 1960 series as it felt as if I had just lived through an episode for real! Walking under the bridge on the Gibraltarian side afterwards, I was kicking myself for not getting their addresses.

Might be a collector's item now!

In Gibraltar, I tried the British Consulate and the Labour Exchange, but neither would give me a work permit. First you found the work, then you made the application. I found a room at the Toc H, a Christian charity hostel where several travellers were staying, and they put me onto Raphael Rodrigues, a Gibraltarian who could act as my agent. Raphael was a short man, always dressed in the same suit but always immaculate. He wanted 10% of whatever I earned. I agreed. Within the day he had fixed me a job working as a receptionist in The Trafalgar Palace Hotel owned by a Mr Frances. Things were looking up. Board at the hotel was 30/- per week (about £17 today). I managed to get 10s (50p) per week for taking a Moroccan resident's seven-year-old son Adibe to school on the bus. He was a well-behaved little chap who was happy to try out a few words of English on me.

The reception work was something of a challenge. At least 50% of the callers were Spanish and the switchboard was the old peg system that you see on British B films of the 50s and 60s. I got into a few Norman Wisdom type scrapes putting the calls through to the wrong people and then not being able to understand what they were shouting at me. Fortunately, I got on very well with the manager, Mr Edge, who saved my bacon many times. (In the films he would be played by Geoffrey Keen.) We went out socially a few times. One night we were sitting in a bar and ended up talking to Taff, a sergeant in the RAF barracks at the end of the Rock near the airport runway and arranged to meet up the following night. We had a taxi from the hotel to the barracks, met his wife then went for a few jars and onto a Moroccan night club. At the cabaret there was an extremely attractive Moroccan lady, doing a superb belly dance right out of the gypsy encampment in *From Russia With Love*. It flowed well that night, intoxicatingly sensual on all fronts. Taff was outraged that the manager wouldn't let the dancer sit and chat with us after we had spent a great deal of money. She was keen, but the manager wasn't! We were escorted out by two heavies from central casting.

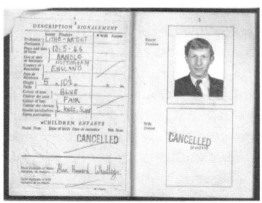

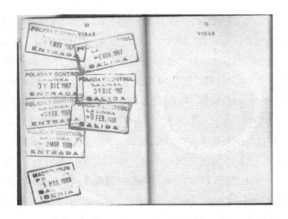

Back at The Trafalgar Palace Hotel, however, things were not going well. Mr Frances had trouble coordinating things. (In the films he would be played by Willoughby Goddard.) He organised a Sunday tea dance for 50 people with food and brought in a band to play. I was booked as a waiter, and Amina a very attractive Moroccan young woman helper organised me to dress in the bowtie, waistcoat and cummerbund that went with my hotel supplied outfit. I fancied her like mad, but she spoke very little English although she seemed to like being with me. I made her laugh. Only 20 people turned up to the tea dance. The reason? Mr Francis had not advertised it enough, beyond a poster in the hotel foyer and minimum advertising around Gibraltar. My own contribution to the cabaret was walking across the empty dance floor taking an empty tray back to the kitchen to fetch drinks, and dropping it with a clang. It rolled around on its edge several times much to the amusement of the local teenagers. At least they had a comedy turn for the evening.

We didn't have many Spanish people staying at the hotel; the workers would walk over the border to get picked up by various lorries and transported to their various building sites, then walk back over at the end of the day. The telephones were busy on reception (in those days ringing someone within Gibraltar was free), but there was not a tremendous amount of work for me. I had plenty of spare time to walk up the Rock, honeycombed with passages and dotted with gun posts, to see the view overlooking Algeciras Bay and the border with Spain. I also spent a lot of time reading books from the library or watching *Coronation Street* (four years behind), *Star Trek* and *Mission Impossible* (shown in Gibraltar before they were shown in the UK). However, my inability to master the switchboard and the language, were making it frustrating for everyone. I suppose you could say it was a lucky escape when I was dismissed. To be honest it was a relief, as sometimes when I went into the bank with the pay cheque it would bounce as there weren't enough funds in the account to pay me. The next day I would then have to return to the bank and get my dinero. But I was allowed to keep renting the room, so at least I did not have to find new digs.

Watching TV in the hotel lounge two weeks later, four locals came in of the street and changed the channel without asking. I clearly remember I was watching *Man In a Suitcase*, a UK thriller series made by ATV/ITC. I shook my head at them and changed it back. This annoyed them greatly and they all started shouting at me. Unfortunately, Mr Frances was walking through at that moment and asked what was going on. When he heard the details, he went apoplectic with rage, turned bright red, and shouted at me to empty my room and leave that evening. I sought out Mr Edge and thanked him for all his help. I didn't see him again, but I heard a few weeks later he had returned to the UK with his wife and ten-year-old daughter. Unfortunately, things hadn't worked out for him in Gib. Luckily some friends witnessed what went on and put me up in the flats round the corner for a couple of nights til I could find somewhere else.

Talking with some lads in a pub, I found out that they were looking for labourers at a block of flats being built by Taylor Woodrow down by the harbour. I was given the name of the site manager and went down to look for him. Notwithstanding my attempts at painting, varnishing and decorating they are still in business today. I went to the second-hand store and bought some hard-wearing trousers and a work shirt from the thrift shop, and started the following week, reporting to Diego, the foreman. Hawk-faced and no-nonsense, in the films he would be played by Horace McMahon from *The Naked City* TV series. I was one of only a handful of English men on site; the other 30 or so were all Spanish, coming over the border every day. It was a huge relief to find some new income. It's not likely to happen today, an unskilled labourer set on immediately at face value and at nearly twice the rate of pay as I had been paid at the hotel.

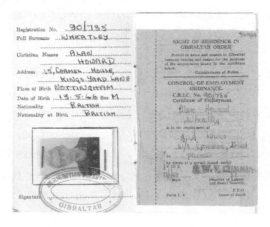

On top of that, I was now there legally. My application for a work-permit had gone through. For some reason Mr Frances had been delaying my application for the Immigration Bond Registration. This meant that if I had fallen ill or had an accident I would be on my own; with the work-permit I would be sent back to the UK. I still have the Gibraltar Registration Card with my photo on it, plus a pristine ten-shilling Gibraltarian note. Luck was with me again because Peter Yiend, a skilled painter and decorator from Hampstead who was working on the site, was looking for a flatmate. It was cheaper than the hotel room, even at staff rates.

My social life took off again. Out and about with Peter, and the flatmate Gerry, a Canadian doing maintenance work on the caves inside the Rock. I never did find the time to go inside the Rock nor around to Catalan Bay on the south side. We met up in a café up a narrow street called Smokey Joes. It was a great place, done up in a soup kitchen style with long tables and benches. The owner was a real extrovert and looked a little like a Spanish Les Dawson. We spoke a mix of Spanish and English, mostly English I am sorry to say, but we all managed to converse somehow, and the banter was brilliant. The meals were cheap and tasty, as long as you liked a fry-up. Even the baked beans had a film of grease on them.

There was another 'Smokey Joe' around at that time. This was an old steamboat that berthed near to La Linea when the wind was in the right direction. The crew would burn oily rags and waste so that the smoke would blow in the direction of Gibraltar. Just Generalissimo Franco's weird sense of humour, making sure that we knew he hadn't forgotten that Gibraltar really did belong to Spain and that we should vacate it as soon as possible. However, it was not to be. I was on an adventure again, in a secure job and making my own way without having to tip my forelock to anyone.

I entered the world of the building trade without a clue. I was left alone to get on with varnishing, so I was able to quietly make lots of mistakes until I got the hang of the job, which was much harder than I had thought. I was in close contact with the Spanish workers. They were incredibly skilled at painting and decorating; fast and very professional. For example, one had to put a heated plastic cover strip on a steel handrail all the way up the eight floors. He had to do it while the plastic was hot so it would mould around the rail. He could tell when I was watching and would finish it off with a flick of the wrist.

It was quite a macho environment, but not the caustic machismo of the printing trade. We all got on well, no English reserve here, and lots of banter but it was all amicable and anyone who did a good job was well thought of. They took a pride in their work which I fell into quite happily. I varnished the wardrobes, doors and windows in forty flats, in two separate blocks of twenty, over three months, without a hitch.

I did have the occasional good night out

I had been going to The Wesley Hall restaurant for lunch and to read the English Daily Mirror compilation that came bound in a yellow cover once a week. In the flat, I found a cupboard with a whole stack of copies of the Daily Mirror and various Sunday supplements over the previous two months while I had been 'on the road', and busy working, filling me in on all the news and showbiz I'd missed. I found one article on a film and TV director who said he planned out his shots on a storyboard. They showed you an example; it was like a comic strip cartoon. Now, that was something I could relate to. I had worked on duplicating strip cartoons in the printing trade and been trying out a few of my own ever since I was a lad. I started to get a notion that this might be something I could get into when I returned to the UK, so I went to the John Mackintosh Library and read everything I could on film and TV directors. After a few weeks I was developing an interest on the interviews with actors. In that time, I read all the thoughts and advice I could from my heroes: Humphrey Bogart, James Cagney, Errol Flynn, Spencer Tracy and Bette Davies, and my modern heroes: Sean Connery, Roger Moore, Steve McQueen, and Michael Caine.

With the build up to Christmas looming, a lot of people were going back to the UK. It was turning out to be a boring seven days. The days leading up to New Year's Eve were spent hanging around with a few guys in a similar situation to me and going on the inevitable pub crawl. 1968 came in and I was alone at The NAAFI watching loads of servicemen getting paralytic. No one said a word or said hello during the two hours I was there, hardly any girls were present, so I went back to the flat around 1.00am. Not a fantastic start to the new year!

During January 1968, we were out on the town and met a chap called Vince. While we chatted, it emerged that he was a steward on Norman Wisdom's yacht, *The Conquest.*

I asked, "Did you ever get to meet him?"

He replied, "Yes, he's often here, he's on board at the moment."

Vince was from Liverpool and great company, and in fact he looked a little bit like Norman himself. We met up with him a few more times because he was such a laugh. After a few jars he was a hoot, going into a bizarre cabaret for us, jokes, and little monologues. One night, we were in a bar full of English squaddies. He was on a balcony overlooking the pub below after going to the loo. He shouted out, "I'm not scared of nobody. I'm definitely not!" We looked around cautiously but fortunately they were all too drunk to care.

One night, he asked if we were alright for jobs, "Because Mr Wisdom is looking for a couple of deck hands."

I looked at Gerry, and we both said at the same time, "Yes! We are interested in that."

Vince said he would have a word with Mr Wisdom about an interview and we arranged to meet up again in a couple of days. Sure enough, an interview was arranged. Mum and Dad had taken me to see Norman Wisdom's first film *Trouble In Store* in 1954. That and *'What's Good For The Goose* 1968, were his best films and my favourites. He had just returned from making his first Hollywood film, *The Night They Raided Minskys*. We met Vince and went straight round to *The Conquest* berthed in the harbour. Vince showed Gerry in first while I waited. Gerry came out full of confidence that he had the job and Vince showed me in. It was clearly the lounge in Norman's own cabin, huge and full of dark shiny wood. I sat opposite him against a large coffee table. He asked what work I'd been doing so I told him I had been varnishing. His eyes lit up,

"For instance," he said. "This table here, would you be able to French polish it?"

I had no idea what French polishing was. I assumed it was a variation on the basic varnishing I had been doing on the construction site, so I said yes.

He said "Well, that's fine then, when can you start?"

I said apologetically, "I have to give two weeks' notice on the building site. I don't want to let them down."

"Not a problem," he said. "Start on Monday in two weeks' time. You can share a cabin with Gerry."

I was very excited by this, thinking to myself that on a yacht I could be travelling around the world. It was lucky that I had had a chance to learn how to do varnishing on the building site. I lacked the confidence to ask him about his life in the film business, but I had hopes that in time I would be able to approach him about this. Gerry and I turned up on the Monday two weeks later and walking up the gangplank were stopped by the captain. I cannot remember his name, so I shall call him Captain Bligh. (In the films, he would be played by Nigel Green as the arch-villain in *Deadlier Than the Male*.) He ushered us into a cabin in the bowels of the boat and told us to be upstairs in ten minutes. Appearing as directed, we were told to go to the engine room, me for painting duty and Gerry to service the mechanics. The kit was already in there. We had no foreman as such; Captain Bligh would come in from time to time to bark orders. Gerry just let it wash over him, but I was on edge every time Captain Bligh appeared. We met up with Vince for meals, which he cooked and served in the galley where all three of us ate together. There were no other staff around and we just got on with it. I worked hard and seemed to pass muster.

Norman Wisdom's yacht, *The Conquest*, 1968

Back in our cabin, I read in The Gibraltar Chronicle about *Play Dirty* being filmed in Almeria about 200 miles further up the coast, starring Michael Caine, who it said was staying at the Gran Hotel, and that Sean Connery was filming *Shalako* in the area as well. However, I felt that things were going well on the yacht and that I might have a chance to meet Norman again, so I stuck with it. A couple of weeks in, Captain Bligh's wife started coming into the engine room to inspect our work. She brought mugs of tea, but was curt, and closely inspected my painting, speaking in a way that was starting to worry me. Sure enough, a further two weeks later, Captain Bligh came into the cabin and said, "You're too slow. I can get a couple of skilled Moroccans for what you're costing me. You'll need to be gone by the end of the week."

Gerry was fine; he had the skills. Good job they never asked me to do French polishing! Anyway, the 4 weeks had been well paid, but it was a disappointment having to give up my notion of little chats with Norman about acting. On the last night, myself Vince and Gerry went out for a farewell drink, which was quite upsetting because we'd had so many good times together. They were sorry to see me leave and it was an emotional farewell.

I left Gibraltar on 3ʳᵈ March 1968. It was a lovely, bright, clear, spring morning as I took a picture of The Rock from the Spanish border. My passport was filled with ENTRADA/SALIDA stamps. I sat in a bar in La Linea. I had come to love those plain bars, always with tiles on the wall and a picture of Generalissimo Francisco Franco. They were good nights, getting blasted on the cheap, and I always got on with the Spanish, even the Guardia Civil and the Policia Municipal. For some strange reason, they took to me too, and it still applies today. I learnt my social skills in Spain and got a better sense of perspective about my background.

In La Linea I was crossing a main road while the traffic was directed by a Policia Municipal officer. I took no notice of the Spanish people lined up on each side of the road; the road was clear of traffic; I took the chance to get across. Not to be. The officer blew his whistle maniacally and summoned me over. Like a good boy I went. In front of about 40 people, he proceeded to give me a good telling off in Spanish. I thought that this was a fine start, but he was right, and I knew it. I apologised. He wished me "Tengo un bueno viaje," and off I went.

The hitching didn't go too well to start with. I was anxious to get to Almeria quickly, thus avoiding spending too much, but the lifts were few and far between. Again I spent the night in a large drainage pipe that Spain seems to have so many of. The next day dawned bright and clear, but lifts continued to be slow. Perhaps weekends in Andalucía meant staying at home. After three hours I had only travelled ten miles and I started to get that *Fugitive* feeling again. It didn't help that there was a taverna on the opposite side of the road, with families and couples hailing each other gladly as they turned up for lunch together. A bit of homesickness started to creep in. By the time the sun set, I had done about 40 miles and dusk was setting in. I was thinking about bedding down for the night when a taxi stopped. He asked me where I was going and offered to take me to Almeria for what was about £40 in today's money. This was extraordinarily cheap to travel 150 miles, but he said he was going that way anyhow. I reckon he had been sitting in the taverna earlier and knew I might still be around, but it was a great deal, so "De accuerdo" I said. I never asked why he was travelling that way, mainly because his English was as good as my Spanish, but nonetheless we managed to 'pigeon converse' over the journey. Arriving in Almeria at about 10pm, I noticed that there had been a storm and a lot of the roads were not tarmacked so it was very muddy. I asked the driver where I might find a boarding house "barato" and he sent me to a hostel off the main drag. I wanted to be smart and presentable next day, to have a hope of some extra work on either *Shalako* or *Play Dirty*.

4

"Bend me, shape me"

1968 to 1972

On my first morning in Almeria, I docked my luggage at the train station and walked to the Gran Hotel, where I waited outside for two hours hoping to catch someone who looked like crew. Noticing the Playboy club next door, I wondered idly if it would be as good as the one I'd seen in Park Lane. Two hours passed by, then a limousine drew up outside the hotel, and from it emerged Michael Caine. I was desperate by then, so I walked straight up to him.

"Excuse me, Mr Caine, could you spare a moment?"

He had what looked like a bodyguard behind him, who squinted at me, but then Michael said, "How can I help?"

"I was wondering if there was any extra work on your film?"

"No, we finished with the extra work last week. But if you go over to the Hotel Mediterraneo the *Shalako* unit are based there, they might want someone."

"Alright!" I said. "Thanks for your help!"

"Well good luck!" he said, "You should be alright. There's a shortage of fair-haired guys around here." I got a quick smile and off he went.

After that brush with my hero, I decided to go straight to the Hotel Mediterraneo. As I arrived, the crew were unloading their equipment after the day's filming. One guy was rolling up a reel of cable on the street, while others went inside, so I walked up to him and asked,

"Excuse me. Is there anyone I can talk to about getting extra work?"

"To be honest mate," he said, "it's practically finished. All we're doing now are scenes with the principles and the whole thing will be wound up by the end of the week. Sorry. You can always try the *Play Dirty* unit; they may be needing extras."

No. I'd had enough. I could be fruitlessly waiting weeks for another film to start up. I went to the train station, picked up my luggage, and boarded the 8pm to Madrid. I sat looking out of the window. There were very few people on the train, so I had a compartment to myself for eight hours. Outside, sunset fell over craggy rocks and barren lunar landscape like the end of a Western film. As we went further north it changed to oil refineries, factories and power furnaces, looking much like Nottingham. I felt like I was in a dream sequence, cut off from the world. It was like the train scenes in Bergman's *The Silence* 1963. I fell into a deep sleep for the final three hours. When we arrived at Station Chamartín in the early hours, it was snowing. I got out to a cold wind that blew right through the light clothing I had worn for Almeria. I queued up with early morning commuters and bought myself a train ticket to the border at Northwest Spain. Luckily, they spoke English at the desk. Back to reality folks. I was the first onto the train and had to wait an hour for departure, so I switched on my transistor radio and searched for a decent tune. I quite enjoyed 60s Spanish pop, so I listened to that for a while. Then I heard a psychedelic guitar. It was *You Keep Me Hanging On* by Vanilla Fudge, too long and drawn-out for me but certainly different and cheered me up no end.

At the border we left the train for our passport checks and boarded the French train to Paris at Hendaye. I decided to think positive, figuring that there could be a lot to look forward to.

Walking through Paris in the snow to the Station Gard Du Nord bound for Dunkirk, I decided not to bother hitchhiking. Time to get back to reality so what did it matter now if I spent all my money? It continued to snow, and I realised my blood had thinned out somewhat from the Spanish sun, as I was freezing cold and hungry. I'd eaten all the snacks in my bag, so I splashed out on a coffee at the train station. Three hours later I was in Dunkirk to take the Dover ferry. By this time, it was night again, a very stormy night so we had to wait for a lull in the weather before we could set off. After a couple of hours, it became clear this wasn't going to happen, so we were herded onto a bus and taken to Calais. By this point, I was absolutely worn out, the weariest I had been since September. The ferry could have taken us anywhere, I didn't care. But it did take us to Dover. I slumped on a bus to Deal and walked up the hill to Uncle Arthur's mid-morning hoping he might be in. Fortunately for me, he was, and Gladys was away at a wedding.

Arthur wanted to know everything I had been up to. I made light of the disasters and told him all about my adventures from going it alone, to Norman Wisdom, who he knew had been a resident of the Walmer area in Deal, and my decision to come home after the extra work fiasco. We talked for a while then I turned in for a couple of hours and then we went for a few jars at the nearby Yew Tree pub. Next morning, while Arthur was at work, I had enough money to see him right for staying there a few days, but nothing more, so I wrote a 1st class letter to Mum asking if I could borrow £5 to tide me over for longer, the equivalent today of about £50. Then I made a beeline for the radio and searched for a decent radio station to listen to. After an hour I gave up. Nothing! Zilch! This didn't improve my mood one iota. I tried again at night when Arthur went to bed, same result. Having lost track of all things Pirate Radio since I left the UK in early September, I assumed that there were no longer any Offshore Free Radio Broadcasts. How wrong I was. Radio Caroline continued in fits and starts right through to Sunday 3rd March when the goods supplier seized the ship along with Caroline North due to a backlog of unpaid bills for the tender company, and both ships were towed to Amsterdam. If only I had been a week or so earlier, I would have been able to catch up with Caroline and symbolically listened to its last broadcasts. Instead, I was fated to be left adrift in a sea of inane Radio One!

Mum's postal order arrived, and Arthur and I went out for three good nights which helped blow away the cobwebs. When Auntie Gladys came back, I decided I would go to Norman Wisdom's Kensington flat in London, to tell him that Captain Bligh was a bombastic idiot, and to fill him in with the details. I had a lift going to Canterbury, and from there walked across town to the M2 for London, where I gained another lift right away. A very attractive lady in her late thirties picked me up in a sports car on her way to Belgravia. We chatted amiably for about an hour while I attempted to impress her with my adventures in Spain. However, any thoughts of further adventures were soon quashed. At Victoria Station, she said, "Well, this is as far as I go. You can get across London quite easily from here to Kensington. Nice to have met you and all the best of luck for the future." I was not sure how to get across London by bus or tube, so I walked, following the signs to Kensington, found the High Street and asked around for Phillimore Court. Arriving there, I asked the uniformed security man if I could speak with Mr Wisdom. He didn't send this rather scruffy youth, without a suit, on his way but just rang through and spoke to Mr Wisdom's wife. He handed over the telephone.

I said, "I've just travelled back from Gibraltar where I worked on *The Conquest*. I would like to tell Mr Wisdom why I had to leave."

"Come up, the doorman will show you the way," she said.

The doorman took back the telephone and she spoke to him, while he stared at me. I was rehearsing my thoughts and by now was hoping Norman would give me another job. Well, I had achieved entry into the flat, and I wasn't expecting that, so why not? The doorman took me up on the lift, next to a wide staircase with light streaming down from the ornate skylight, like something out of a British film of the forties or fifties. A very stylish lady met us at the door and brought me in. She completely took my breath away, that and the fact that I was starving hungry by now. She introduced herself as Freda. (In the films she would be played by Barbara Shelley.) It appeared Mr Wisdom was at his club, so she called and asked for him, but he didn't come to the telephone, so she left a message. I thought that must be it, but then she asked if I would like something to eat while I waited, so I ended up eating a couple of poached eggs on toast, cooked by Freda Wisdom, in Norman Wisdom's spacious apartment. After about twenty minutes he rang back. I told him all about Captain Bligh. He was very polite about it, but he said ultimately, rightly or wrongly, he had to leave the decisions to the captain. He thanked me for taking the time to call in. I asked him if there was any other kind of work going that he knew about. He said no. I thanked him, thanked Freda, and left. All the while at the flat, I had been staring at a plaque on his wall, "With grateful thanks from the Rank Organisation for ten years of success and contribution to the film industry, 1953-1963."

I walked up to North London until I came to Swiss Cottage and then the M1 Motorway where I had a lift after an hour which luckily took me up to Leicester. A couple of hours and two lifts later I arrived in Arnold. We usually used the back door to enter and receive visitors, but I couldn't find my key, so I knocked on the front door for convenience. Dad opened it and his first words were, "I thought you were getting bloody well fed up!" Welcome home Howard! Clearly, 'I ain't no fortunate son'. Mum was pleased to see me though, and cooked me a huge supper. I filled in for her the gaps missing from my letters over the last six months.

Now that I was back in Nottingham, I thought I was ready for anything. Don't get the wrong idea here. I knew I wasn't going to be another Michael Caine, but I had survived going it alone and spent five months reading about actors and directors, so why not me? At school we never had any of the creative subjects: drama, contemporary music, nor art or even languages. I cycled over to Mr Swindell to pick up the *Photoplay* plus *Films And Filming* he had saved for me. He was a soul mate was Mr Swindell. We always got on really well and had many discussions about cinema over the years. I hadn't anticipated my dad's reaction though. He barely registered I was there and, when he did, he said things like "Where are you going from here then?" in a 'jokey' fashion. I suppose it was understandable. In the 60s, it was not difficult to get some kind of a job and there was me lounging about the house reading magazines and chatting about the film business and pop music to friends. He had been brought up in times when jobs were difficult to come by and had escaped the family path into mining or factory work. I had turned my back on the career he'd thought was a bit out there anyway, and now I wanted to be an actor. You know the kind of words he used for actors and those in the industry. The idea of a 'year out' and any kind of Swinging 60s vibe had not made it as far as Arnold. I was a time waster, he said. I did eventually pay back Mum all the money I'd borrowed from her but to him I was a disappointment.

I went off to the Labour Exchange. There, they decided I would be good for a job loading bags of flour for Be-Ro, a flour mill in nearby Daybrook Square. "OK," I said. Before he turned to films, J Arthur Rank, the boss of the Rank Organisation and Film Production at Pinewood Studios started off in the flour business. Well-known and respected throughout the UK, the Be-Ro name stems from 'Bells Royal Flour' and was eventually taken over by Rank Hovis McDougal. All day long I loaded big sacks of flour onto pallets, then ran the pallet on a trolley up a ramp, loading the sacks into the back of long lorries. Although I had done a fair amount of labouring work in Spain, it took me a while to build up the muscle for this job. Every morning I woke up aching all over and had to start up again. It was more like the dramatized social documentaries of the time, *Up The Junction* springs to mind – the same thing, day in, day out. Everyone knew each other and most of them knew my family. The majority of people lived within walking distance and had worked there for a long time. They were friendly enough, even though they knew I had been off to work in 'foreign parts' and thought I was an odd ball. However, it was just down the road from our house and got me fit. It also had an office where the walls were pasted in Be-Ro archive advertising posters and flyers from the past four decades. I used to volunteer to take invoices up, so I could look at the amazing photographs and classic designs.

Meanwhile, Mum had been looking out for me. She walked past the Nottingham Academy of Speech, Dance and Drama every day, on her way home from her part time job at Fords The Drapers in Nottingham and saw they were looking for students. I called up and asked for an interview to study there. On a hot day in May 1968, I took a day off to go in. I was impressed by the very attractive principal, Mavis Hoffman. We chatted about films and how I had tried to get extra work in Spain. I was excited at this point, as my mate Gordon Wood Junior had spotted that they were taking extras on D H Lawrence's *Women In Love* and had driven me to the Holiday Inn, Derby where the unit was based, to sign up. I proudly explained this to Miss Hoffman.

"You know my dear," she said, "you'll never be taken seriously as an actor if you do extra work, what you need is the training."

Miss Hoffman said she was prepared to sign me up for the new term in September.

"The other students are a little younger than you," she said, "but then you are a more fully formed character and will make up for your deficiency in dramatic experience. Classes are from 9am to 1pm Monday to Friday. Are you able to take this on board?"

Miss Hoffman was very attractive. In the films she would be played by Barbara Stanwyck. There was a picture of her on the wall in the performance area at The Academy as a gypsy, dancing in front of Oliver Reed in the 1961 film *Curse of the Werewolf.* I fantasised briefly having an affair with her for some free study time. Back in the real world, I told her I would find a night job and join up. She offered to let me come in and watch rehearsals and try some classes out for free before the new term started.

I wasn't about to ask my dad about night shifts at Raleigh. However, the Plessey Works at Beeston, a suburb in the West of Nottingham, was a huge factory that made electrical components. In the 60s, you could walk out of one job and into another, being trained up to do all kinds of unskilled work if you could stand the pace. I just swung by and asked if I could interview, told them about my interest in laser work and was made an offer. I handed in my notice to the secretary at Be-Ro and started the night shift at Plessey turning out small pieces of electrical whatnots on three different lathes. This was life imitating art again. I was Albert Finney playing Arthur Seaton in *Saturday Night And Sunday Morning.*

Come September, when I started at the Nottingham Academy of Speech, Dance & Drama, it became an exhausting schedule. I would cycle the six miles to Beeston, work my shift from 10pm to 7am, then cycle four miles to

Nottingham, drop the bike at John's father-in-law, Gordon Wood, have breakfast at a café, then study from 9am-1pm at the Academy. After a few days of this, I had a wander about the Academy building and found that there was a landing at the top of the main stairwell which no-one went up. After breakfast, I would slip up there and get an hour's kip before starting lessons. Come 1pm, I'd cycle home to Arnold and sleep about five hours until 7.30pm, have dinner and at 9pm I cycled to work. Dinner and my sandwiches were both provided by Mum. She was known all her adult life for being a very stylish dresser, well turned out and in high heels well into her late 80s. She was quite reserved herself but was the one who encouraged me to keep trying for a career in the arts, and prepared all my food and did my washing every day whenever I was at home. Later on, after Dad had died, I would visit her at least once a week, and with my cousins' help and that of my partner Diana we were able to keep her living at the home she loved for 75 years.

The Nottingham Academy was a primer for applying to the major drama schools in London. It was also my first experience of ballet, 'movement and dance', girls in leotards, and of young men my age who didn't need to work. The majority of the students' fees were paid by their parents, and they all seemed very young to me for late teens. Equally, although I was that bit older, everything seemed to be an embarrassment, including going to a theatrical supplies shop with another student (chaperoned by her mum), to acquire ballet slippers, tights and a jock strap. However, it was not really the other students' fault that I didn't have the time to make many friends there.

I was on the go from morning to night. Along with working full-time I also took up horse riding at Bestwood Country Park, thinking it would add to my skills as an actor. I also took up voice-coach lessons, having noticed that the others spoke more confidently and resonantly than I did. I asked about finding a voice coach at the shop and they gave me the number of Mr Walter Crane at Redhill, not far from Mum and Dad's house in Arnold. (In the films he would be played by Miles Malleson.)

I set up some lessons with Mr Crane, who informed me I was a 'basso profundo'. Good for singing Elvis songs, apparently. His small front room was amazing. A grand piano was surrounded by piles of sheet music with just enough room to squeeze in and out. The weird thing was my horse riding mate Richard Williams' father was also a music teacher and his front room was exactly the same. Since those days, it has become more acceptable to speak with a regional accent yourself, and for some parts, just as long as you can lose it for other roles, but in those days I had to lose my Arnold accent right away. Dropping aitches, short A's and deep U's were my bug bear. But I worked at it, listening to the posh boys and copying them. It helped that Mr Crane invited me to the choir at Cross Street Baptist Church (where I used to go for Sunday School). Singing is easier without a pronounced accent. To be fair to the other students, later on a couple of them had part-time jobs, but none worked full-time like me. It really was a profession for those who could afford it. Education has changed now, much for the better; although later on, in my DJ days, I noticed that students in the 90s and 00s nearly all had full time jobs while doing a university course.

Steven and John Emberton, with
yours truly and Robin Reliant, 1969

Once I got into my stride, my weekends were packed out meeting up with friends from Arnold. Saturday mornings after work, I would cycle home and sleep until noon, then meet at the Druids Tavern in Arnold to play Koo Kan, a card game I wasn't very good at it because I had trouble remembering what had gone before. It's a bit like Gin Rummy, but with ten cards plus an imaginary one! Back to bed for a few hours, then out for drinks around Nottingham with John, his brother, and Brian Marsh and the farming stock Jones Brothers, Alan, Arthur and Steve. I got up at 10am on Sunday for swimming, which I'd been told would help with the voice, secretly hoping I would turn the skinny muscles I had developed in Spain and Be-Ro into muscles like early Sean Connery! It never quite worked out that way, but it was good for my breathing, which helped at the voice classes. Then on to Basford Miners Welfare to be entertained for two hours by a pop group, bingo and two strippers. There was one particularly attractive stripper, called Gypsy Rose on stage, who went by the name Rose. In the films she would be played by Susanna Hoffs of The Bangles. She always gave marvellous performances to some unusual music. On one occasion she finished her act with a cracking jazz/soul instrumental. I was keen to find out what it was called and went backstage and asked to see her. She came out with a dressing gown on and was understandably a bit suspicious about what I was after. I asked her what the last tune was called. She brightened up straight away.

"It was *Music For Gong Gong* by Osibisa. I'm glad you like it," she said. "I'll write it down for you, it's one of my favourites."

"Well, it certainly puts your act in a different league," I said. "I fancy buying that for myself."

Which I did. Every time Rose saw me in the audience from then on, Osibisa's *Music for Gong Gong* was played. In the 90s and Millennium I played it in DJ sets regularly around Nottingham and London, and it never went by without me thinking of Rose.

Basford Miners Welfare was a great place to go in the 70s. The nameless resident trio played standards and bluesy numbers. Kenny Ross the compere had a deep rasping voice and every Sunday he would sing *Good morning world it's a brand new day, I'm packing my bags and I'm going away!* by Elton John. Then we had a stripper, a pop group that played really good covers of the top ten, and another, different, stripper to finish off, all for 25p, the equivalent today of about three pounds. Sluicing back three bottles of cold Newcastle Brown made it all feel nicely alternative and great fun. Occasionally there were hen nights for the ladies. Mum and John's wife Margaret used to go.

After the Miners Welfare it was horse riding through the woods at Bestwood, then round to Mum and Dad's for tea, followed by voice training at Mr Cranes. By the evening, I was out with mates at either The Cherry Tree in Calverton, a mining village or The Maid Marion pub in Arnold, which sometimes had a band on. I felt like life was grand again.

However, at the Plessey factory I sometimes fell asleep at the lathe and the foreman would have to come over and reset it because I had crunched up the drill. More Norman Wisdom than Arthur Seaton. I was paying my bills, including giving Mum a third of my wages, but I was tired out and was not really giving the Academy as much attention as I should. Then I had a stroke of luck. John's father-in-law, Gordon Wood helped me out again. (In the films he would be played by Sam Kydd.) He worked night shifts at the Nottingham City Council maintenance garage at Eastcroft Depot on London Road and told me they had a vacancy. An interview was arranged at 10am the following Saturday. It lasted just 15 minutes.

I remember two managers from the day shift, Tom Schoolar and Doug Galley, saying, "You know lad, it gets a bit rough down here at times, especially in winter and you'll be working outside, cleaning vehicles, the whole council fleet in fact."

I replied: "Well, I've roughed it before. Worked on a building site in Gibraltar and had to sleep rough hitchhiking and travelling back."

Doug said, "Well that's alright then. When can you start?"

I gave two weeks' notice at Plessey and that was it. A huge relief, because it meant that I wouldn't have to cycle to and from Beeston, and I was still on a night shift, Monday night until Saturday morning, plus it was much better money. Gordon Wood and the Eastcroft Garage team turned out to be my saviours. I couldn't have continued at the Academy without that job. On the first week, I cycled into Nottingham, and then walked with Gordon over to London Road. Eastcroft Depot was an amazing place. Old Victorian buildings were set like a village on cobbled streets in a dip just off the main road on the east side of Nottingham. I only planned to stay there for three years until I finished drama school, but I felt at home immediately.

Gordon was a mechanic. He took me round the garage and introduced me to Baldy, who looked the spitting image of the Northern character actor Bert Palmer. They showed me how to use the equipment to clean and carry out simple maintenance on the vehicles if necessary and then left me to it. I had a set amount to get through and eventually became my own boss. That first night, I joined Baldy and Gordon to 'have me snap/grub' with them in the room where spare tyres were kept. Having tea and sandwiches in there, I realised that there were stairs to another small room which no-one went up to. In time, I would work non-stop until 2am to complete all my work, grab a bite to eat in the tyre room, then get my head down for three hours upstairs. A very comfortable easy chair had been pulled out of the refuse vans and taken up there. With the lights off it was dark and fairly quiet. This was where I was able to get my naps in thus charging my batteries! Magic!

The American Forces Radio Station signal was really strong at night, so I was able to keep up with the music scene, and often heard top tunes before the records were released in the UK. I became a great fan of DJs Bob Kingsley and Wolfman Jack, years before the latter made that charismatic appearance in the film *American Graffiti*.

I was 22 years old. All the other blokes on the night shift were in their mid to late fifties and had been on active service during the war. They wore flat caps with a collar and tie to work, and each of them had a metal 'snap tin' for food. Everybody smoked, usually Park Drive, except Gordon, who smoked a pipe, and me, who rolled Old Holborn with liquorice papers. These took longer to go out if you put them down. As long as I completed all my jobs, no one was bothered about my taking a nap.

Thus, I left *Saturday Night and Sunday Morning* and entered into *The Dad's Army Garage* – where I would be Pike. In reality, those eight blokes had a strong sense of duty about getting things done properly. They too 'got their heads down', always making sure they completed their jobs first. They had survived World War II on active service and had been through the great Depression of the 30s. And in some bizarre way they resembled my dad, mode of dress, mannerisms and the way they spoke.

Our foreman was a great guy called Harry Crackle. He spoke with a throaty rasp not unlike the older men I had met in Spain. (In the films he would be played by Peter Vaughan in *Straw Dogs*.) I hit it off with Harry straight away. He was interested in films and very knowledgeable about those from the 40s and 50s. He allocated me the five large electric school meal vans to wash inside and out. Knowing that I had one to do each night made the job quicker for me, especially if I had a play to rehearse. I didn't skimp on the job, but I had it finished in time to get my head down. On Friday nights, Harry made certain to allocate me the petrol bowser vehicle to clean.

"Time to do your Friday night favourite, lad," Harry would say.

I would scrub the petrol bowser down with a bucket of paraffin, and then wash it off, along with all the dirt, which was immensely satisfying and took no time at all. Another job was emptying the bottom out of the Paxit refuse vehicles, removing the dust that had built up during the day's collections, then shovelling it up into the refuse vehicle. There were about 25 of these and the time allocation to do them all was three hours, but you could do it in half that time if you worked at it. A large hanger-like garage housed the refuse vehicles. The numerous highway lorries and vans were kept out in the yard. We also cleaned and maintained vehicles from other sections, including lighting, salvage, scrap paper vehicles, school meal vans and housing repairs.

As well as the crews on refuse, I eventually knew most of the drivers on other sections too. Whenever I walked through town, there would be plenty of beeping and waving at me from the guys on the road. Fame at last! I also had lifts across town, or even home to my flat in Carrington. As late as the mid-90s, long after I left the Eastcroft Depot, I still kept up with them. However, there was one incident that nearly finished my time at the Eastcroft. I had been washing down a refuse vehicle and was driving it into the garage for a monthly service. I wasn't going very fast, but my wellington boot slipped off the brake and I hit the garage wall entrance. I rolled out, shaken but unharmed, to find that I had caved in half of the driver's cab. It had just been refurbished after a previous collision. Harry Crackle ran up none too pleased and rasped at me for a bit. Worst of all, from his point of view, we had to fill out an accident form, which brought management down the following night to say how disappointed they were, and not to do it again or a disciplinary would follow. You didn't attract the attention of management if at all possible. Luckily, Harry didn't hold it against me. He was a grand bloke. I took some ribbing for a while, but it settled down, although occasionally Gordon and Baldy would bring it to mind when we all sat down for a brew.

"Well, things are looking up, aren't they? You managed to get that bin lorry in the garage without dust pouring off the rafters when you hit the entrance. Only just been done up hadn't it, Howard?!"

One of the fringe benefits of working down 'The Croft' was the 'tatting', which basically means looking for useful items in the refuse vehicles. It was really surprising just what people would throw out. Anything and everything turned up. Clothes, cutlery, crockery, and wood which was handy when I acquired a flat with a coal fire. The Wastepaper Collection put paper and cardboard upstairs in a large Victorian building known as The Destructor for recycling. I used to enjoy sorting through the paper because there were always plenty of magazines to pick up: films, TV and pop music. It was also good for picking up shopping vouchers and for years Mum and I saved a small fortune at Tesco. In those days providing they sold the goods the vouchers could be used to reduce the bill. When I drove back to Kent on a visit to Arthur in 1972, I took down six pairs of shoes I had 'tatted' with very little wear. I knew he was short of cash what with Gladys taking a lot of his earnings.

On 11th February 1970, Pirate Radio North Sea International began illegal broadcasting from the Dutch coast and the signal at night was so much stronger. It really made my night shift work a lot easier and I carried my transistor radio all around the yard with me. I felt cleansed! I hadn't had so much Pirate Radio fun for three years! On the night of 23rd March 1970, it set off for the East Coast of England, anchoring in International waters five miles off the coast from Clacton at 9.00am. And I followed it every wave of the way! It was just like the good old days before The Marine Offences Bill.

On 15ᵗʰ April, RNI responded to the Labour Government's jamming them by broadcasting pro-Conservative political messages for the general election on 18ᵗʰ June. RNI changed its wavelength, but the jammers found them and continued regardless. It must have cost a fortune. Unfortunately, the new wavelength was close to Radio One who were also affected by the jamming! On 13ᵗʰ June the name was changed to Radio Caroline International with the full support of its founder Ronan O' Rahilly. "Vote for the Conservatives and you will keep Free Radio," was the clarion call and of course I loved every minute of all this. I vote Labour nowadays, but the Labour government of the 60s had really upset me. The Tories won the election, and it has been proved that the RNI/Caroline campaign greatly helped them. However, the jamming continued regardless, so RNI returned to the Dutch coast on 23ʳᵈ July. The next few years were really traumatic for poor old RNI, with hijacking, enforced radio silence, the return, bombing in 1971, continual jamming – heaven knows how much this cost the British taxpayer! Then Radio Veronica joined the Dutch Pirate Radio Station wavelength calling it RNI 2. All jolly good fun. However, just as in the UK seven years before, the Dutch government then made pirate radio illegal and on 31ˢᵗ August, 1974, Radio Veronica, RNI and Radio Atlantis were closed down. A not so Jolly Roger conclusion.

My nights at The Croft continued apace. They all looked out for me, and I wish deeply that I had been more appreciative of their company, but I was so self-centred and caught up with my acting. I'd like to take this opportunity to thank them in that Great Council Depot In The Sky for being really sound men who gave me the chance to grow up in their company.

There were only two jobs I didn't like very much and luckily they didn't occur very often. Occasionally, a refuse crew might take a chance and do more on their round than they should, or they might save time by not going to the tip to empty their vans out at the end of the day. This meant that when we got it the vehicle was overloaded with refuse and jammed up. If left overnight it could smoke and start to combust, so me and Baldy had to prop the back up and shovel out the refuse until there was enough room for the mechanism to operate. This delightful chore took us about an hour and a half, although fortunately it only occurred five times during my twenty years there. I counted. It was character-building stuff.

The other chore was steam cleaning the chassis of lorries and refuse vehicles prior to having an MOT. At first I had to get the help of one of my workmates to guide me with the vehicle up on the five-foot-high ramp in order to steam clean, which was a bind because I had to wait for them to come over, and as you may have gathered, time was of the essence if I had acting the next day! After a while I noticed that whatever vehicle I drove onto the ramp, minivans, trucks or refuse vehicles, I found that if I lined up the right-hand edge of the ramp with my crotch, I could drive any vehicle up there on my own. I was really proud of myself with this manoeuvre. Even the skilled men on both days and nights were puzzled as to how I managed this feat!

One night Harry pulled me to one side and said, "Howard, do you mind if I ask you summit. What's a bright lad like you doing on a job like this? With your skills you could get a job anywhere instead of wasting your time down here?"

I told him not to worry, and confessed I was really enjoying the job and wouldn't change it for the world. I'd never been so happy.

He laughed and said, "Well that's OK then, as long as you're alright that's the main thing, see you later."

The first fifteen years at the Eastcroft were undoubtedly the best. I never ever dreaded going to work – so much fun! The only downside was having to work on the Friday night when everybody else was out and about round the town enjoying themselves. It's a shame we couldn't work on Sunday nights which were quiet, and have the Friday nights free, but it was a minor drawback.

I loved my time there and I miss you Gordon, Harry, Baldy, Tom Bright and Tom Maltby. Plus Ernie Dennis, who prepared shop front blinds stretched out over the garage floor, and last but not least Jack Soar who was my foreman for the last eight years and who I met up with for a few drinks from time to time, meeting Eunice his lovely and attractive lady friend. As Joni Mitchell sang, *You Don't Know What You've Got Till It's Gone.*

Towards the end of 1968, something happened which brought me down again. Upon returning home in the afternoons to get to bed, I started to have trouble getting into the house. My key just wouldn't open the door. I managed to stand on my bike, squeeze through the bathroom window and clamber in. It happened about four times. I told Mum and Dad about the problem, but when I showed them, the key turned in the lock just fine! With my limited grey matter, I was thinking that the wood had swollen around the lock because it was winter or something like that. After a while, I realised that it only occurred when my dad was working afternoons. He must have locked the back door putting the night lock on, then gone out of the front door. Mum gave me a front door key and the lockouts stopped. When I tried to talk to him about it, he just grunted.

I kept my head down because Dad hadn't been keen on me since I returned home. Although I had a proper job, he didn't think much of it, and of course my being home meant he had competition for Mum's attention. When Dad returned home after four years of being a prisoner of war, Mum understandably felt sorry for him and really looked after him. The trouble was she kept on spoiling him for the next 55 years. Then I came along, and she spoiled me too. When I'd left in 1967, it was the first time that Dad had had her to himself for 22 years, so it was understandable that he resented my return six months later. He became more and more fractious with us both. Once he turned on her angrily when he had boiled the kettle dry. She usually left it full of water ready for him when he came home from work, but she'd forgotten just this once. He didn't check first, and he told her off big time. My mum was a lady about it, of course, and he never touched her, but I know the atmosphere upset her.

On another occasion, one Sunday night, in early January 1969, I was watching the *Farewell Cream* concert on TV, held the previous November at the Albert Hall. Mum and Dad came in from the club. Dad, fuelled by a certain amount of alcohol, went straight over to the TV and switched it off.

I leapt up and said, "Hey, I was watching that!"

Dad came over and gave me a forceful shove.

"If you don't like it, you know where the door is. In fact, why don't you just bugger off!"

He pushed me again, even harder. So I wacked him with my fist as hard as I could, and he fell over backwards. He was a little shorter than me but broader and had always been willing to bring me down, so it was only fair. Mum came in between us as he got up, shouted at me again to clear off, and stomped off to bed. It was clear I would need to leave 19a Church Street very soon.

From 1965 to 1967, the Pirate Radio stations frequently played tracks from the first four albums by Simon and Garfunkel, and they were absolute magic; so many haunting tunes which they never really matched after *Bookends* in 1968. Another fine example of it being just the right time and place for it.

As Mary Wilson of The Supremes always said, "The music of the mid-60s was the soundtrack of our lives."

In the autumn of 1968 I saw *The Graduate* with Dustin Hoffman and I was totally hooked. My favourite tunes were on the soundtrack It couldn't have come at a better time, and of course I identified strongly with the character of Benjamin. It was also good for me seeing someone who wasn't particularly handsome have the lead role. And he had a large nose too! I went to see it four times over the next few weeks.

Meanwhile, I was still trying to nail the characters for some scenes in *Richard the Third, Macbeth,* and *Two Gentlemen of Verona,* which were to be performed at Christmas, my first public performance.

We never had drama at school and certainly never read Shakespeare. Others were really confident with the text, particularly those like Janine Duvitski, who eventually went to E15 Acting School, and Sherrie Hewson who went on to RADA. They were willing enough to help, but I was adrift, not really understanding what was being said. Miss Hoffman was directing. After several mumbles from me, she took me aside and asked whether the notes at the back of the book had been any help? I didn't realise there were any. From then on it was easier. I also occasionally had the advantage of a canine co-star. When you walk on stage as Launce with 'Crab' the dog in *Two Gentlemen of Verona*, no one is looking at you, only at Crab. That suited me fine, as it meant I could get out the words, and eventually I felt comfortable in all the parts. The Academy won an award at the Derby Arts Festival in early 1969, which was great for my confidence, and Crab got a lot of dog treats.

I moved out of Arnold and took a 25-foot square loft flat on Sherwood Rise in a converted Victorian house. It had one small wardrobe, one bed, a chest of drawers, and a long worktop on which was a very expensive Belling electric stove. It was too expensive to use so I purchased a Camping Gaz stove and ate out. No TV. I had a three-bar electric fire which was also expensive to use. So, playing safe, I tried putting on just one bar and plugging it into the continental adaptor I had brought back from Gibraltar, fixed onto the overhead light, as this was on the house supply and not running through my meter. That little dodge saved me a small fortune and saw me right through to the spring, by which time it started to give off a burning smell so time to call it a day. I used the showers at the Eastcroft so there was another saving. I would meet up with Mum for lunch to catch up at a café opposite Ford The Drapers where Mum worked next door to the Academy, very convenient. One time, she told me that her boss was going out with a zany local actress called Sue Pollard. Mum was a regular viewer of *Crossroads* and had been on the lookout.

She said, "You've done bar work before. There's a vacancy for a barman on *Crossroads*. Why don't you send in a letter applying for the job?"

Was that how you got TV work? I didn't know; we had no classes about how to find any kind of work at drama school. Sitting round a table in a pub that night with my mates, I mentioned that I knew about this opportunity for an audition at the ATV studios off Broad Street but had no idea how to go about trying for it. John's brother, Steve, came to the rescue, and said, "No problem, pal. I'm installing lifts around that new Spaghetti Junction in Birmingham next week. Why don't you come with me in the van, and I can drop you off? Job done."

Job done indeed. I took the morning off drama school and went with him at 7am the following Monday. Spaghetti Junction was the first huge concrete jungle I had ever seen. It was not yet finished, so the amount of traffic jams on all the roads leading up to it were also a first. It took us two hours to get through 50 miles, a taste of things to come. Steve dropped me off at the ATV Studios about 9am and I walked into Reception.

"Could I see someone in casting about a job on *Crossroads* please?" I asked

"Certainly sir," said a burly, friendly security man. "What time is your appointment?"

I thought, oh right, maybe I should have called first. If I had the telephone number.

"I'm afraid I don't have an appointment," I said. "I was hoping to audition for the barman role."

He looked at me with a bit of a smile, but said, "Just a moment, take a seat and I'll see if there's anyone free for you." He rang through and said, yes, someone would come down in ten minutes to see me.

I wasn't even in *Spotlight*, the directory of actors. I had no agent. But ATV were like a family in those days, so if they were free, casting would come down. Two very pleasant ladies, Margaret French and Barbara Plant, emerged ten minutes later. It seemed they were impressed that I had come over all the way from Nottingham on the off chance of getting an audition. Margaret said that, unfortunately, the barman role had already been cast and recorded two weeks previously. But there may be other opportunities eventually. However, when I told them that I was still at drama school and didn't even have an Equity card yet, they said they were sorry but there wasn't much they could do for me. I thanked them for seeing me and got up to go, my heart in my boots.

Then Margaret said, "But we are really impressed you made so much effort to get here and that you're enthusiastic about working on *Crossroads*. We don't have many actors from the East Midlands on our books. Look, as soon as you get your Equity card, let us know and there may be something we can do. We're expanding so there will be other shows besides *Crossroads* in due course."

I shook hands, thanked them both, and left. I walked across Birmingham to the train station elated. I didn't expect anything out of meeting them, but it was gratifying to find that they were so friendly, none of the stand-offish attitude I had been expecting from people who could make or break your career. Or, in my case, having any career at all. I knew all about the owner of ATV, Sir Lew Grade and all the TV series he had produced at Elstree near London. I desperately wanted to be a part of it. I had something to aim for now and it made me want to go right back to drama school and get that Equity card. I then fell victim to my first bout of corpsing while rehearsing a scene from *The Old Curiosity Shop* by Charles Dickens. I was playing Quilp, of course, while a lovely girl called Lesley Prior was playing Little Nell. Lesley was 17 years old, though she looked a lot younger dressed Victorian style. I was swinging from the spiral staircase as the scene started and leaping about the stage, while speaking with a squeaky voice. It was exhausting. Lesley looked up at me from under her bonnet and we both cracked up into giggles. Every time I swung about, and she looked up at me innocently, about to speak her part, we couldn't help but laugh. Lesley was great, very funny but really professional, and we got through it eventually.

At the beginning of December, and with the weather turning colder, John offered to help sweep my chimney in my new ground floor Victorian flat on Ebers Road in Carrington. With all the wood and coke I could obtain from the Eastcroft it was a good idea. However, the fireplace covering sheets weren't good enough and the soot went everywhere. I bet it hadn't been swept for years. It took me all that day to clean the flat. About a week later I started to go down with flu. I barely managed to perform some scenes in The Academy's Christmas Show. I had to paste on a false beard for Macbeth which I hadn't done before. When I looked at the end result in the mirror, I realised I had missed a bit, so I coloured it in with a brown felt tipped pen. When Lady Macbeth came out of our snogging clinch I looked on with horror when I saw that I had left her with a brown moustache. Luckily it was upstage from the audience so they couldn't see it. I had also picked up a gallon of blood from the local abattoir, to get that proper aura of death for the knife wielding scene. I didn't know about fake blood. We kissed, and grasped each other's gory hands as we embraced. By the third night it had all coagulated, but I'll give Janice Fell her due she was a proper trooper and really went for it.

That weekend I was leaving Mum and Dad's after tea when Dad shouted after me, "Me, your mum and grandma are having Christmas Dinner in The Musters Hotel. If you've got nowt on you can join us if you like?"

I said yes, I'd love to meet up and thanks. These were the first words we had spoken in 20 months. However, come Christmas Day my condition had become much worse and all I wanted was to stay in bed. I struggled there not wanting to let them down, but when I did get there, they were understandably disappointed at my lack of appetite. That three hours was a nightmare, I felt as if I was going to black out. We went back to Mum and Dad's, and I rolled into my old bed, and that was it. I slept through the rest of the day and most of Boxing Day. On the 27th I made an appointment to see the doctor. She diagnosed severe tonsilitis mixed up with a double virus – flu and flue from the chimney soot. I had to have a month off work and I also developed a deep red rash on my arms. Turns out that I am allergic to penicillin.

During the summer of 1971, after my three years at the Academy, we put on a performance of *Richard the*

Third as the end of term show. I was playing Richard. I really got into this one and after all I did have the nose! Looking back, I can see that I was relying very heavily on a combination of Peter Sellers and Lawrence Olivier, rather than putting my own stamp on it, but it was a learning curve. The Nottingham Evening Post gave it a good review, and I passed out as planned with my Bronze Acting and Silver Speech awards from the London Academy of Music and Dramatic Arts in July 1971. Miss Hoffman wanted me to stay on to try for Silver and Gold Acting, but I was ready to try my luck. This didn't go down well, and she said I would never get an Equity Card without her, but apart from that rather heated exchange, I still fancied her and look back on my time there with fondness and gratitude. Thanks a lot Mavis. I did see her one last time later that year. A film company was in The Meadows shooting Alan Sillitoe's *The Ragman's Daughter* with one of her pupils in a small role. I watched the proceedings from the opposite side of the street, but I couldn't be bothered to go over and chat to Mavis. With hindsight I wish I'd made the effort.

Mum had seen a documentary about the community in a town called Costacabana on the outskirts of Almeria, full of British people being employed as extras on Spaghetti Westerns. Ignoring Miss Hoffman's advice about never doing extra work, I decided it would be a way to get my Equity Card and some real experience. Free from the Academy, I took on another part time job as a delivery driver for Flewitts the Bakers to help me save some money and buy a van. It was the perfect part-time job. I could leave Eastcroft at 6.30am, start work for Flewitts at 7am, finish at 12 noon and there was often a Cornish Pasty going spare for my breakfast. Cousin Dick contacted me to say he'd enough of plumbing and wanted to try something else. (In the films he would be played by Rodney Bewes, from *The Likely Lads*.) I told him about my plans for Almeria and he asked if he could come along, suggesting it would help out with petrol costs. Trouble was, neither of us had a car. One dark rainy Monday afternoon, I went to a fortune teller in Forest Fields in the back room of a Victorian terraced house. There were five women in there waiting to start a séance. Yes, it certainly did resemble a scene from *Séance On A Wet Afternoon* 1964. She said the trip to Spain would be a successful one. Later that week, I took Dick along to meet John Emberton and the other lads for a drink, to tell them all about the plan. Next thing I knew, John had found me a second-hand Minivan from the early 60s for sale. You could drop the rear seat down to make space for sleeping in the back. Once I'd bought it, John also saved me the cost of an expensive RAC Overseas Rescue service by doing it himself. The next problem was the Eastcroft. I loved my job there and didn't want to give it up. Luckily, Harry really wanted me to give it go, and persuaded the big bosses to let me take all my annual leave plus some unpaid time making it a two-month leave of absence.

By the end of March 1972, we were ready to go. I said goodbye to Mum and Dad, and we set off down the M1, the first time I had driven on a motorway. We stayed overnight at Uncle Arthur's as a pit-stop (ha!) on the way to take the ferry at Dover next day. We went out for a drink round Deal. Arthur was always keen to meet new people and he and Dick got on very well. We had a lively night in the pubs while in the background the wind was blowing up a storm and we could hear the sound of the waves crashing on the beach as we walked along the seafront. Luckily it had calmed down next morning. Arthur came to see us off at Dover. When we reached Calais, all I had to do was remember to drive on the right. Unfortunately Dick didn't drive but it wasn't a problem. I had some very entertaining moments when there was a particularly spectacular piece of French driving. Dick would shout "Aaargh, look at that split arse!" or similar. He was also really good at looking out ahead beyond long vehicles, to tell me when to overtake, because we were in a right-hand drive which made the manoeuvre difficult for the driver. I took it steadily at first, but after an hour I had settled into it, and we made good time so four hours later we were in Paris. We spotted a camping site, right in the centre of Paris, and paid to stay the night so we could use their showers. First of all, though, we walked around the Champs Elysée bars and had a few beers and snacks. I think I might have been trying Spanish rather than French, but we stumbled through. The trip was turning out to be in marked contrast to the one I had endured five years before. On our first night sleeping in the van, we stuffed our luggage onto the front seats and had a good night's kip, warm and dry, in our sleeping bags on a carpet in the back. Next morning, there was ample hot water for showers and shaving, and after this luxurious start we went on the Metro and had a look at Paris from the top of the Eiffel Tower before we set off again. There weren't as many motorways in those days. I found us cafés and translated 'Jambon' into 'Jamon', no problem. As it was getting dark, we spotted a quarry from the road. Turning off the lights, we drove slowly along the sand and found it

Waiting 'on hold' up the road
at Tabernas, Almeria

Then my turn came. Except the weather turned for the worse, with monsoon-like rainstorms pounding down. The company decided not to play a waiting game with the elements because, not only did it make things really hard work for them matching shots, the colour of the landscape would change with the weather. They moved the production to Madrid for interiors over a couple of weeks. So I was on hold. I remained optimistic. I still had quite a bit saved up, while Richard had earned his pile. We set upon a few adventures here and there. In a convoy of three or four cars with other extras, we drove into the mountains stopping at bars. One of them had turned his car over leaving San Jose but the red volcanic sand acted as a cushion, so we just rolled it upright and carried on. On another drink-fuelled night, halfway back down a mountain, we were ready to go home in the early hours, but all of a sudden there was no sign of Dick. The others tootled off into the night while I drove around, stopping to look into people's yards and gardens, trying to call out loudly enough for him to hear and softly enough not to wake anyone. As I rounded a corner, in the headlights I saw Dick being propped up by two Guardia Civil officers. They rolled him into the van smiling, and rolled their eyes at me, which fortunately was all they did.

I was starting to run out of money and time, trying for some more gardening work without success. One day I drove up to Garrucha Harbour at Vera to see if there was anything happening on the *Treasure Island* shoot but it was totally deserted, just the galleon Hispaniola in the harbour. I also kept going into the Gran Hotel looking out for new productions. Nothing came up, although one evening as I sat in the reception area with a drink, a voice boomed out, "Good evening, I would like to have the key to my room please."

I just couldn't believe it. I was ten feet away from Orson Welles! He was there to play Long John Silver in *Treasure Island*. I'm sure the timbers shivered with his voice. He was in his late-fifties, dressed in a smart cream suit, a big man, craggy and tough-looking with a large cigar, dark beard and moustache. I watched as he was taken over to the lifts by the concierge, frozen to my seat. These days, I would've gone over to him and said, "Excuse me Mr. Welles, may I buy you a drink?" Who knows what might have happened.

Round the corner from the Gran Hotel, I struck up a friendship with the owner of a great little bar called El Barril. I went in because all around the walls were pictures of film sets and stars. It turned out that the owner, Ginger was a second unit director in the area and hired himself out to various companies who had come to film. He was very knowledgeable about film, although not so knowledgeable about the availability of extra work. I took along Dick and a few of the lads from Costacabana for a night out there. As the evening wore on, I began to hear Dick talking about his prospects of regular plumbing work and that he was intending to stick around for this. We chatted for a while about our plans, and I realised that I couldn't really afford to wait for the work on *Reason To Live – Reason To Die,* the casting man's two weeks mention had long gone. Dick said he was happy to take on the bungalow alone. At the end of May 1972, I left him my Grundig radio as a parting gift and drove off into the sunrise.

The trip back was traumatic to say the least. Driving through a sleepy village on the road to Madrid in the height of the day, I was flagged down by a Guardia Civil officer. This was Franco's Spain where the Guardia Civil made their own rules. He stood in the middle of the road with his hand up and when I stopped, he walked around to my open window. He was obviously asking me a question, but I didn't know what it was. He scowled and went over to an old man, slumped on a chair at the door of a house. He practically lifted him up, then brought him around the car, opened my passenger door and bundled him inside. It became obvious that I was being asked to provide a taxi service for someone who had a bit too much sun, drink or both. I eagerly nodded away and established that I had to take him to the next town. Rolling along, I was happily anticipating perhaps there might be a coffee and Jambon in it for me. Then the radiator blew. Steam was pouring out of the engine. It had been a hot day and having the numberplate over the grill probably hadn't helped. I stopped and pulled up the bonnet to let it cool down, when it occurred to me that the old guy might be a bit concerned. I went around to his side, only to find he had got out, flagged down another car, and was pulling the door shut as it sped away. So much for my coffee and snacks.

I took the front numberplate off and used the gallon of water I had stashed to top up the radiator. However, the overflow of boiling water had dissolved one of the distributor leads, so I only had three. I crawled to the next town at a snail's pace. There was a telephone booth with a directory and luckily the address of a nearby British Leyland garage. I asked the way by stopping near anyone I could find to ask for "Calle" something, until I drew into the garage. It was about 6pm and luckily still open. Two older guys, and what looked like a couple of apprentice mechanics around my age, looked at the burnt-out electrics and scratched their chins. One of the apprentices must have seen I was somewhat crestfallen and said, "Tranquillo hombre, tranquillo. Sentarse."

Which means, "Alright mate. Keep calm, just take a seat."

One of the lads was sent off somewhere on his bike. I guess he had been sent for coffee and sandwiches. Half an hour later he came back with a bag and out of this bag, like a magician with a rabbit, produced four spark plugs and four distributor leads. It was huge relief, and I will forever be in their debt. After an hour, I was on my way.

¡Me encanta España! Muchisimas gracias!

I was intending to get the Bilbao/Southampton ferry in two days' time. Just to be on the safe side, I pushed on without stopping for a snack. I had been driving for quite a few hours, so it was around 10pm as the night closed in, when I started to hallucinate. I can still see those white knights on white horses riding across the skyline. I just had to pull over and sleep. Fortunately, there was a small park just off the main highway out of Madrid. I woke up fresh as a daisy in the dawn, and with a snack and a coffee in a bar I was on my way. Ah Madrid! Again, I was only passing through and didn't have time to get to know this magnificent city, but I've been back since and, along with Andalucía, it's my favourite part of Spain. When I cleared the northern suburbs there was suddenly a horrible banging noise coming from the engine. When I looked under the bonnet, I couldn't see anything wrong, then I noticed that the suspension arm had broken away from the bracket and was hanging loose. Another wave of panic hit me, but then I had a brainwave. Out of the tool kit John had packed me, I pulled out some rope and threaded it through the bracket then onto the walls of the engine to keep it secure. Luckily, it had come away in a vertical position, enabling me to do this. I drove for a while, and it was fine. It banged occasionally depending on the road surface, but at least I was mobile. In much of the previous seven weeks, that old minivan had taken the brunt of some lengthy driving on rough roads. I can still remember the registration number CWK 513C which was made in 1965. The suspension arm was on the driver's side, thus taking the heavy gutter knocks on that side of the road. The ferry was 250 miles away and ran every two days. Unfortunately, I didn't make it in time, the ferry had left and was way over on the horizon.

Parked next to me on the harbour side at Bilbao was the VW Dormobile of a British family who had also missed the ferry. Mr and Mrs Johnson and their 10-year-old daughter were from Streetly near Birmingham. In fact, they had had hoped to get the ferry that day but had missed it because Mrs Johnson had to be taken to hospital. Apparently, it was something fairly minor, but they had kept her in overnight for observation. He invited me to walk to the hospital to fetch her, then we ate together at a small restaurant nearby that they liked. Mr Johnson was a policeman and should have been back at work the next day. On our return to the Dormobile, he telexed back to his station from the harbour office to say he was going to be late. I was fascinated by the Telex Machine; to think that you could type in at one end and that someone was able to immediately read it off a sheet at the other! After a night in the van, I decided that I didn't want to twiddle my thumbs by the harbour for two days. I said goodbye to the family and set off driving through France to Cherbourg. Two days later, I was on the UK ferry. At Southampton customs, they wanted to look inside the van. To be honest, I looked a bit rough. I hadn't done a lot of washing in the past four days and had also grown a big curly ginger beard. The van was a tip inside. After a bit of rummaging around, the customs officer gave it up as a bad job and asked, "Alright. That's OK. Where are you going?"

"Nottingham," I said.

He looked at my passport and obviously could see I was, indeed, from Nottingham, land of Robin Hood and the Sheriff.

"Anything to declare?" he asked.

"Yes," I said, "Two hundred Embassy cigarettes and four tins of Old Holborn."

The Embassy were for my dad, hoping that he would enjoy these as he also collected the vouchers.

He was not impressed. "I'm sorry sir. You're over the limit. It's either one or the other, not the two together."

"My apologies," I said, lying my socks off, "I thought it was one of each. I'd better pay you the difference. Sorry, how much do I owe you?"

"Go on, clear off," he said. "Have a good trip back to Nottingham."

This cheered me up. At least something had gone right.

I had a lot of trouble dealing with the one-way system in Southampton. In driving 2,500 miles through France and Spain I hadn't gone wrong at any time. But Southampton?! I went round the one-way system in the city centre twice and ended up back at the harbour! Eventually I had to ask someone how to get out. After that and a further hour on the road, I was too tired to continue. I pulled down a quiet country lane and set my alarm for two hours' time. It was a nice warm sunny afternoon, and I was out like a light. Ah well, at least the suspension arm lasted through to Nottingham. In those days Mum and Dad didn't have a telephone so it was another doorstep surprise for them from me. That minivan had quite a few miles on the clock when I bought it. It had done me proud, and with John's invaluable help I did it for a quarter of the price quoted by the RAC European Rescue Service. I had managed to get a constant fifty miles per gallon at a steady sixty miles an hour and no leakages of either brake and clutch, fluid or oil that the RAC said it had.

For a while I thought the Forest Fields fortune teller had got it wrong. I hadn't come back a success at all. But now, on reflection, I think I had. Not much to do with films but a lot to do with having a good time, surviving all sorts of adventures, and developing a great love of Andalucía and Spain, which has led to many more visits and adventures. As Arthur Seaton said,

"Yo think yo've got me weighed up, but let me tell you summat, I ain't got mesen weighed up yet!"

5

"Shut it!"

1972 to 1977

Back in the UK, I still had to acquire an Equity card. I auditioned for The Playhouse Roundabout Theatre In Education group. However, as soon as I arrived, I knew I had made a mistake. Anticipating posh, middle-class types I had dressed like Simon Templar. At that point in my life, I didn't know that the posher you are, the more likely you are to dress as if you are about to do some gardening. I didn't get the job, but that was fine as I didn't have any dungarees anyway.

Next was an audition for the Limbo Fringe, an alternative group dealing with social commentary issues. I dressed down and was successful. Two productions in two months meant I now had two of the three contracts required to get an Equity Card. When Limbo folded, I was at a loss about what to do next. Then I had a bit of luck. Mum was still working at Fords, and her boss, Andrew Pink, was still going out with that zany actor called Sue Pollard. Mum asked Andrew if he could ask Sue for advice about getting my final contract and the Equity Card. He suggested I go round to see Val Terry, the local Equity representative who had an office on Bridlesmith Gate in Nottingham. In the films, Val Terry would be played by a more robust Peter Wyngarde in the style of Jason King. He was an expansive man with long dark curly hair, always in a three-piece dark navy-blue suit and had a cigar in the ashtray. His office was in an old Georgian building at the top of some creaky stairs. It was reminiscent of the scene in *The Wrong Box,* where Peter Cook meets up with Doctor Pratt and his kittens. Behind a desk was Val Terry who motioned me to sit down. Around the walls were photographs of magicians, comedy acts, and singers, with heaps of posters and programmes piled up around him on a similar theme. The actor's trade union, Equity, had merged with the Variety Artists Federation in 1966. My heart sank. It was clear that the East Midlands branch was focused on the Variety side. I told him what Margaret French had said when I turned up at ATV on spec hoping for a role. He said, "I'm glad to find a Nottingham lad who wants to be an actor," he said. "We could do with some local actors in the branch."

I explained how I had gone through my drama school training by working at the Eastcroft. We had a laugh about how dressing down had acquired me a couple of contracts at Limbo, and I asked him how he thought I could obtain the third contract that would get me an Equity Card.

"Just between you and me, fill out the application form now and I'll leave a gap for that third contract. "I know Margaret French at ATV. If she says she's interested in using you, she'll get you the work."

He leant back and smiled at me and said, "Let me know as soon as you have confirmation of the type of work you'll be doing and I'll put that down as your third contract, and send you the Card."

Two weeks later, Barbara Plant, Margaret's assistant, rang to say I had a walk-on as a teacher in a children's programme called *The Kids From 47A.* I was worried that I didn't have the Equity Card yet, but no one asked for it. Barbara asked me to send in some professional photographs with my height and weight details. I sent in full colour photographs showing me as I was, still with a full beard, long curly hair and the heavy framed black glasses. I also sent some soft focus black and white ones to Lew Grade's office, as I'd heard that they were casting for *Jesus of Nazareth*. (To no avail – Robert Powell got the job.)

By the time I was given another couple of ATV walk-ons, one as a hospital visitor in *Crossroads*, the other lurking in reception, I had a brand-new Equity Card in my wallet. It was a Red 'Provisional', but that just meant I couldn't work in the West End.

ATV asked if I could send them some new photographs without the beard and the glasses as they needed to see my features unadorned!

Early in 1973, I was looking at getting another flat closer to Nottingham when I noticed an ad in The Evening Post for a flat going in an old Victorian House opposite the cemetery on Mansfield Road. I arranged to see Mrs Grimes the landlady who certainly didn't look like a Grimes type person! She was a very attractive lady in her mid-forties, very fashionably dressed. In the films she would be played by Lilli Palmer.

"Actually, I generally prefer to have ladies here at 208 so I'm uncertain whether I'm able to make the flat available to you."

I loved this house and felt very comfortable there immediately. I almost pleaded with her to have me as a lodger.

"I have some ladies to interview over the next 24 hours. Would you give me a ring tomorrow evening and I'll let you know?"

I rang a couple of times but there was no answer. That's it I thought, the tedious job of searching is to be resumed. However, the following evening Mrs Grimes rang full of apologies. She had two more women to interview who couldn't make it the evening before. However, she didn't find them suitable: one wasn't working and the other couldn't supply references. But I had some great ones from my two bosses at the Eastcroft and that clinched it. "Well, Howard, the flat is yours if you want it." Hurrah!

208 Mansfield Road was a godsend to me. It was a large house in which I had a small single room at the top of the house, with a separate kitchen down a corridor and a bathroom shared with the other nine flats. John had a spare aerial he wasn't using and as I was at the top of the house, he suggested I rent my first TV. He was right yet again. The outdoor aerial was perched on top of the window pelmet and gave a good picture. With a bit of experimentation, I found that if I turned it at right angles I could obtain Yorkshire TV as well as Midlands. In those days the regions had different programming.

After I'd been there a year or so I found out there were caves below the property. Martin, Steve and I went with torches through the entrance off Mansfield Road, turning a corner twenty steps down and found ourselves in total silence. There were eight white walled toilets looking as if they'd just been painted as this was one of the 86 air raid shelters scattered around Nottingham during the Second World War. We were actually underneath the foundations of 208, and in a hundred metre rectangle. There were doors cut into the sandstone walls and foundations which led to the cellars of other large Victorian houses. A few years later

I had moved to the ground floor flat and found to my horror that someone had gone into the caves via a small hidden entrance on St Andrews Road, 200 yards down Mansfield Road. They found their way down into the main rectangle and gained access into my cellar by forcing the door, going up the steps and trying to break through my kitchen door. Luckily, I'd remembered to bolt the door. When they heard me approaching, they scarpered through a grating into the yard.

In fact, Nottingham is honeycombed with 800 sandstone caves underneath the streets, dating back to the dark ages. Quite a few of them are open to the public and I can strongly recommend a visit.

Around then I hit a lull in my acting career. As I didn't have a telephone, while 'resting' I rang ATV every Thursday from the local phone box, but there was no work forthcoming. I remembered that Dave Pidcock, the photographer I had used before, had invited me to join Wollaton Drama Group, which he said was a semi-professional theatre company. I went along to the venue, a barn at the rear of a pub called The Admiral Rodney and was impressed by the rehearsals of various comedy scenes mixed up with some singers led by director Mike Ridley. I also hooked up with Andy Davis and his parents Wynn and Pauline, who went on to become my adopted drama parent mentors.

To begin with, the company were only doing sketches. I joined in a two-hander with a woman from South London, playing pensioners reminiscing in a graveyard, which gave me a chance to try out my South London accent. Mike asked me to read a play, *Stringer's Last Stand* by Stan Barstow who also wrote *A Kind Of Loving*.

"I want us to put on a full play," Mike said. "Have a read of this and see if you fancy playing the second lead."

I certainly did. I played the boyfriend of one of the daughters in a working-class Yorkshire family, who had been 'sent to Coventry' by the domineering father because she refused to join in a factory strike. She discovers a packet of condoms in his pocket, then she and her sisters took revenge on him, showing him up for being all mouth and no trousers.

I drew on The Method sense memory technique playing angry Bob the boyfriend, sparking me up nicely for the part. It was a great rehearsal schedule with lots of comforting bonhomie from the rest of the cast, a gathering of very talented teachers, civil servants, architects and accountants. The play ran for five nights from Tuesday to Saturday. The applause at the end of each night signalled to us that we were going down well and by Saturday it was really tight and polished. The difference between amateur and professional is not just that you are paid for the latter, but also professional stage productions have at least twice the rehearsal time.

That final night, as I went into my diatribe about coming out in support and refusing to join the strike, my dad spoke from the audience in a way that was clearly audible throughout the auditorium, "Yeah, and he's like that in real life an' all!" I took that as a sign of success. We submitted the play for the Nottingham & Notts Drama Association (NANDA), and I won my first and only award – for best supporting actor.

One of the cast was a very attractive girl called Fiona who smoked Gauloises in an impressively nonchalant manner. We started going out together on a regular basis. It was great fun being with Fiona, although I don't think it was particularly brilliant for her because I was working at night and in TV, as well as taking on plays at Wollaton Drama Group. She shared a terraced house just over the River Trent in West Bridgford. She was a music librarian and through her I made many friends with her colleagues. Those parties were wild affairs and exactly the opposite to the reserved and studious image librarians project for the public. Fiona also had two friends in Canterbury, who we went to visit staying the night at Uncle Arthur's en route. We visited frequently and over time developed a fondness for Scrabble with three boards, smoked cheese and Asti Spumante.

In the summer of 1975, ATV gave me five days' work as a hippy called Zap on *Crossroads*. I wanted to save my holidays, so I drove there and back doing five 18-hour days. Rehearsals were done in old warehouse on Bradford Street just south of the city centre. I was working with Jack Watling's son, Giles, who was also playing a hippy and is now the Conservative MP for Clacton. He came from a great acting dynasty with Dad, Jack, Mum, Patricia, and sisters Deborah and Dilys. My part consisted of grunting, saying "yeah" while rolling my eyes and pulling out bubblegum. I was only in a few brief scenes and had close-ups. For me, being featured on screen was enough of a thrill, along with having three days of rehearsal with all the cast and crew. Our lunches at the pub nearby were paid for. I managed to get something wrong of course. In the Green Room, Ronnie Allen who played Mr Hunter the manager of the *Crossroads* motel and garage spotted that I was sitting in the most comfortable chair.

"I wouldn't sit there if I were you," he said. "That's Nolly's chair."

I leapt out of the chair. 'Nolly' was Noele Gordon, who played Mrs Meg Richardson, the owner of the motel and garage, a presence both on and off the screen. In his memoirs, David Jason also mentions a 'Chair Reserved' scenario. Miss Gordon and Ronnie Allen were very pleasant to me though, as were all the cast, who involved me by allowing me to give them their cues while reading their scripts.

Recording the programme in those early days was quite tense because it went straight onto videotape. *Crossroads* was recorded in two halves of about 13 minutes each.

Imagine a semi-circle of various sets on the perimeter of the studio with two camera crews in the centre, each one operating alternately. While scene one was being recorded, scene two would be set up ready to go. When scene two was being filmed by the second camera crew, the crew from scene one would move silently across the set for scene three. If anyone fluffed their lines or if any kind of unwanted noise occurred, we all had to go back to the beginning of that half of the programme and run through it again. When we had completed the first half the camera would focus on a board that stated "END OF PART ONE." On the broadcast, the adverts would be rolled between the two halves of the show, then when we had completed the second half of the programme, two boards showing a list of the cast and crew would be recorded. One board went vertical. Someone stood behind it and moved it upwards, so the camera gave the effect of moving credits. The other board was moved horizontally, thus creating a cross effect.

Giles was staying next door at the Holiday Inn, which I thought was a very posh hotel, as it had an indoor swimming pool with bar on the top floor. On the final day of filming, we finished in the early afternoon and went for a drink there. I only had a couple of shandies because of driving, but I was so tired afterwards that I had to have a doze in the car on the A38 before I drove home and had my usual three hours' kip prior to starting at the Eastcroft. The next day, I was so tired I didn't join my mates for a Saturday lunchtime session and instead slept right through to the evening. I managed to catch up with them that night though so we could celebrate! I soon got the hang of catching a few hours' sleep before going on to Eastcroft. About a month later, I was back as a hippy without Giles, this time in a group sitting cross-legged on the floor listening intently to some poetry being read, with the camera zooming in on yours truly, for a close-up. Hey man, in those days I certainly looked the part! In the late summer I also had some work playing 'The Hawker' and 'The Specialist' in a live version of the rock opera *Tommy* by Pete Townsend, being put on by Bill Smith at The Palace Theatre in Mansfield, 14 miles north of Nottingham. Bill had acquired special rights from Mel Bush and Pete Townsend to put on *Tommy*. It was excellent experience for me – six weeks of rehearsal with a professional company and a full-on production. Bill even put the music on a Quadrophonic Sound system, rare in those days. It pulsated around the auditorium where it was a sell-out success. A Leeds-based agent put some extra work my way on *Dickens of London* for Yorkshire Television. I went to the Harrogate Theatre, where I was kitted out in wardrobe with about 50 other people.

"And you'll have to have your beard off, and your hair cut," said the matriarchal supervisor.

"Strange," I said to myself, "I figured my appearance was just right for a random Victorian bloke. Maybe they're going to give me something significant to do."

After a shave and a hatchet job of short back and sides on my hair, I found myself at the back of a darkened theatre crowd. There I stayed for both days; my face not even seen by the camera. I realised then that Marvis Hoffman had been right; for extra work they see you as cattle, don't even think of you as a person never mind an actor. I was even more annoyed because I had already paid for 30 photographs of me with a full beard and sent them off to repertory companies and TV studios, including Yorkshire Television. Still, I had some more extra work on *Raffles* and then the Casting Team at Yorkshire Television responded to my request for an interview to see if I was eligible to join their register of actors. I went up to their office during *Raffles* to be faced with a couple of severe women with cold eyes.

"So, you're applying to join our register here then?" said one. She eyed my haircut, perhaps she recognised the handiwork. "Where are you based?"

"Nottingham," I said, "but I've been doing work at ATV in Birmingham," I added hopefully.

"Ah I see, so you're a Northern actor."

"Well no," I smiled, "Nottingham's in the Midlands."

Normally there is a very important distinction to those of us from both sides of the Midlands/Yorkshire borders. However, not for these ladies.

"It's still the North as far as we're concerned. We've plenty of Leeds-based actors on the books. Unfortunately, there's no work available at the moment, but we'll let you know."

I tried my best to smile gracefully as I left but there was no response. Those eyes. Yikes!

The last job I did for Yorkshire TV was *Raffles* starring Anthony Valentine. The call time given by the agency was 7am. When I arrived, they said I'd got it wrong and it was 7pm. Oh well, I'll just have to hang around for 12 hours, I thought. It was only when I was talking to the other extras from different agencies that I realised that they'd been told 7am too! So from 8.30am onwards I was on the phone to my agent before Yorkshire TV could contact her to say I'd got it wrong. At 9am the agent answered, and I proceeded to tell all so that hopefully I would be paid some kind of recompense. I spent the rest of the day asleep in a storeroom, leaving a message for the Eastcroft night foreman that I was going to be an hour late.

You know what? I never did receive that recompense. I decided then that Yorkshire TV and I weren't suited.

In the early Autumn of 1976, Margaret French rang from the ATV Casting team in Birmingham. A speaking part was going as a mechanic for the motel garage in *Crossroads*. I had already met Sam Kydd, who played the garage boss, and admired him very much, knowing that he'd thirty years of experience playing character actors in films and TV. He always looked as if he'd just come from the bookies, flat cap on and a newspaper sticking out of his pocket.

"Of course! When do I start?"

"In two weeks' time," said Margaret. "Monday, Tuesday and Wednesday are rehearsal days, and for you recording days are Thursday and Friday, and just to make sure you look different from your hippy days could you please not grow your hair too long and be clean shaven?"

What a welcome contrast Margaret and Barbara were to the Yorkshire Television approach! Two weeks later, I was walking through the *Crossroads* garage rehearsals with the rest of the cast, being told to slow down a bit because I was rushing across the set due to excitement.

It was bliss. I removed my green overalls at the Eastcroft, drove to Birmingham and pulled on blue ones for *Crossroads*. The pale green walls of the motel garage were identical to those at the Eastcroft!

On *Crossroads* my face appeared on the screen all over the nation. Some of the critics were not very kind about *Crossroads*. The chairman of the IBA, Lady Plowden described the programme as "distressingly popular". Indeed it was. It had 15 million viewers per week and was in the UK's top ten ratings most of the time. It might not have been as slick as *Coronation Street,* because we had a hectic production schedule. I was really comfortable at ATV and loved being in *Crossroads.* Back in 1968, when Thames Television dumped *Crossroads* from its schedules, there was a public outcry including the Prime Minister's wife Mary Wilson, to such an extent that Thames put it back on again some six months later. How they caught up when *Crossroads* was fully networked in 1972, I don't know, perhaps they showed episodes every night! First studio rehearsals were for the actors, second were with the technicians, and the third would be a recording. The main mechanic in the garage was 'Jim Baines' played by John Forgeham, a well-known character actor who was at The Royal Shakespeare Company in Stratford and on films and TV. I wish I'd known he was a driver in *The Italian Job*, I would have loved to hear his stories about the filming. A great bloke and quite a character whom I watched carefully to see how to improve.

After six episodes, he said: "Howard, you keep turning up here and we have these scenes together, but they still haven't given you a name." He smiled at Sam Kydd. "I know, let's make it Nobby," he said. Sam laughed and agreed this was an excellent idea.

John shouted up to the Director's box. "Alright with you if we call him Nobby, Jack?"

Sitting in the Director's box was Jack Barton, the producer along with the director of that particular episode – they had several directors. Jack gave a thumbs up, and I had a named speaking part – occasionally! I was happy with 'Nobby'. It was right up there with the kind of names we called each other at Eastcroft. The atmosphere at ATV was every bit as easy-going and just like Eastcroft with the banter. What's more, I could leave Eastcroft in Nottingham at 6.30am and arrive at Birmingham in time to visit the best canteen in showbusiness for breakfast, grab my overalls from wardrobe, then head off to one of the dressing rooms for a doze, while I listened out for the tannoy to announce my scenes. Over the next nine years I would do approximately 12 episodes per year at ATV in Broad Street, Birmingham. I respected Sir Lew Grade and all those marvellous series he financed – *Robin Hood, The Saint, Danger Man, William Tell, The Invisible Man*, etc.

I was introduced to Peter Palmer at a classical music concert by Fiona. He was a classical music reviewer for the Nottingham Evening Post; a softly spoken, reserved man in old fashioned clothes (on TV he would be played by Patrick Malahide). When I went to see him at The Park in Nottingham, I had never been into this kind of 'gated community' before, nor seen up close these large Georgian and Victorian houses in huge, well-tended gardens along leafy avenues. As I walked up the hill behind the castle, the sound of Nottingham fell quietly behind me and turning around I could see all the city laid out. The Park hasn't changed much since and has been the backdrop for many episodes of filming. As Peter ushered me into his pristine bijou flat, I could see Brambly Hedge pottery laid out and I felt it was like something out of a Jacques Tati film. We had tea and chatted. Peter asked if I could give him some driving lessons. He had purchased a Volkswagen Beetle and his plan was to get a few driving lessons with me before he started out with an instructor. I had a brainwave and suggested that I teach him early in the morning on my way home from work at 6.30am, in The Park, where it would be doubly quiet so early and in a secluded area. We went out twice a week over a month. The Park was perfect for hill starts, and had its own little roundabouts to navigate, plus with so little traffic he could practise reversing, and doing three point turns without being beeped at. A couple of months later he reported that he had passed his test first time. Maybe I should have set up as a driving instructor, as one of my aspiring actor friends did. "Save Time And Money The Jacks' Way on Toff's Hill The Park Driving School!"

Regardless of being somewhat like the 'Odd Couple', Peter and I had beer, cigarettes and snooker in common, and met up regularly at the Nottingham City Council Social Club for all three. Neither of us were any good, we would take a shot or two, have a few swallows of ale, and a draw of the ciggy and then go for a shot. In the main, we talked about his work. Peter had reviewed for the Nottingham Post for thirty years, spoke fluent German and was a specialist in classical musical notes, a music director and translator of German manuscripts. He also told me about film extra work he had done, including *Inspector Clouseau* on location in 1968, where he can be seen behind Alan Arkin at the Zurich Hauptbahnof train station.

By 1974, it was time for a change from my minivan. Seeing a re-run of the hour-long episodes of *Danger Man* reminded me that Patrick McGoohan as John Drake drove a Mini Cooper, the antithesis of James Bond's Aston Martin DB5. Luckily for me, my chum John Emberton liked working on cars. He shunted coal wagons at night for Calverton Colliery, would sleep until midday and work on cars during the afternoon. He found a Mini Cooper in Gedling, about 14 years old because there was no registration letter after the number e.g., PTO 646. After 1962 the letter A would come in after the number. If you are an avid film buff like me, you will be able to see if modern TV series set in the 60s and 70's get the car registration plates right. For example, I saw GNN 602G in a *George Gently* episode that was set in 1966, which made it wrong by about three years. This Mini Cooper had been used as a rally car and had yellow flashes over brown paintwork. The bodywork was not in good shape. However, it had some unique fittings with a small, sporty steering wheel, a short shift gear change, trendy black bucket seats and twin carburettors. Inside was a roll bar with seatbelts that stretched from the back – before seatbelts became a legal requirement. It had a removable bonnet which made it easy to work on, and a really unusual matt brown vinyl roof.

"It's great John," I said, "but it's really too flashy for me."

"No problem," said John, "I can do a spray job on it."

"I never knew you did spray jobs as well."

"Well, you do now pal."

I bought it and named it 'Drake'. John went to work on it, and a month later asked me to go over to Arnold and view the finished product. He had done a brilliant job. It was just how I wanted, plain Post Office red, looking like a standard Mini, although with the matt brown vinyl roof still intact. John had gone to a scrapyard and taken off the Austin Cooper lettering on the boot and replaced it with 'Austin Mini'. By that point, I had seen enough at the Eastcroft to know the basics and had attended car maintenance, but John's skills were way out of my league, and he had given it a complete service – yes, of course I paid him for his labours. I would have been totally lost without John during the years 1966 to 1976. I still say he is more like Arthur Seaton than Alfie, and he would protest vehemently – but this is my story! You would have had to look carefully to notice the slightly chunkier exhaust straight through the middle, but boy could it move. It had instant zoom upon acceleration, very quick on the uptake with a friendly, purr-like roar. People thought they could overtake me, but they were wrong. On motorways, I had all kinds of vehicles coming up behind me flashing their lights to get out of the way. "Who me? You flashing at me?" Then it was foot down and roaring away off into the distance. They didn't stand a chance. Very John Drake. What you see is not what you get.

I was hoping to go camping that summer. John was too busy but his brother-in-law, Gordon Wood junior and a mate from drama school, Paul Matthau put their hands up for it. I scrubbed out the Mini and cleaned up the battery terminals which were looking a bit corroded. Three of us in a Mini with camping gear, I don't know how we got it all in, but we did. We set off early afternoon and did just two miles when on the Western Boulevard in Nottingham the engine cut out, totally dead. Peering into the engine I couldn't see anything wrong but looking into the boot I remembered cleaning up the battery terminals, and that I hadn't been able to get the terminal tops to tighten up, so I thought it must be that. I was determined not to give up on celebrating my good fortune with mates. I walked to a garage on Raleigh Island and bought a new battery. It worked and we had a great time camping in Llandudno. No radio but one of them had my cassette player on their lap, playing music I had recorded from vinyl with a microphone in front of the record player!

Drake behaved himself for a couple of months, until one evening in West Bridgford the same thing happened again. This time I went straight to the boot. The battery terminals were intact, but I did notice that the metal jack handle had straddled the terminals. Could this be what had happened before, a short circuit? I moved it out of the way and the engine sprung into life. Come December, I had made plans to drive down to Kent and visit Uncle Arthur for Christmas, while my mum and dad were taking the first of their many holidays abroad. The engine kept going dead, and I was blowing fuses. I went to a scrapyard and tatted a fuse holder, replaced the original then went for a drive round the block. Everything seemed to be working fine: wipers, lights, indicators, etc, without any fuses being blown. However, when I came to park up and I pulled out the ignition key there was something not quite right – the engine was still running! I tackled the fuse holder again and tested everything. This time everything worked fine, and the engine switched off when I turned the ignition key. I decided to play safe and delay my trip to Kent. I went to work and when I had completed my shift, I washed Drake and drove it into the Eastcroft garage. The foreman of the time, Jack, came over to see how I was doing, and I told him what I had done in the engine, so took a look out of curiosity. Thank goodness he did.

"Ahh," he said, "I can see you put the fuses back in the holder wrong. I'll sort them out for you. But the coil's red hot, Howard! You'd better leave it outside the garage."

John eventually fitted me a new coil and off I went. A week before Christmas I started blowing the odd fuse again. I still hadn't made it down to Kent. No phone in those days, so I sent Arthur a Christmas card with a note saying I was unable to make it. I booked John in to take another look at the engine, but the earliest he could do was 28th December. I was able to travel short distances until Christmas day when I went to check Drake over prior to driving 13 miles to Farnsfield to see Lynn Turton, a friend from the 208 flats. I removed the bonnet and went to the boot to get the anti-freeze to top up the radiator. A wind sprang up seemingly from nowhere and knocked over the bonnet smashing the headlights. Drake was now firmly disabled, and I was no longer able to drive up to visit Lynn. So that was my Christmas 1974 – up the Brussels sprouts! I went back to my flat and mindlessly watched the rubbish Christmas Day programmes for a couple of hours, but I was so fed up that I eventually went out to the phone box to ring a taxi to go to Lynn's. I was up in Farnsfield within half an hour. That taxi must have cost the earth on Christmas Day, but I didn't care. I'm glad I did it though, because I had a great evening with the Turtons and managed to get my mind back on an even keel.

On December 28th 1974, I drove Drake round to John's house for him to check out what was wrong with the vehicle. He brought the car round the next day.

"It wasn't the fuse holder that had been causing your problems, or the battery or the jack handle," he said. "There's a spade clip missing on the milometer fitting. The wire was just hooked through. Every time it was jogged it would blow your fuse. Didn't you straighten the milometer just before you went to Wales?"

I confess I was then in a state of shock, lost for words as my mind flashed back to my 'getting the car in order' for the Wales holiday. The milometer was off-centre, so I had straightened it up, losing the spade clip in the process, so I hooked the bare wire through the hole. I have never really enjoyed Christmas, and this was one of the worst.

"You prat!" said John.

In the summer of 1975, Paul Matharu and I went down to Hertfordshire to see Cliff Richard playing Bottom in *A Midsummer's Night's Dream* at Cliff's old school, the Cheshunt Secondary Modern.

It was great drinking down there, a perfect, balmy mid-summer afternoon, and a great evening watching Cliff shine as Bottom. No doubt about it, he could act. After the show, we did a detour to the MGM studios at Boreham Wood, at least, where they used to be. It was such a shame that the studios were now derelict: it had been a thriving MGM when I first visited in 1964. In 1975 the building was demolished to be replaced by a cold storage plant. The last production filmed there was the TV series *U.F.O.*

By now, the Mini was using a lot of oil. In the 120 miles from Elstree to Nottingham I used a gallon of oil. I saved up enough to have a full Gold Seal Engine refurbishment, which improved matters no end, plus I could really put my foot down. Fiona lived in a great, cosy terraced house on Portland Road in West Bridgford and when her housemate said she was pulling out, Fiona asked if I wanted to move in. However, I found West Bridgford too quiet for my liking and the rent was considerably more than I was paying. I'd heard that a ground floor flat at 208 Mansfield Road on the other side of Nottingham was available. It had a large kitchen and lounge with coal fire, small study, large bedroom and a cellar for storage and coal deliveries; and was 20 minutes' walk from the city centre. I convinced Fiona to move in with me. However, in the long run, it turned out to be a huge mistake. There was one shared bathroom between ten flats. As time went on, I realised that it was not fair on Fiona to have to share with so many other people. It was alright for me; I was used to roughing it and I could do my ablutions at the Eastcroft. Plus, we both started to miss the peace and quiet of West Bridgford. But I selfishly wanted to stay there, because it was so cheap and convenient. Eventually, the situation got to us both and after five years we agreed to split up. For all of the grief and stress I gave you Fiona, I would now like to apologise. My fault totally!

One morning in early 1977 on the way to *Crossroads*, Drake's fan belt snapped just outside Derby. I was in the 7am rush hour traffic and I panicked. One episode missed by yours truly and that would be the end of Nobby the mechanic. Luckily, I had forked out for RAC membership and there was a phone box nearby, so I rang. They said they would get to me in half an hour. All the 15-day episodes I had completed up till then didn't require my presence until about 10am. The RAC were prompt, they replaced the fan belt, and I was on my way by 8am with 40 miles to go. By now, I was running an hour later than usual, and the traffic had really built-up, but I made it for 9.30am. Would you believe it, this was the only time I was ever on first call in the ten years of *Crossroads*. The tannoy was red hot.

"Final call for Howard Jacks to studio one, Howard Jacks to studio one."

I just made it, without any of the hierarchy noticing, phew. Unfortunately, this meant the end of Drake. I couldn't risk that type of thing happening again, plus the bodywork was starting to go and that would have been more expense. Sometimes we would be working on the car until 9pm at night and then we would both have to set off to a grim night at work. And it always seemed to be winter! I would miss having Drake, it had been a helluva lot of fun for three years, and I have John Emberton, my special agent for cars to thank for all that. I went round to the TSB and arranged a bank loan for a Fiat 127 (the precursor to the

Uno.) My first hatchback and, luxury, it had a radio, the first one I ever had in a car. I chose this one because my girlfriend Giovanna had one, so I was familiar with it. Ahh Giovanna, the spitting image of Candice Bergen. We met at car maintenance classes.

With 'Candice' on my minivan

Owning a car got me in the end though. From 1977 to 1995 I had had four Fiats without any mechanical problems. Come 1995, I decided I wouldn't need a car and would sell it in due course. For the first time in 23 years, I paid for third party insurance rather than fully comprehensive. I had been hired for a day's extra work on *Peak Practice* at the Law Courts in Derby. When it came to lunchtime, the assistant director came over to us and said they had all the shots they needed and we could go, still being paid for the full day. Central knew how to run things. He did however ask me to stay as I may still be needed. At about

3pm he came over to say that it was a wrap, and I wouldn't be needed anymore. Up till that point it had been a nice sunny day but as I drove off it started to rain. The A52 is a dual carriageway and I remember getting up to 50mph when suddenly there was a car stopped in the fast lane, no flashing warning lights or indicators. I learnt later that a few seconds earlier a dog had run out and the car in front had hit it. At 50mph on a dry road I would have braked in time, no problem, but instead I slithered into the back of the other vehicle. I put on my hazard warning lights immediately. My bonnet was dented into a V shape and the car was not driveable, so it was a matter of getting my stuff out of the car and waiting for the police and the RAC. The breakdown truck came and gave me a lift to Chilwell where I had arranged to see a girlfriend, Joyce. I walked round to her flat in order to get drunk and forget. I had guessed it would be a write-off and I was right. It never dawned on me that third party meant you get absolutely nothing! Twenty-three years of fully comprehensive and no claims to one month of third party.

Adios Fiat the fourth. I never owned another one!

6

The Stripper

1980 to 1989

Towards the end of the 1970s, the lease was up on The Barn Theatre used by the Wollaton Drama Group. They had to move out to the Sheila Russell Centre in Bilborough. This meant that at the end of rehearsals each night, I had an extra ten minutes added to my race back to the Eastcroft to clock on for 10pm. I tried hard to keep up, but in the end I did only one more play with them, *The Golden Pathway Annual.* As it turned out, it was one of the most rewarding theatre pieces of my career. My parents' names in the play were George and Enid. Easy to remember, since my parents were called George and Edna, and what's more it was my own history being played out on stage. A working-class lad brought up at the end of the 40s, his daydreams and fantasies moving from planning to be a missionary, to wanting to be James Bond. I never managed to be seduced by a French language tutor as the character was, but otherwise it was spot on. A great play, directed by my good friend Mike Ridley and an excellent way to exit from The Wollaton Drama Group after six years. Unfortunately, Mike passed away in March 2021 after a long illness, and I will miss his company and easy-going humour. I wish I had kept in touch with him in later years more often than I had. Thank you for all those many rewarding and happy drama times. Vaya Con Dios, amigo.

I had been going to watch plays at the Lace Market Theatre in Nottingham, another 'amateur' group that regularly put on plays. In the bar afterwards, I saw you could put your name down for auditions. The theatre location was perfect, being a five-minute drive to the Eastcroft. My first play at the Lace Market was *Death of a Salesman*, by Arthur Miller. I was playing Bernard, a neighbour of Willy Loman, the salesman of the title, and a bit of a nerd compared to Willy's butch sons Biff and Happy. Happy was played by Steve Mills who became a good friend, and Biff was played by Ian Smith who went on to create and direct the Central Television Junior Workshop. I managed to upset the director of *Death of a Salesman* early on. During our rehearsals I noticed that 'Arkansas' was being pronounced as written – Arkan-SAS – and pointed out it is pronounced Arkan-SAW, but she was having none of this: "I know what I'm doing thank you" and told me to look to my part and let her do the directing. That was fine by me, I thought I was right, but I kept my head down. However, not long before the first night, one of the stalwarts of the theatre group called in and listened carefully to our rehearsal. She was a polite lady and didn't make a fuss, but immediately after the show she took the director aside for some quiet words. She was advised to pronounce it my way. No word of apology from the director. I knew it was right, you see, because I had grown up on all those Westerns on TV.

♪ Sugarfoot, Sugarfoot ♪
You'll find him on the side of law and order,
♪ From the Mexicali Border to the rolling hills of
Arkansas. ♪
(Arkan-SAW)

She got her own back, however. At the dress rehearsal she changed the staging so that I came on with a table and chair, setting the scene. I have never been good at changes being sprung on me; I need to rehearse a lot, so even though I knew the lines, I dried and needed a prompt on the first night. I made sure that I got it right the rest of the week though!

Ian Smith and I were then cast in *Hamlet*, done in a futuristic style. I was Guildenstern and he was Rosencrantz. It was a hugely enjoyable production and Max Bromley was superb as Hamlet, deeply morose one moment and then doing a lively and impressive sword fencing scene the next. Meanwhile, I had auditioned for the boy Alan Strong in *Equus*, but I lost out to a lad who, I was told, was dyslexic and so he had memorised all the lines before the audition. My next venture at the Lace Market Theatre was Launcelot Gobbo, servant to Shylock, in *The Merchant of Venice* directed by Gordon Parsons. We'd done Shakespeare at the Academy, and I'd learnt to read the explanatory notes at the back. It turned out to be great fun to play Launcelot Gobbo because he argues against his own conscience, making nasty remarks about Shylock as his master and as a Jew, so even I was able to spot he was meant to be a young man of poor taste with only the odd flash of wit. I was learning the tricks of the profession. At one point, I had to pull an envelope out of a briefcase, but I kept fumbling it in rehearsal. So I put three in there. As James Garner said, "Acting is all about common sense." Gordon let me be really extravagant in playing the clown in this part and we had a lot of laughs.

In the Autumn of 1980, I was offered a days' work as an extra on Yorkshire Television's, *The Good Companions*. At least it wasn't going to be filmed in their Yorkshire homeland headquarters so nothing could go wrong, or so I thought. It was well paid, so I decided to do the job, despite having grave reservations about being scalped again. When we arrived at the location in the Peak District at The Crich Tramway Museum, we were instructed to change and go to make-up. Which was...... yes, take off! A very uneven short back and sides. Then we waited three hours to be used. It's not uncommon to wait around but I wasn't impressed. I had a hat and scarf on, so just for stubbornness I pulled the hat down and pulled the scarf up, turning up the collar of the overcoat, so you couldn't see my hair. The next day I had to go to Michael Dockery The Barbers on Mansfield Road to get it evened out. A traditional hairdresser, even he thought it was a hatchet job. I cancelled the agent who provided me with the work and never worked for Yorkshire Television again. By contrast, during the summer of 1981 I had a day's work as a 'special skills' dancing extra in *Great Expectations* at Pebble Mill BBC in Birmingham. Those dance classes with Roy and Mary Knight, plus Sid Wildgust and his sister at the Arnold scout hut came in handy after all. The choreography was intense. We had to waltz around the studio set, but in a certain stylized Victorian way. It was a long day, but I enjoyed every minute of it. For many years, I was paid £1.50 repeat royalties every year for *Great Expectations*! There was always a great atmosphere at Pebble Mill and it's a shame it had to close. If ATV/Central was 10/10, Pebble Mill was a close runner-up at 9/10, and Yorkshire Television 0/10.

When in 1981 Peter Palmer formed the Nottingham Music Theatre, I had the pleasure of working for him on four opera productions. I was very surprised, and relieved, to find that most of those singing opera smoked and liked a jar or two. I came to sing on stage in *Love Scenes From Shakespeare*, in a scene taken from the Merchant of Venice, it was *Tell Me Where Is Fancy Bred* and I was able to come out with a fair baritone. I was also the roadie, driving the van bringing scenery on and off stage and helping to assemble it. The final performance was in the round, at The Catholic Hall, the rear of The Cathedral on Nottingham's Derby Road, after which we all retired to The Strathdon Hotel across the road to celebrate the end of the run. It was at this gathering in 1981 that I met that glorious, formidable lady Elizabeth Porges Watson.

"You missed two lines from one of the speeches, you know," murmured Elizabeth, cigarette holder in one hand and a large whisky in another. (In the films she would be played by Valerie Hobson out of *Kind Hearts And Coronets*.)

I replied that I did realise this at the time, but it had been a mental block and I'd not done it in any of the previous five performances. For the next hour and a half, we chatted about Shakespeare and the book she was writing about the legend of King Arthur. Meanwhile, I was giving Elizabeth some close scrutiny. She had that noble lady look about her with long dark hair scraped back Spanish style. To my mind, she looked like the flamenco dancers I remembered from Andalucía. I was in my late thirties around this time. Elizabeth was in her mid-forties. She told me that she was the head lecturer for English at Nottingham University. When we had a break in the conversation, I asked her if she would like to meet up sometime for a few drinks and she agreed. We met up several times over the summer. Then she told me it was, "Jolly pleasant and good fun going out with you, but it cannot possibly go any further, because I happen to be having an affair."

With a married man, as it turned out. I made a strong case for this, meaning she could have other affairs if she wanted, after all that's what he was doing. However, she was true to her word and wouldn't talk about it further. I was fascinated by her and not at all minded to give up. She lived in a large Victorian House on Hope Drive in The Park behind Nottingham Castle and was what my mum would call a 'dirty toff', which I knew enough by then to pronounce as 'bohemian'. I set out to impress her. About ten minutes' walk away was a club called 'Part Two'. Gay clubs were not all that common in those days, but this one was well known for celebrities turning up there. Membership was very strict. However, I had my Equity Card and thought maybe it would get me in. I knew she would treat it as an adventure to make into one of her anecdotes. One Sunday night, as I began to walk her home along Canal Street. It was only about 11pm.

"Surely we are not going home already?" she asked.

"No, we're going in here," I said, as we entered the foyer of 'Part Two'.

The doorman had a good suit on and was very big indeed. "Are you a member sir?" he asked.

"No, I'm afraid not," I said, "but will my Equity Card suffice?"

He looked me up and down and said, "Step this way sir."

Inside, in the dark and through the cigarette smoke, I could see that a cabaret band was playing surrounded by couples at tables. Elizabeth was most impressed. I sat her down and went to the bar. There was Lionel Bart. I'd heard that he was in Nottingham to do some work at The Playhouse. As well as being a dancer and writer, he had numerous musical hits including Cliff Richards' *Living Doll* and the theme song for my favourite Bond film, *From Russia With Love*. He looked over at me and I would have loved a chat with him about the business. I didn't go up to him, though this was not due to a lack of confidence on my part. I generally feel it would be an intrusion, and that they would have heard it all before. What do you say "Oh, I just loved *Oliver* as a film? Tell me etc....?" Especially in a public place, where you couldn't have a proper chat because it wouldn't be long before someone came over to interrupt. I went back to the table with our drinks to watch some comedy sketches on the little stage. By the end of the night, we were talking to a musical quartet, three lads and a young woman who were planning to drive through the night in order to perform at the Edinburgh Festival.

"Oh no, we can't have that, can we Howard?" said Elizabeth. "Put your props and scenery into the van and park it up outside my house. It's just down the road and you can stay the night there, then you'll be fresh to drive up tomorrow."

So, they did. While I lost any chance of canoodling with Elizabeth that night.

Once, she asked me during the hot summer of 1981 if I would be kind enough to feed her six cats the day after she had gone away. When I entered the first-floor kitchen where they were, the toxic smell was so overwhelming she should have supplied me with a respirator. The felines gained access by walking along a ledge to the narrow opening of the kitchen window. Elizabeth had easily gone away at least two days before. I had to come out, take a deep breath and go in a few times, emptying the litter trays and spooning out the food.

Our next activity together was going to Munslow in Shropshire.

"Howard," she said, "May I borrow you for a long weekend?"

My heart lit up.

"I need a chauffeur. It's high time I paid a visit to my dear mama, and you'll be most useful in breaking the ice between us."

I had heard that 'dear mama' was herself quite formidable, so I was looking forward to seeing how this went down with Elizabeth who is herself quite a strong character. We arrived at Munslow mid-afternoon, where Elizabeth requested we had a couple of drinks at the local Swan Inn before going up to the house. We arrived just as the sun was setting. I realise I have watched far too many films in my life, but my, it was dramatic. As the autumn sun was setting in a welter of reds and oranges across the sky, we drove up to a large old parsonage in the Georgian style. Mama came out to greet us as we were unloading the car, accompanied by Mabel, who I had been told was her companion and housekeeper, and had been for 20 years. The lounge had a large coal fire, brightening the room and casting dark shadows across the gothic features up above. Mabel brought tea and scones and we all sat together to scoff them. Elizabeth was more on edge than I had ever seen her. She introduced her mother as Emily, although I didn't get much of a chance to find out about her as she was the one asking questions, politely, but without pause, about what Elizabeth had been up to "these past six months." She didn't leave me out, turning to me with a definite twinkle in her eye as they talked. When Elizabeth decided she would go upstairs to unpack I stayed behind. As Elizabeth went up the stairs, Mrs Porges Watson turned to me to say, "I wouldn't mind guessing that she has a bottle of whisky in that case." She was a man's woman alright! I sat happily with her and Mabel until Elizabeth came down again, talking about what we had been up to. Dinner was roast lamb served with a very up-market Rioja wine. I was pleased to see that Mabel joined us. I had brought a white wine which was pleasantly received, but which disappeared into the kitchen and didn't emerge again. I didn't mind. I'm not a big fan of white wine these days, wouldn't touch it now. After dinner, we were both offered a brandy in the lounge, and eventually to bed – in separate rooms.

The next day, mother, Elizabeth and I went for a walk over to the Long Mynd. We climbed up a steep valley and around the bottom of a couple of massive hills. I had never seen anything like it. I later saw it featured in *Gone To Earth* a film adapted from Mary Webb's book by two of my favourite film makers, Michael Powell and Emeric Pressburger. After a late lunch at the Swan Inn, Mrs Porges Watson and Elizabeth felt the need to have an afternoon nap. Me? I was on a high, unable to sleep from the excitement of yet another new environment. Before they went up, I asked if they had any photo albums I could look at. Elizabeth looked at me curiously, while her mother brought out four large albums. I sat on the floor, in front of a roaring fire looking over photographs taken in the first 60 years of the last century. 'Papa', as it was written there, turned out to be captain of The Queen Mary during the thirties, although I couldn't find his name on the list of captains, so I can only assume it was a previous husband. He appeared in idyllic photographs, in cap and medals, accompanied by his daughter and wife. Vintage cards, holidays on the south coast and in the West Country, days on ship. It was another world of time gone by. As the sun set, I dozed in front of the fire and only woke when I heard footsteps on the stairs. Mabel prepared a salad for our tea, when I took the opportunity to regale all three of them with a host of questions about everything I had seen in the photographs. I was genuinely interested in the stories behind them, but I was also plotting to warm Elizabeth up in the hope she would drift across to my room that night. However, Elizabeth became more tense as the night wore on. A couple of bottles of red wine were opened and I did carry on somewhat, caught up in my own interests. It was a cold night alone in my bed. I was still hopeful, though. It was a most unusual weekend, and I loved every minute of it. I would've loved to keep in touch and gone back again to visit The Parsonage at Munslow, if other events hadn't occurred.

In 1981, Elizabeth invited me over for Christmas Day dinner. When I arrived, she introduced me to a friend, Yvonne, and her daughter Rachel who was six years old. It appeared that Yvonne was staying after splitting up with her partner, Bernard. After dinner, the four of us sat round the coal fire in the lounge chatting. Elizabeth didn't have a television but none of us noticed. Rachel went to bed early as she was tired out and the three of us were absolutely blasted on drink. Yvonne was humorous and witty. We spent several hours putting the world to rights while I enjoyed the company of two fabulous women. About 10pm, Yvonne said it had been a long day and retired up to the spare room. "That's it," I realised, "No menage a trois for me. It's either blankets on the settee or a trudge home." Elizabeth returned to the lounge. Slowly and somewhat dramatically, I thought. She sat down and poured herself a large brandy, picked up her cigarette holder and placed a cigarette into it, gazing into the fire.

"Is everything alright, Elizabeth?" I asked. It looked as if I would be walking home through the snow.

Still gazing into the fire, she said, "Yvonne has asked if you would care to share her bed tonight."

I was lost for words. Then I said "Elizabeth, what do you think of that?"

She said, "Howard, I don't mind at all. Have a good time. See you in the morning."

I spent a few minutes with her, kissed her on the cheek and retired to the spare room and Yvonne. It was quite romantic in that spare room, with just the glow of an electric fire. Without going into the details, I may say that I didn't have very much sleep and then only when the light came through the window at dawn. Breakfast was an uncomfortable affair, not least because I was hugely hungover and very tired. I left late morning and went straight to bed. The best Christmas present I'd ever had! A few days later, Yvonne confessed that the turkey Elizabeth had placed in the bath to defrost had been assaulted by those pesky cats. They managed to rescue it in time, salvaging half. They cleaned it up and decided it was better I wasn't informed. I asked her out for another drink on New Year's Eve. Although it was snowing, people were larking about in the fountains on the city centre known as 'Slab Square'. Yvonne was very funny indeed, recounting stories about how she had to go to masonic events with Bernard and that she had met Elizabeth on one of their 'Ladies Nights'. Before Bernard, she had been married to Peter Tomlinson, a six-foot three-inch-tall policeman, in the mould of Brian Blessed playing Fancy Smith in *Z-Cars*. He was Rachel's father. Bernard had been physically abusive to Yvonne, building up to the climax at Christmas, when she left him. With this background, it was a surprise to me that Yvonne was prepared to take up with me, and of course a delight. Yvonne and Rachel continued to stay at Hope Drive for a short time and I visited occasionally, staying overnight in the very cold front lounge with blankets in front of the log fire. After an hour or so I had to struggle out to put more logs on. Eventually they moved into a women's refuge. Looking back, I was a bit of a sod to Elizabeth for not staying away from her house until Yvonne was able to move out to the refuge, but I was entranced. Yvonne was Israeli in origin, a beautiful dark-haired woman resembling the young Tracey Ullman and with a similar sense of humour. She and Rachel did mad things together. One morning returning to the flat from the Eastcroft, I found that overnight they had totally filled the room with balloons for my birthday!

In October 1981, I had one of the most hilarious jobs I'd ever had. Still working on *Crossroads* and at the Eastcroft, I received a phone call from Central TV Casting. They asked if I would be one of four pantomime horses on location for an insert on *TISWAS*, a Saturday morning children's show, which stood for *Today Is Saturday Watch And Smile*. It was the first anarchic children's show on UK television. Don't eat beans they joked. At 9am prompt, on the Monday morning, I turned up at the running track in Aston for the 'Pantomime Horses Race'. Happily, I was the front of a horse. For the next hour and a half we frolicked around the track. We were given some basic direction about which horse went where but were given a 'free rein' for the larking about. After a break for lunch at the ATV stables, it was 'Pantomime Horses Shopping At Tesco', just up the road from ATV. Strangely, shoppers carried on as per normal apart from the fact that four pantomime horses were running up and down the aisles. After that, we went to a playing field. At first, the director Bob Cousins was annoyed to find that a local youth football team were playing on the field, but after a quick chat with them he sent us in as the opposing team – all completely improvised. Except for the opening shot, where we had been told to run down the hill and onto the playing ground. "Cut, cut, cut," he shouted. "Howard! You're going the wrong way!" I had gone right instead of left, of course. I nearly lost my place as front of horse, but it was fine. The ten-year-olds on the playing field fell in with it, messing around with the Panto Horses who were trying to steal the ball from them. By now, it was about 4pm and rush hour. Off we went to a zebra crossing in suburban Birmingham. The Panto Horses trotted over the zebra crossing one way then another, while the traffic beeped at us. In the end though, cars were stopping just to watch and wave. Brummies have a great sense of humour. A week later, we went to Hollywood, a village near Birmingham. There we picked up some extra shots of Panto Horses grazing and some horsy facial reaction shots. There were small controls in the head that made the eyes and mouth move. A couple of weeks later, I went into the canteen for lunch and sat down at Bob's table.

I said, "Bob, I've got an idea for doing another Pantomime Horse sequence. Can't they be trotting through *Crossroads* Reception?!"

Bob replied, "Been done mate, I thought of that very thing last week. I went to see Jack Barton, the producer, and put it to him, but he didn't think it was a good idea. He thought it would hold the show up to ridicule."

I can see it now. We focus on Noele Gordon playing Meg Mortimer in reception, talking about admin policy to Jane Rossington as her daughter Jill and Tony Adams playing Adam Chance. Backs to the entrance. The Panto Horses come in behind the three of them, one after another, mugging to the camera while the actors are totally oblivious.

I am proud to say that I also appeared as a Phantom Flan Flinger in the *TISWAS* cage. We filmed it in the same studio as used for *Crossroads*. I had been in there the day before, playing Nobby. There were six of us, dressed in the black leotards and tights of a Phantom Flan Flinger, with hats or headdresses for the most stereotypical of nationalities. There was a US Cowboy (Stetson), a Native American Chief (feather headdress), a Mexican (sombrero) among others, and me, with a wide coolie hat as a Chinese Phantom Flan Flinger. With the hat on, I looked like a great big nail. We were placed in a cage then Sally James and Lenny Henry came past, acting the fool. I did my best to appear like the sweetest puppy in the cage for Sally. She turned and walked away. I pawed at the cage bars and whined. A huge bucket of gunge fell on our heads. Great fun, and for this I was paid quite well thank you. Bob Cousins went on to direct Bullseye, Spitting Image and Dale's Supermarket Sweep. He is a great bloke, very funny and easy going. I really enjoyed working with him on those two *TISWAS* sessions.

On 13th October I was asked to take part in the *Crossroads* Motel bonfire night party at Long Marston airfield 25 miles away near Stratford on Avon. Strange I thought, why go that far? When we arrived for the cast meeting at The Masons Arms pub, we were informed it was for security reasons. It was to be the final episode featuring the death of Noele Gordon in a fire at the motel. Other endings had already been filmed to confuse the press, who were seen flying around the area in a helicopter all afternoon till sunset. Heck, I thought, is this marking the end of the series? After a hearty tea we all went out and performed various activities around the bonfire, fireworks etc. If you don't blink, I can be glimpsed, briefly. They put some inflammable jelly around the set erected on the airfield and, luckily, used three or four cameras, because when they set fire to the set it blazed up in a furnace a lot quicker than expected! Yet again another great night shoot I didn't want to end.

Yvonne never seemed to want a job, even after she settled down in a council house in Sneinton. I did my best to help out. I had my TV work, the odd play and an active social life, so we really only saw each other at weekends. I went with her and Rachel to visit her parents in Mablethorpe a few times. One night I had to take a back seat when she decided she wanted to enter a disco dance competition at some function rooms. I was reluctant so Yvonne asked someone else. They matched each other really well and building up to the climax Yvonne finished off their set by 'limboing' down to the other chap's nether regions. They won first prize for the most original dance sequence! No doubt about it, Yvonne and I were soul mates. She had a black cat, a lovely, delicate creature called TC (Top Cat), who I got on with very well, often playing together in the grass weeds at the back of Yvonne's house. She went in and out of the house through Yvonne's bedroom window, by jumping on the low roof below it. One morning, Yvonne told me, she had woken up to find four cats on her bed. TC had brought three of her mates round after a night out. Of course, Yvonne gave them a slap-up meal for breakfast. When TC was about to give birth, I'd arranged to meet up with Steve and Martin, so Yvonne said she would keep an eye on the proceedings. I came back four hours later to hear Yvonne shouting for me to come upstairs, whereupon TC gracefully gave birth to two mini TC's. Yvonne said she was convinced TC had held back until I returned home! Once TC ran up a very tall tree and stayed there. Yvonne and I did all we could to bring her down, but she wouldn't budge so Yvonne rang the fire brigade. I don't know how it works today, but in those days, you had to pay for the fire brigade if it was for a tree-stranded cat and, unfortunately, TC decided she would come down after all, just before the fire brigade arrived. Luckily, Yvonne was able to charm them into excusing her from the fine. TC was very adventurous, and one day she was lounging on the road underneath an electric milk cart which started instantly when it set off, crushing her. TC somehow managed to hobble down the road and clamber up through the bathroom window, even though her back end was crushed. Yvonne rang for a taxi and went straight to the PDSA in Dunkirk, near Nottingham. She stayed with TC all afternoon while the vet worked on her. She told me later that TC was so badly injured that her inner eye and third eyelid had emerged, which the vet had told her was a serious injury reaction. Luckily, TC survived the operation. The vet placed a thin steel rod through her haunch to help knit the fractured bone together and Yvonne brought her home in a borrowed cat bed. I was horrified not to have been there as I had spent a lot of time in TC's company. The steel rod came out only a couple of weeks later and TC was soon back to her normal self, although I think she must have used up all her nine lives.

Steve Mills and I were still meeting up for a drink regularly. He was taking a similar route to mine – packing in a good job at the council Planning Department of Leicester City Council to go and study at Mountview Theatre School. Around this time, I also met Martin Goddard, who was promoting the Wollaton Drama Group productions, which I still went to see regularly. (In the films, Steve would be played by Dennis Waterman and Martin by Robert Powell.) Later on, they could easily have doubled as the leads in *The Detectives*, the BBC comedy show of the mid-nineties. I've had some great mates in the past and will give most of them eight out of ten. However, with Martin and Steve, it was a ten out of ten right from the start. We knew where each of us was coming from and had funny times winding each other up. We shared a great fondness for the first four

Bond films, 60s music, Indie pop, TV and films. Martin was involved professionally in marketing with great social skills, and was really good at meeting people. Through him, a whole network of new acquaintances sprang up. Other people I admire also turned up around this time. I had read Quentin Crisp's *The Naked Civil Servant* and seen the TV drama with John Hurt. I liked his Bohemian philosophy very much: "After three years the dust doesn't get any worse." When in the summer of 1981 he was doing his one-man show at Nottingham Playhouse, I immediately booked myself a ticket and bought the book he was promoting: *How To Become A Virgin.* Strangely enough, when reading through the book, lo and behold there was his London telephone number. I rang it and he answered, I asked him if he could spare half an hour before the show to chat about life and the acting world. He said yes, and to meet him at the Green Room at 2.30pm prior to his matinee. I asked for his advice on things, agents, etc, and we chatted merrily for half an hour as if we had known each other for a long while. I remember one thing he said was that when acting and mixing socially in this world, "Don't try to be someone else, be yourself." "This above all else, to thine own self be true," he said, and laughed. Just before he went on stage, he said if ever I wanted to meet up again in London to give him a call. I would have loved to but had too much going on to pay him a visit. It was a kind offer and I really regret not finding the time to meet up again.

I made some other good friends too. During 1981, I was walking down the corridor at Central TV on my way to rehearse a scene, when I noticed a black guy walking towards me. It was his Radio Caroline T-shirt that caught my eye. It had been 15 years since most of the 60s pirate radio stations had been axed, so I just had to stop him and ask how come he was wearing it. "Ronan O'Rahilly, who ran Radio Caroline, is a close friend of mine. Why do you ask?" Out it all came: my interest in Free Radio and the many times I had heard the best of tunes for the first time from the pirates in the 60s. We bonded over a love of good toons. This was Carl Andrews, who was taking on the role of Joe McDonald, a garage mechanic. Obviously, I was envious that he had a substantial part, but I couldn't have wished it to happen to a better bloke. We began to chat whenever I was doing episodes and meet up in the ATV bar occasionally. It was as if we had known each other for ages. He mentioned once that he had a liking for cowboy boots and was on the lookout. A week later, in the 'tatting area' we all sifted through at the Eastcroft, I found a pair, size 10, quality red leather, as good as new. They looked handmade. Why anyone would throw them away is anyone's guess. I polished them up and took them along to Central TV. They were big boots though, a size ten. When I bumped into Carl two weeks later, I asked, "Right then Carl, what size shoe are you?"

"What kind of question is that then Howard? I'm a size ten."

I pulled them out of my bag – you should have seen his face! He was over the moon at the style and asked me how much I wanted for them, which was nothing at all. He was a FAB bloke and even now I miss him loads. Carl Andrews 1947 to 1990. Vaya Con Dios amigo.

"LITTLE WILLY"

All will be revealed!

In the first part of 1983, Yvonne and I had a row and split up for nearly a year. It was the only serious dispute we ever had and for the life of me I can't remember what it was about. I moped about for a bit and then decided I needed some more activity in my social life. A friend told me that if I wanted to try something different, I could always apply to a stripping agency to chauffer ladies about at weekends. I got in touch with them and offered my services. The managers – let's call them Tom and Sue – asked me round to their house for a chat first. When they started talking about the Working Men's Clubs and Miners' Welfare Socials, I was happy to tell them that I was already familiar with that culture. They were a down to earth couple who were keen to help out their charges. They set me on using my own car. By that time I had a telephone, so they could call me a week or so beforehand with instructions.

It was great fun, driving to the different venues on a Sunday lunchtime with some very attractive ladies. A couple of months in, I was invited by the 'Silver Lady' to her house. She lived in an old Victorian terraced house near Bulwell, which I drove up to for tea one Saturday afternoon. Downstairs, we went through subdued lighting to a back room where a coal fire was blazing. She produced salmon and cucumber sandwiches, with home-made scones and jam to follow, all in the romantic glow of the fire. My heart soared when she asked me upstairs. As we rose out of the stairwell, I could see into the bedroom and a living room on the first floor. Both were a mass of dolls. Hundreds of dolls, some of them in glass cases. Silver Lady took me round each room, pointing out her particular favourites and giving me their names. Spooky it certainly was, but I realised that she was confiding in me, showing off her pride and joy, and trusting me to understand why she had invited me into her home. I took an interest, asking about the history of a few of the dolls. We had some more tea and she let me know that her brother was coming round that evening, which was my cue to leave. Ah well!

Mum and Dad gave me the best ever birthday present in May 1983. It was a Grundig Video 2000 recorder. This was going to make working at night a lot easier. The recording quality was leaps and bounds ahead of VHS and Betamax and it was certainly original in that you could record on both sides just like an audio cassette. Eventually, they produced cassettes on which you could record for eight hours either side! But it didn't survive the 80s consumer war for various technical reasons and because it never managed to acquire the library of films that VHS had. But that didn't bother me anyway, I was always recording the TV programmes I had missed due to my night shift and social life. I loved that machine; it was like an old friend and it was a sad day when seven years later I dumped in the back of a bin lorry in lieu of a new VHS model.

In the summer of 1983, I had a call to do a day's work at Central Studios on *The Country Diary Of An Edwardian Lady*, an autobiographical drama about the life of Edith Holden, the West Midlands artist and author of *Nature Notes 1906*, which became *The Country Diary*. They drove me to the location, which was a field in rural Dorridge in the West Midlands. After lunch at the site, I was issued with a waistcoat, baggy trousers and a shirt without a collar, and told to walk over to the other end of the field and start to scythe some wheat growing there. Pippa Guard, who was playing Edith Holden, and Isabelle Amyes, would be walking towards me and at a certain spot I would say "Good afternoon, m'lady" in a Dorridge accent, and touch my forehead in salute. After three different set-ups, it was in the can within an hour and a half, and I was driven home. The route was idyllic, a balmy afternoon through trees and past wheat fields. Marvellous! A few weeks later, Central TV rang and said they were sending me a copy of the book that accompanied the TV series. They said to open it in the middle. It was a very glossy coffee table book, with lots of colour photographs. I opened it in the middle and there I was. A double page, colour spread with the two actors, me, a scythe and a wheat field. Cracking.

I went to as many parties as I could find during 1983. One Saturday evening, I was at a party in Hyson Green in Nottingham and shared a couple of spliffs. Even in my youth this was rare for me as I am generally already chilled out. The next thing I knew it was 2am and I had to be chauffeuring two ladies up north to Sheffield at 10am that morning. I bundled myself out of the door and walked along Gregory Boulevard to my flat on Mansfield Road. Instead of taking just 20 minutes as normal, it took an hour. Four paces forward, four behind! I hit my bed and forgot to set my alarm, woke up at 10am on the dot. I ran out the door and fell into the car, drove to the pick-up point at Raleigh Island on Western Boulevard. The ladies were not too happy with me, because if they missed a set, they didn't get paid. I apologised profusely and did my best to catch up some time on the motorway. I dropped the first lady off outside a Miners Welfare in Darnall just 15 minutes late. After that, I set off for The Attercliffe Steel Workers Federation & Welfare Club – CIU Affiliated. I tootled around a ghost town of empty steel mills, dark foundries and boarded up houses, trying to find the Welfare Club without success. No one around to ask. My passenger, 'Lady Lashes' gave me to understand that she was hugely annoyed with me, which helped me come round completely. I got her there 45 minutes late, which meant she had missed her first spot. In today's terms, she had lost about £80. As I opened the door for her, I told her the fare both ways would be free. She stomped into the venue without replying. Lady Lashes looked the part: she was dressed up ready in a leather basque, stockings and suspender belt, thigh high boots and a whip, so she made a fantastic entrance. I had to wait in the audience, not normally a chore, but unfortunately for me her act was not on stage but in the round. The steel works had closed down recently. Fifty-odd ex-steelworkers probably didn't understand why she kept cracking the whip in my direction, but I did! Later I dropped her off at the Midland Train Station back in Nottingham. She had calmed down by then. I think she enjoyed frightening the life out of me. After that incident, I never went out the night before chauffeuring again!

In the spring of 1984. I had a night shoot as a soldier at Ferry Meadows, Nene Park, near Peterborough. It was for a BBC dramatised documentary on the war hero Airey Neave who was the first man to escape from Colditz. The unit was based in the Ferry Meadows Visitors Centre. I just love night shooting. We were filming as an army unit waiting for Airey Neave to come in from across a lake or The Channel in a rowing boat. My job was to flash a Morse Code signal across the water to let him know where we were and that it was safe to come in. "Action" was called and I flashed away. Immediately came the cry "Cut!" The director came over and asked, amiably, what I was doing.

"I'm signalling safety to Airey Neave that it's safe to come in, is that right?"

"Ahh, very good Howard, but that was more like disco lights. SOS. That's what you're SUPPOSED to be doing."

This brought out chortles of laughter amongst the crew and made what was a very easy going shoot even more light-hearted. I loved working for the Beeb.

"OK Howard, we'll go again and it's three short flashes, three long flashes, three short. Can I see that please?"

Take 2 was a success and that was it. All finished for 1.00am with a hearty buffet. Even just doing that little bit, I was on a high and would have liked to have carried on til dawn, but they were the last shots of the night. Everything was being packed away. All I had to do was to wait for everyone to go and I would be sleeping in the back of the car. It was *Crossroads* next morning. Then came a pleasant surprise. A club pianist I had met on BBC's *Sons and Lovers* called Stan Holt was visiting nearby the next day. He had a word with the Production Supervisor and asked if we could both kip over in the Visitors Centre. The all clear was given just as everyone else packed up and left. Stan and I got our heads down about 2:30am, me in my sleeping bag on a large, cushioned settee. Stan must have done this before; he was well prepared on a collapsible bed with blankets. In the films, Stan would be played by Charles Hawtrey. We were sleeping peacefully, when at about 6am, I heard the outer doors open. In came a woman in a cleaner's overall, carrying some buckets. As I sat up, she saw us and let out a shriek and ran outside. You see it in films, but this was for real. Stan leapt off his put-you-up in his long-johns shouting, "It's alright, we've got permission!" He didn't manage to catch up with her and came back. We decided to grab another couple of hours and then go on our way, Not so. Just as we were dropping off about 20 minutes later, the police arrived, "Allo 'allo," etc. We explained. By this point, I was wondering if I would make it to *Crossroads* and that if I didn't, would they take Nobby away from me? Stan practically forced the telephone number of the production supervisor on them. They gave him a call and he was up, fortunately, so we were given the all-clear. The roads were surprisingly empty for rush hour at 8am, so I managed to arrive at Central TV for 9am with time for a shower and the usual hearty breakfast.

One day in the summer of 1983, Tom and Sue rang me. "You're a bit of an actor aren't you Howard?" asked Tom.

"Well yes, Tom, I am a bit of an actor."

"How do you feel about taking on the role of a stripper?" he said.

"I'll try anything that gets me noticed," I replied. "Is it a TV drama or a play?"

"Neither Howard," he said, "It's for real."

Tom explained that they were very short of male strippers. I thought, no lines to learn and maybe I'll get lucky after the show! Apparently, it doesn't matter how well 'equipped' you are. They gave me a mentor called 'Gentleman Bob'. He was a miner who lived out at Hucknall. I drove him to a gig he had just outside Bedford, where he was the support act for 'King Dick'. I did my best to concentrate, but it was a bit disheartening to watch a rather well-endowed King Dick and I was more interested in what the women in the audience were saying.

"Hey Mary, I bet he'd make your eyes water!"

"It's not my eyes I'm worried about!"

After the show, I called Sue and said I really didn't think I could compete in this particular arena. She asked me to come over to Wollaton, an up-market suburb and have a chat. In the office, she told me all about the strippers she had worked with. She explained that the difference between hen and stag parties is that women mainly go out to have a laugh, perhaps to cover nervousness, while men simply lust. I was very 'personable' and I should give it a go. I thought, "I'm happy to make women laugh, as long as I don't have to live up to any expectations." I decided to call myself 'Little Willy' and dress as a schoolboy. Sixth Form of course! For my first spot, I stripped to the tune *Little Willy* by Sweet, *Breakaway* by Tracey Ullman and *Wake Me Up Before You Go Go* by Wham. and went around the audience putting my besocked foot up women's skirts and dresses. The second spot was heavier, and I was more comfortable. Dressed as a rocker to *Bring on the Nubiles* by The Stranglers, *My Sharona* by The Knack, and *I Need You*, by The Kinks, dressed as a rocker in leathers. What did they do? They laughed. They giggled, they snorted, they roared and tried to pinch my bottom. I was fine with that too. I had some postcards of me printed up (clothes on) and gave them out at the next show. Gentleman Bob later politely told me off. I was supposed to charge 30p each. That would be about a pound in today's money. It turned out that postcards were part of his regular income, so he didn't want me undercutting him. I was fine with that, especially as the ladies often wanted a kiss with it. It pays to charge apparently. Bob himself was a big hit with the ladies. I once went with him for a gig in Manchester. At the end of the night, we stood by the exit signing autographs and selling the postcards. Bob signed five to my one – well, he was the star. Two women cornered him chatting away about the business,

"And what do yo do ma duck, when yer not cavortin' on stage?"

"I'm a miner down Hucknall pit."

"Are yer ma duck, well done. Good lad!"

Yes, I thought, well done for grafting away in the bowels of the earth. In their eyes he was just a regular bloke. I have had a few friends who were miners. It's a skilled job where you have to rely on those you are working with, especially if you want to come out uninjured. I was never questioned about my proper job, which was just as well. After a gig at Ashfield Working Men's Club, the owner asked me for

a show just for her and the staff: "For a whip-round like."
At last, I thought, it's going to end up in an orgy. I gave it
my all. When I'd finished, she came up with £10 – a very
respectable amount for 10 minutes work, but all I got apart
from that was a pint and "thanks very much", while they
started cleaning up. I had done ten shows by that point
and turned down more than that to take on acting roles.
One I definitely turned down was Arnold Working Men's
Club CIU Affiliated. It was five minutes' walk from Mum
and Dad's house!

"Eyup George and Edna, seen your lad last night tekkin'
his clothes off in the Wockin' Men's!"

No. I decided to call it a day. Being invited to a posh
house in the suburbs where a select gathering of ladies
present to see me perform just wasn't going to happen.
I had one more gig to do, at a Working Men's Club in
Birmingham in the spring of 1984. I was booked to work
a half-day on *Crossroads* the next day, so this fitted in
perfectly. I was more than usually full of trepidation when
I arrived, because it was my last gig and I didn't really want
to be doing it. I can't remember the name of it but this club
in the suburbs turned out to be quite a good size with a
smart crowd drinking at the bar. It was one of those sunny,
early spring days and I was the only act on the bill, before
and after the bingo, I started to warm up to the idea and
I wasn't disappointed. I did the two slots and the crowd
were great, the best ever. Good old Brum! Well alright,
not wild, but they were very appreciative, clapping away
and shouting out to "get 'em off." I look back with great
fondness on that night. Afterwards, the staff and a handful
of customers stayed on for a lock-in. I got to know them

better and the landlord said I could stay in the car park to sleep. I even told them about the acting, although I didn't go so far as to mention *Crossroads*. The next morning, I joined the rush hour traffic going to Birmingham. I went straight to the studio refectory at Central TV and packed in as much food as I could, found a dressing room to have a shower and off to wardrobe for my overalls as Nobby. By call time at 9.30am, I was fed, washed, brushed and exuberant. As I sat in the dressing room waiting to be summonsed to Studio One, I reflected on how lucky I was. I had a council job that paid my bills, which also fitted in with the acting, and allowed me to do a stint on whatever job I fancied. Yvonne and I were back together again, and that evening I was due to meet her and some mates at the pub. Life was great!

There was an epilogue to the stripping saga. About six months later, Gentleman Bob contacted me and asked if I would be interested in joining him for a hen night.

"I'm sorry Bob," I said, "I don't do it anymore. I don't even have the schoolboy outfit anymore."

"Howard," he said, "Central TV are doing a documentary on male strippers and have asked if they could interview me and film my act. Can't you come along, it should be fun, your world meets mine, eh? You can bring your lady friend."

Yvonne was over the moon with this and was really looking forward to it. Bob's wife drove us to the Miners' Welfare at a town in South Derbyshire. I was pleased for Bob. He deserved the fame; he was a great performer who could really get the crowd going and had been kind to me and we got on well despite my not being very good at it, or a burly miner from the pits. As we arrived the TV crew had just finished setting up. The crew were from Birmingham and recognised me straight away.

"Eyup Nobby, wot yo doing 'ere? Is this how you got your name in the garage? You're not going to take yer clothes off as well are yer?!"

"Oh, I've taken me clothes a few times in the past, just to please the ladies of course!"

That caused a ripple of laughter. We had a fantastic night. Yvonne later said she had very much enjoyed the film of Bob taking his clothes off.

In July 1984, I had a day in a walk-on role in a sit-com I can't remember the title of, but I do recall that my days' work was thoroughly enjoyable. I was the only male in an aerobics class all of us jumping about for three hours – and for this I get paid? After the filming that teatime, I drove down to Dawlish to meet up with Martin and Andy for a week's holiday. The Yorkshire miners were taking industrial action about pit closures, which seemed to have a knock-on effect, so the roads were really quiet. It was a glorious, warm sunny evening. I had Pirate Radio Station Laser 558 playing some tunes I knew, such as *Smoke on The Water* by Deep Purple which made me drive faster! They let loose with a load of obscure but fascinating LP tracks, you never really knew what to expect next which made it great fun. The journey just flew by, absolute magic! Laser only lasted 18 months due to poor advertising revenue which was such a shame. The same old reasons.

In October 1984 I was booked for two weeks extra work on *Jenny's War* which was a co-production from Columbia Pictures and Harlech TV, based on a true story about an

American woman who during WW2 goes into Germany to rescue her son from a prisoner of war camp. It starred Dyanne Cannon (who was previously married to Cary Grant for three years), Elke Sommer and Hugh Grant. A prisoner of war camp had been set up at Thoresby Hall next to a compound where the police were storing personnel and vehicles in case the NUM striking miners were to come over the border to harass the non-striking Nottingham UDM. I was hired to be one of the prisoners of war. I knew we were in for a spot of déjà vu as, when I drove up in the dark to the location at 6am, a production assistant flagged me down with a torch. "Go straight ahead and it's the second on the right. Oh, and your hair needs cutting, and the beard comes off!" The makeup and wardrobe team were probably on loan out from Yorkshire TV just 50 miles up the road. This time, though, I was ready. Firstly, my hair was the same length as Steve McQueen's in *The Great Escape* and secondly, Dad was a prisoner of war for four years and he had verified that they rarely had shaving equipment, so it was easier to just grow a beard. We were shown into a barn to change into uniform, then sent off to wardrobe, in a nearby caravan.

As I entered, they said "Go through to that side to have your hair cut and beard off."

"I'll be okay thanks," I said. "My dad was a prisoner of war and they had beards."

"Well it's not suitable for *Jenny's War,* it'll have to come off."

"There was minimum shaving equipment in the camps!" I said, "and anyway, my hair's just like Steve McQueen's in *The Great Escape.*"

223

"Are you refusing to get it cut?" she said.

"Oh yes," I said, "Don't forget, *The Great Escape* was a classic."

She tut-tutted, got on the radio to the assistant director. "Follow me" she barked, and I was frog marched round to see the assistant director. He came out of a Winnebago and looked me up and down.

"The hair will have to be cut and the beard comes off," he said

I repeated my little speech.

"Look, if you want to be on this production just do it. You either do as I've instructed, or you can leave."

I didn't say anything, just turned and walked way. I couldn't help but whistle the theme to *The Great Escape*.

I had passed up the opportunity to earn about £800, but I didn't give a hoot. Friends who were in it said that it was a miserable experience. They were treated like cattle and had to wear uniforms that were still wet from the day before and the food was cold. Stan Holt, who I knew from *Sons and Lovers*, said that he hid out in the toilets for most of the shoot just to keep dry only coming out at mealtimes, and they never noticed he was gone. About an hour after I walked out, I drove round to Mum and Dad's, who were just preparing breakfast. When I told my dad he became really angry.

"When you've had your breakfast, you can drive me up to Thoresby Hall," he said. "I'll tell 'em a thing or two about what it's like to be a prisoner of war!"

"Show-biz, Dad!" I said, "I wasn't bothered anyway, but at least they don't mess us Wheatleys about!"

Dad grinned. "Get your breakfast, son," he said.

When *Jenny's War* was broadcast the reviews were very poor and I was really pleased to notice that it was panned. No one had a good word to say for it. I was still doing the odd play at the Lace Market Theatre. In 1985, I joined the cast of a one act play called *Ashes*, about a young woman who wants to have a baby but cannot conceive, and the lengths she and her husband go to get pregnant. I played a GP, an eccentric Scottish gynaecologist, and a Brummie ambulance driver, and was giving each of them a touch of Peter Sellers. All went well during the rehearsals. When it comes to the dress rehearsal, everything should be sorted out: props, lines, the lot, so that it mirrors the actual performance. My scene as an ambulance driver from Birmingham was my final part in the play. I came on-stage, helping the young woman into a wheelchair, had a few lines of dialogue then wheeled her off through the black curtain backdrop. At the dress rehearsal all went well – patient, wheelchair, dialogue, and a quick exit through the curtain with a swish as it flipped back after our departure. In between the dress rehearsal and the performance, someone tacked down the curtain, so it was a fixed wall, with just a small gap to manoeuvre through. Now I'm very short-sighted, and of course it was already quite dark on stage, so to put it simply, I couldn't get her off. I lunged at the curtain as usual, but it wouldn't budge, so reversed back down stage. After another two attempts the audience were in stitches. A friend in the audience had to leave to visit the gents. Yvonne fell out of her seat. On the fourth attempt, the curtain gave way and we exited, to great applause!

While rehearsing, I had met up again with Ellie Smith, a young woman attending the sixth form at Nottingham High

School who had been in *Rosencrantz and Guildenstern* with me. She introduced me to her mother, Thea, who was an English teacher, and we had some fine chats about drama productions. She was a lovely looking woman with long black hair and a confident manner, with deep mellifluous tones in her voice, who should have been an actor herself. I spent as much time as I could with her, but unfortunately she had a husband. They had this large Victorian house on Sherwood Rise and put on some great parties, with brothers Tom and David Symonds. The gang played cover versions of 60s hits. Ellie had discovered my interest in the Indie music scene of the time and invited me to meet up with her sixth form chums at the rockers' pub The Salutation on Maid Marion Way in Nottingham. On the night I turned up, Ellie was sitting with four lads who were also musicians. Very much into 60s music, as well as the Indie scene, of course we talked about the tunes and musicians of the 60s and current favourites, which at that time were The Smiths, Orange Juice, The Primitives among others – the greater Indie boom had yet to come. Musically, I was closest to Tom and David Symonds. David was the older brother and was forming a band called The Rio Snappers, and Tom was jamming with others in the group at different venues, with an excellent series of 60s cover tunes from Tom and his friends.

During this time, in the spring of 1985, I successfully auditioned for two Smithland Motors adverts for the new Yugo car. They said they would pay me a lump sum above the usual Equity rate, but that as it was not an Equity contract, I wouldn't get paid royalties for the first six months. I agreed to everything straight away, figuring I would at least get a few weeks' exposure on national television. The ads were shot over two days at Loughborough with the catchphrase "Find Out Why Wally Fainted," based on my character swooning when he found out the bargain price of a Yugo. The Director drove me into Loughborough and picked out a knitted tank-top, tie and shirt, with turn-up trousers from a gentleman's outfitters to make Wally into a nerdish character. It was shot on film with full production values over two days. You can see one of the ads on You Tube under the title 'Cheesy Car Ads Of The Eighties – Swithland Motors'. It was a shame that they cut my first line on You Tube – "Another new car Jane?" To me, it was just another little gig. What I hadn't understood was just how often they would show the ads. They were on ITV and in cinemas across the country. Wally was everywhere. People would stop me in the street and wave at me from cars. It was a good job I enjoyed the fame. When the ads were still being shown after six months, I asked Equity to help me get the royalties, but once Equity contacted the production company, they stopped showing the ads completely. My visions of building up a profile as The Nerd faded before my eyes. Swithland Motors have never tried to use me since. Still, it was great fun, and I would do it all again. They attempted to re-vamp the ads along the same theme, but with Samantha Fox, actress and Page 3 model, who sensibly insisted on royalties being guaranteed in her contract. Predictably, the ads were only on for a couple of months.

Shortly after this, I was told that the garage scenes in *Crossroads* were to be axed. Nobby the garage mechanic appeared in just a couple more episodes, in the autumn of 1985. The last garage scene with Stan Stennett and Carl Andrews was broadcast on 31 December 1985, after which they dropped the shutter down and walked away. It was the end of an era, and I wasn't there! I reckon a new production group had taken over and I definitely wasn't on their list of priorities.

Meeting up with Ellie and her fellow sixth formers at The Bell Inn in Nottingham one night in late 1986, they suggested going on to a club called The Garage, so we strolled over to the Lace Market area of Nottingham and spent the night dancing to Indie tunes in the basement. Of course I was the only one in the club who had already been there thirty years before when it was The Beachcomber and Ad Lib. Martin and Steve were not really into this kind of music so I would do the pub scene with them, then after midnight would stagger round to The Garage til 2.00am. Alongside meeting up with them, I also found myself going along to the lads' gigs and band nights out around Nottingham. The Garage was ten minutes' walk from my house. One Friday night, I did a detour on the way to clocking on at work at 10pm and asked Dave and Erroll the door staff if I could see the manager. We had chatted before, and Dave ducked in the back to see if the manager was available. Out came a young man in his early twenties. Quietly spoken, he introduced himself as Shaun and asked how he could help me. I said, "I've been here a few times and like the basement scene a lot. I know I'm older than the crowd here, but my teenage friends can't always make it. If I came on my own, would I be able to get in?"

Shaun laughed and said, "Yeh, no problem." He nodded at Errol and Dave, and said to me, "If you should have a problem just ask for Shaun. It might help if you shave off the beard though!"

"No problem. It's starting to get a bit of grey in it anyway!" I said. Thus began a beautiful friendship with the Indie scene.

I had free time for another reason as well as the end of my *Crossroads* part. Yvonne had laughed me willingly into her bed on Christmas Day 1981 and continued to do so for nearly five years. During that time, she was keen for us to move in together, but I was in my flat and saving hard for a place of my own. In the October of 1986, she politely gave me an ultimatum. Either I gave her more commitment or she thought it would be better if we called it a day. It was going to be at least six months, I said, before I could buy a house. She wasn't prepared to wait. It was sad and unfortunate, but we agreed to end it. After a weekend of merrymaking, I drove Yvonne into the city centre to drop her off on Clumber Street, a busy thoroughfare at 9am on a Monday morning. We kissed our last goodbyes and as I walked off, I'd gone about 20 yards when I heard a shout of "Howard! Howard!" I turned around to hear her shout back as she walked around the corner, "Thanks for the orgasms!" No word of a lie. Ten weeks later she rang me to say that she was going to get married to a neighbour on her street. Yvonne was a unique personality. She invited me to the wedding, which was to be early in 1987, but I decided not to go. It was early evening of Christmas Day 1986, and I was walking the mile or so to Sherwood to meet up with the High School sixth formers at the Robin Hood pub there for the 'Anti Christmas Session'. Nothing stirred in the quiet evening; there was no traffic, nor any other person walking about. As I came to Carrington, half-way to Sherwood, I saw a policeman booking a solitary car. As I got closer, I recognised the officer. It was Peter, Yvonne's ex-husband.

"Hello Peter," I said, "not bothered about Christmas either are you?"

"No, never have been so drawing the short straw doesn't bother me!" he said.

He sent his victim off back onto the road and asked, "You going to the wedding?"

I hadn't really wanted to go, and I felt more rapport with Peter than the new guy.

"No," I said, "I think I'll give that one a miss, are you?"

"No, I feel the same about it as you do Aitch. Anyway, a happy new year buddy."

"Thanks a lot Peter," I said, "let's hope it's better than the last one, eh?"

Fifteen minutes later I was walking through the doors of The Robin Hood Pub. Laid out before me like a scene from Charles Dickens was much merriment. Not only were there some blokes from the Eastcroft but Ellie, David, Tom and the High School lot, and so were Carl Routledge and his entourage Vera, Miriam and Keith. More about Carl later. The rapport and bonhomie were really good among the thirteen of us and I didn't want the night to end. We could have carried on til dawn. I felt suddenly that 1987 was going to be a great year. What a FAB way to celebrate Christmas. By January 1987, I was signing a contract to move into a house on Cliff Road in Nottingham. I wasn't doing much drama at that point but saved enough to put down a deposit and was still doing night shifts at the

Eastcroft. I was lucky with Cliff Road. When I moved in on Easter Sunday 1987, I found that some of the families loved it so much they had lived there from the early 30s, when they were first built as council houses.

Cliff Road, 1930s. The one with the smoking chimney would eventually become my house.

Before 1930, it had been Red Lion Street in a notorious area called The Narrow Marsh, with ten pubs in an area about the size of a premier league football stadium, along cobblestoned streets honeycombed with cramped and rickety tenement housing. The police were frequently around, always in twos.

From my living room, I could hear the
commentary on the Nottingham Experience
Tourist Bus that drove past my house,
saying "This used to be the biggest slum in
Europe....."

Cliff Road was enclosed on one side by Canal Street and a Victorian railway viaduct, which now hosts the Nottingham Tramway. On the other side, out of my front window, I looked up at a tall cliff on which was built a 19th century prison. Now it's the Galleries of Justice, where you can go and pretend to be a prisoner in the dock or a washerwoman, as well as viewing the extensive collection of artefacts. I loved the place. Enclosed behind the cliff it felt like a village, but with it being central I was now able to play host to my friends. Ten minutes' walk away was the rock and goth scene at The Salutation, there was Rock

City on a Saturday night, and best of all was Pete Beckett playing Indie in the basement at The Garage, owned by Brian Selby. In 1966 he had opened the first Selectadisc record shop on Arkwright Street. Weirdly, it was but ten years ago that I found out that my mother's neighbour, Frank, was Brian's brother. They were adopted to separate families but met up and ran a record stall together at the market in Mansfield.

At The Garage, I used to stand next to the DJ turntables to see how Pete Beckett went on. One night he said, "You come here a lot mate. I've a lot of donated beer here, d'you want one?" Thereafter, I would help him carry the records up the stairs and out to his car at the end of the night like an apprentice! While The Garage was being refurbished to become the Kool Kat in 1988, I went to see Pete play at Eden, another club, and that's where I met his mate, Steve Butler. The pair of them had been firm friends for many years and were very keen on Indie. My learning curve about Indie music was just beginning.

One snowy night, Steve Mills and I lost Martin walking back to Cliff Road from the city centre. But when it came to walking down the long steps of Garner's Hill into my road, we were suddenly pelted with a barrage of snowballs.

"Who's doing that?" slurred Steve.

"Who do you think?" says I.

Martin had gone to the trouble of running ahead to stockpile a heap of snowballs in the courtyard overlooking the steps. Ahh Martin. I think he never quite had enough of the childhood games that are an essential part of growing up! From school to boarding at Trent College then to South Staffordshire University, and of course, out into the big world of marketing, he was always on the go. From 1980, though, he was determined to make up for lost 'Free Spirit' time. courtesy of Steve and yours truly.

Gearing up for a night out

Three grown men in their thirties, OK, forties in my case, romping around like it was *Just William* or *The Famous Five*. It's a wonder we weren't arrested. We were in each other's pockets, always out and about: films, theatre, TV, lectures, and trips down south. Martin was originally from Exmouth, so we went there on holiday a couple of times. We found it to be quiet and traditional, with pub bars clad in dark wood, and it felt very much like the 50s.

One long weekend in 1987, the three of us travelled down to Kent to check out the locations in the novel *Moonraker* by Ian Fleming round the back of the White Cliffs of Dover, near Kingsdown. The film fiasco bears no resemblance to the book. I knew the area very well from my childhood holidays and also knew that Fleming had a house nearby in St Margaret's Bay and played golf at the Royal St Georges in Sandwich. He went to great lengths to represent his favourite part of the UK in the novel, including lending his car to his stepson Raymond O'Neill to time the journey from London to Deal, as research for Bond in Moonraker. Up we clambered to the top of the Kingsdown end of the cliffs looking for the rocket-site location. After about a quarter of an hour of walking along the top, they started to doubt I had my facts right, but then … there it was. Not a rocket site of course, but a house called 'Moonraker', set back from the cliff path. Our next stop was focused on the film rather than the novel, this time the setting for the golfing scenes in *Goldfinger*, the Royal St Georges club house. However, arriving there on a Saturday afternoon, the buildings didn't look too appealing. They certainly didn't resemble the luxurious mansion that was the club house in *Goldfinger*. The place was deserted so we reversed round in order to leave, when a smartly dressed man strode out of the club house towards the car.

"Can I help you chaps?" he asked.

"Well yes actually," replied Martin, "We're looking for the Royal St. Georges club house featured in "Goldfinger" – but this doesn't look anything like it."

"Ahh, that's an understandable mistake," he said. "You see as written in the book the location was right here, but when it came to the filming the producers felt that the club house and its buildings were somewhat nondescript. So they cast us aside and came up with the idea of using a golf course near to Pinewood Studios up in Buckinghamshire at Stoke Poges."

That explained it. We'd booked into a hotel next to Walmer Castle in Deal, so we settled in for a few drinks along Queen Street. These days there is now a Wetherspoons called 'The Norman Wisdom'.

The next day we set off for Buckinghamshire, drove past Pinewood Studios and three miles along we went down the drive to Stoke Poges Golf Course club house which had stood in for the Royal St. Georges in *Goldfinger*. We discovered that we couldn't drink in the members only bar, but we could walk around so we took photographs.

With my new VHS recorder in place, I was able to purchase the first four Bond films. It's easy to remember, as they are in alphabetical order, D.F.G.T. I will leave you to fill in the gaps! Once a month, for about a year, we would gather back at my house, nominated 'Jack's Bar and Grill' and watch a Bond film after a night out on the town. It was a rich and heady mix with those two, charging round the estate in the early hours of the morning after several beers, reliving Second World War 'Bocage Country' skirmishes round the gardens. It's a wonder the police weren't called.

Martin and Steve's parents were very reserved, traditional and middle class; I was the odd one out. Going to their houses after a weekend jaunt, tea would often be served in china cups and saucers. We had cucumber, salmon and ham sandwiches, although not cut in triangles! My mum was herself very respectable, but she had a good idea of how to feed you up. Martin said she did the best mixed grill he'd ever had. His parents had a large cottage in Wollaton, set back from the road and unlike any of the other houses in the area. It was like a Rupert Bear house. When you look back years later you see things through rose-coloured spectacles but with those two, it was rose-coloured spectacles at the time. Martin's mother had a fine wit. When a brunette girlfriend of his turned up at the door unexpectedly, his mother called up to him and then said to her, "That's funny he usually goes for blondes." I loved hearing Mr and Mrs Goddard's stories of life in Exmouth and adjusting to life up in Nottingham during the 60s.

At Cliff Road, I had to tackle gardening for the first time ever, as it had a large lawn and six-foot-high privet hedge around it. The hedge was the length of a luxury coach next to a narrow, four-foot-wide walk-through that we would call a 'twitchel'. The other side of it was the same but the council was not very reliable at cutting it. I had to keep on top of it, otherwise the locals would complain about the flying insects and wet leaves. The wildlife was good though. I had a lot of pleasure from feeding blackbirds and robins and giving an occasional treat to passing cats. Two cats I never fed were Whisky, a black and white tom and Smokey who was a blue grey. They lived with Taff and Bett at the back of me. I swear Whisky was telepathic. He was so bright and perceptive. I would not see too much of him from November to March, as my back door would be shut then, but every spring he would renew our acquaintance in the garden, as if to say, "Thank goodness that's finished for another year." Whiskey would never come into the house or ask for treats. His housemate Smokey was of a very different nature, always meowing for a treat and having to be shooed out of the house when I had the back door open.

There must have been ten cats I knew quite well in the thirty years I lived at Cliff Road, but Smokey was the only one who, during winter, would wait for a car to park up, then jump onto the bonnet, curl up and go to sleep until the engine had cooled down. When it did, he would move onto another one. He didn't like Volkswagen Beetles though! Eventually Whiskey started to look fragile and I feared the worst. I kept in touch with Taff who told me he wasn't eating well. One bright summer day, for the first time ever, Whiskey came into the house and struggled up onto the settee next to me. We sat together for about ten minutes. I offered him some water, which he drank. I wrapped him up in a towel and took him round to Taff. We were both very upset, especially Taff, as Smokey had already left us, and Whiskey died soon after this. Both were twenty years old. He had been a much-loved friend.

Martin and Steve eventually warmed to The Garage plus the odd visit to Nottingham's Rock City. We had been wanting to go upstairs to the rock/goth nights at The Salutation Inn for a while but thought we didn't look the part. Goth girls have to be the best raunch ever! I'd shaved my beard off by then and usually wore a battered black leather jacket, Three blokes approaching middle age might have been a stretch, so we stayed downstairs in the bar. One night, waiting to meet up with them at The Sal, I recognised the doorman sitting at the bottom of the stairs letting people go up (or not) as one I had met at Rock City. He didn't look the part either – more like an uncle wearing a very respectable cardigan – but I knew he loved the music and was part of that scene. We had a chat and he said to go upstairs when Martin and Steve arrived, and so up we went. I must admit, we were very pleased with the amount of raunch on view and from then on made it one of our regular haunts. Fab music and a great crowd who really made us welcome.

Martin was bringing along an ever-increasing variety of friends for us to meet. It was fascinating how steadily the network grew. There I was, in my forties and in theory supposed to be settling down. It was never as varied as this in the 60s! One character Martin lined up for us was Trout, the nickname we coined for him from his real name, Carl Routledge-Wilson. What a larger-than-life character he was. Suited and booted, topped off with a waistcoat and bow tie. (In the films he would be played by Ronald Fraser along the lines of Michael Edwards in *Lovejoy*.) In the cricket season he wore a straw boater and striped jacket. We were in awe of his head boy manner. He was so knowledgeable with an extremely intelligent mind. Here is a list of his previous careers: actor, priest, radio personality, freelance journalist, food critic, reverend, psychotherapist, physiotherapist, American studies, law. When we were on holiday in southern Spain, his likeness was everywhere. Engraved in manhole covers on the sidewalk and even a sculpture of him on a plinth in the corridors of The Alhambra in Granada. What a wealth of material he provided for our over-enthusiastic vivid imaginations. He could be El Capitano Trout with a captain's hat and a bandolier of bullets, slung sash style over the shoulder, a gun holster and jackboots, cod – Mexican style – "Badges? Badges? We don't need no steenkin' badges!"

Then there's Field Marshall Trout, Goering style, with a white uniform and masses of military badges, more jackboots – "We haf vays of making you talk."

Prince John – "Bring me the head of Robin Hood!"

Ming The Merciless – "You pitiful fool! My life, Flash Gordon, is not for any Earthling to take!"

We were very surprised he didn't take up acting professionally. He had the charisma and confidence. I can guarantee he would always be in work. Most certainly he would have made an excellent Poirot. On You Tube, there's a good British B film made in 1954 called *The Diamond Wizard,* and 33 minutes in it features Frances De Wolff playing a pub landlord pouring out ale from a barrel on his shoulder. This is so much like Carl, and he most certainly would have been able to take on this part. Carl runs an excellent up-market bar called the Pillar Box in Sherwood, Nottingham where he can be found holding court. If you are lucky enough to catch him in, please buy him a drink and say, "Howard Jacks sent me!"

7

Even The Bad Times Are Good

1988 to 2015

Steve Mills was getting a great deal of driving instructor work, but he still hankered after some more acting. He contacted me to ask if I would be interested in doing a school workshop on *Of Mice and Men* by John Steinbeck, which was on the GCSE curriculum in schools. Calling ourselves *Just Two*, we formed a Theatre In Education company and adapted the play which featured two main characters, Lennie and George, who were hitching around California looking for labouring work in the Great Depression of the 30s. Steve played Lennie, who was big and blundering but liked to cuddle small creatures like mice. I played George, who made all the decisions, kind of Lennie's guardian and a bit of a wise guy. We rehearsed it and the whole thing fell into place nicely – forty-five minutes long with a workshop Q&A session at the end. County Hall gave some basic promotions for us, and we did ten schools throughout 1988. We had a lot of fun doing it. In Lennie's pocket would be a large rubber mouse.

"What yer got in your pocket Lennie?"

It's only a mouse, George."

"What ya doin' with a dead mouse?"

"I was just pettin' it, George."

"Well, ya ain't pettin' no dead mouse when you're walkin' with me. Give it here!"

I would grab the plastic mouse from him and throw it at the curtains, to squeals all round, then it would bounce on the floor. I don't know what it was about this piece of business, but we had great difficulty in keeping a straight face when the mouse went plop to the floor. Lennie also has a dream sequence, where he conjures up his Aunt Clara and a huge rabbit. From off stage, I did the voices. A high-pitched old lady's voice, southern style, and an impersonation of Bugs Bunny for the big wabbit, sorry rabbit!

"Naaah! You crazy bastard!" I said, making chomping noises on my invisible carrot.

The students loved hearing us swear and would crowd around at the end with questions. Most of the girls would be feeling sorry for Lennie and in our Q&A workshop at the end would come up with all kinds of scenarios about why he was a slow thinker. However, the school funding dried up for drama workshops like this. I made endless phone calls, knocked on doors and had meetings with people in many different schools, but no one had the funds to take us on board. Two months after we wound it up, teachers and even County Hall contacted us about some schools, but it was too late, we'd moved on. We wound things up with a fab holiday in Almeria, Southern Spain.

Back to Tabernas, 1988

At Eastcroft, the day manager George Thomas popped in one night. He gathered us together and told us that the night shift would be closing down at the end of 1989. I didn't fancy the voluntary redundancy on offer, so I stayed on. Most of the night shift took redundancy, like Frank Hodgkinson, who had been on the night shift for many years and was a dab hand at art. He had never been trained, but he could do fabulous portraits and caricatures, which he taught me to do, brushing up my early attempts at comic strips although my efforts were not a patch on his skills.

Things were not looking good. That said, Christmas 1989 was the best I'd have ever had at 'The Croft'. I was the only one left from the original night shift crew. The six of us were planning to sneak out for a couple of hours. George turned up as we arrived to start work. "Don't bother about the work tonight lads," he said, "just switch the light out when you go in the morning." No hesitation, we went along with George straight to the Norfolk Hotel on London Road until the early hours!

I was twiddling my thumbs on the day shift, so I took a reception job at Eastcroft, in the Clock Tower building, taking calls from Nottingham City Council customers frustrated with their rubbish collection, greeting members of the public and councillors attending meetings. I had very few calls though, and eventually was made supernumerary (surplus to requirement – I had to look in the dictionary to find out what it meant). This was quite interesting, as it meant staying at home on full pay and occasionally attending meetings at Personnel to talk about my 'career development'. After six weeks, apparently on the strength of my 'people skills', I managed to get an interview with Design and Property at Lawrence House in the city centre. Although that was a day shift too, it meant that one of the sections I would be working for dealt with tourism and public relations, and I had a vague notion that I could do some artwork for them. The interview went well, until they asked me to start the next week. I'd already booked a holiday with Steve and Martin for a fortnight at Roquetas, Andalucía in Southern Spain and was not going to give it up. Fortunately for me, Norman Charlton, one of the team leaders, was good enough to offer me the job anyway.

The holiday in Roquetas was great, despite a tense afternoon watching the penalty shoot-out in the England v Germany semi-finals on 4th July 1990. At that time, Stuart Pearce was playing for Nottingham Forest, most of it as captain, and he was playing for England. When it came to Pearce's turn at goal, Martin said, "Ahh, we'll be alright now with Pearcy. He's on the ball!" Pearce sent a low ball down the middle, but unfortunately it was saved.

Steve turned to Martin and did a slow burn a la Laurel and Hardy.

"Why don't you shut up?!" Steve growled.

Germany won 4-3. Also watching the match in the bar were a group of three German couples. I turned to them and politely applauded. Martin and Steve were appalled.

"Come along lads," I said in my best posh voice. "We're gentlemen, aren't we? Let's maintain a modicum of style and class. Smile and applaud please!"

We hired a car and travelled all around the Almeria province. I took Martin and Steve to all my old haunts in Almeria, including, of course, Tabernas where the Spaghetti Westerns sets had been maintained as a tourist attraction. I was used to the traffic lights being at the side of the road and driving back to Roquetas I missed a set overhead, and went through on red. Sod's Law, there were two motorbike cops nearby. They had seen my error and gave pursuit, flagging me down. Those two cops looked straight out of Central Casting for an episode of CHIPS. White helmets, dark glasses, boots and guns.

"Documentos!" one demanded.

I knew it was pointless looking for them, having left them behind in the apartment safe. In my pidgin Spanish I indicated that this was a problem.

"Vuelve a tu apartamento y te seguiremos!" he ordered.

I got that one, although the way he looked at me anyone would think I was a Basque Separatist!

"Soy Inglese," I said, but then I could not work out how to say, "We don't have our ID with us." All those times visiting Spain and this was the first time I had come a cropper. We drove back to the apartment two miles away with CHIPS close behind.

"You prat Jacksy," the lads were saying, kind of enjoying the moment too. "We're in trouble now."

The coppers followed us along the winding road to Roquetas and then... and then, I looked behind and they weren't in the mirror. I pulled over just in case they'd taken a wrong turn, but no, they'd left us. The next day, Martin and Steve kept winding me up by saying that they would have taken down my registration number with a view to bringing me in at any time. On the third day, at the swimming pool the lads came over to me in a strange, crouching movement. Martin said that two police officers had turned up and were asking for me. I looked over at the entrance to the pool area and sure enough, there they were. The next bit is straight out of a Peter Sellers film. I clambered out of the pool grabbing the documents as the officers were walking towards me. I walked towards them and... they walked past me! The officers had come to see someone else. This was a classic wind up on the part of Steve and Martin. In fact, I never heard from the policia. Perhaps it was because I was English, as we did get let off quite a bit in those days, or maybe because it was Friday and they couldn't be bothered with the paperwork when they were hoping to clock off early for the weekend. For a while I considered living in Spain, but I would have to stay indoors from June to September and the blinds shut from 11.00am to 6.00pm. Me and the sun just don't get on.

I got my own back on Martin later on in the year. Steve and I were calling round to Martin's house for a night out, in Steve's car. I was in the back covered by a blanket under the front seats:

Martin – "Where's Jacksy then?"

Steve – "He had to finish something off, so we'll pick him up."

The car set off and after about five minutes, I quietly moved out of my horizontal position into one where I clamped my hands round Martin's neck: "AAARGH!" he cried, squirming with horror.

Revenge is sweet!

Thanks a lot, Martin and Steve, thanks a lot for those 25 years of good times and mayhem.

"Here's lookin' at you kids."

Back in the UK, it was nerve wracking for the first six months at Lawrence House reception. They were quite a close-knit team, and I was the only man, plus everyone knew that I'd come from the Eastcroft Depot, urrgh, smelly bins refuse and greasy engines... However, the ladies were hesitant when it came to dealing with the more volatile members of the public, so I was handy for a summons when it came to dealing with frustrated and sometimes angry customers. We had around thirty members of the public calling in per day. I also became familiar with the other departments including Tourism and Public Relations. I had some good chats with the Director, John Haslam, who knew people at ATV and Central TV because they had part-funded the refurbishment of Nottingham's Theatre Royal, and with Bob White who played in pop bands during the 60s. They began to call on me to help with the distribution of promotional material across the city, and from this I set up an information section in Lawrence House Reception and kept it stocked with leaflets about gigs and drama events in Nottingham. The Theatre Royal and Nottingham Playhouse gave me complementary tickets for performances. While I was not doing any drama, watching others on the stage helped me keep my hand in. I did what I could to pay them back by trying to encourage people to visit Nottingham.

I planned a visit with DJ Pete Beckett to Expo 92 in Seville to catch up with Jeremy, a friend who was doing role play at the English tabernacle, and when I looked through the official brochure I saw there was absolutely nothing from Nottingham. Nothing about Robin Hood and His Merrie Men, The Trip To Jerusalem Inn being a stop on the way for the Crusades, the ladies of the lace industry, *Saturday Night And Sunday Morning*, or the fact that it's the geographical centre of England. I popped up to Tourism and asked them for promotional material, posters, leaflets, keyrings etc. When I arrived at the Expo 92 site with a suitcase full, I went straight round to the English tabernacle and persuaded them to publicise the city; luckily, they were only too pleased to do it. I enjoyed my week in Seville Expo 92, mixing with Jeremy's work mates and others from all over the world. I really didn't have the time to visit all the countries and their exhibitions, but I was fascinated by the Israel tabernacle because it was part of Yvonne's heritage. I also made a point of visiting the Andalucía tabernacle. It was amazing. They had constructed a sensurround type of screen to show the delights of the province, which made you feel you were really there. There were all the places I had known and visited over the previous 25 years; the sound was so real and wow, there was Almeria and the desert with the Spaghetti Western town. It lasted an hour, but I could have sat there all day. When I came out, I rang my mum and dad to let them know how great it was. That also gave me the opportunity to ask if they would record the repeated episodes of *The Prisoner* on Channel 4. Jeremy had told me about this. I had never seen *The Prisoner*. Every time it had been televised from 1967 onwards, I had been working at night and missed it. Better 25 years late than not at all!

The Tourism and Public Relations team gave me a great welcome when I came back to the office, and I started going out socially with them. In 1993 there was a reorganisation, and they were moving out to another building. I had high hopes of going with them, however, my job banding was too high for their receptionist and general duties role. I was really upset about this, especially as the removal upheavals, new business cards and letter headings seemed to be a complete waste of time and money which didn't really gain anything. However, Environmental Health moved in, and I bonded well with the staff, bringing back my social life. They were all surprisingly cheerful and positive, given the negative aspects of their work, which included Public Health, Pollution, Food And Licensing, Health and Safety, noisy neighbours and lost dogs. I went out with them round the estates of Nottingham, chasing stray dogs with a net and a grabber. They were taken to the pound, where they were looked after very well, even having their photograph taken which would be kept in reception to show people looking for their lost mutt – mostly these were happy occasions, although not always, when they realised they had to pay to get the dog back.

My time at Lawrence House had its Norman Wisdom 'Mr Grimsdale' moments. Early one morning the cleaner went into the Health and Safety offices and saw some sticks of dynamite on a desk: A BOMB! The whole building was evacuated two streets away where we had to stay while the police and fire brigade came over to investigate. Rather them than me. After three hours we were allowed back into the building with the all-clear. Turns out the dynamite was only a dummy. It was on the desk of an officer who used to work down the pit. He had left the dummy dynamite out from the night before after showing a colleague how it would be used by a 'shot-firer'. Except, a shot-firer has a dynamite bag to keep it in, and he didn't, so there it was on his desk to frighten the poor old cleaner in the morning. I too had my own 'Everybody Out' moment. On Wednesday mornings I would do the fire alarm test, easing out the flap from the little red box on the wall, setting off the alarm for ten seconds and pushing back the glass flap to switch it off. One morning the glass fell out and I couldn't get it back in again. The alarm went on and on, with all the staff evacuated again two streets away. Ah well, it was useful practice I suppose.

My second incident didn't involve any staff but yours truly, the door security man.... and the Director. At the end of the day with everybody gone I was working late. I already had an agreement with the doorman that if my corridor light was off, he was to assume that I had left.

One evening I switched the corridor light out and headed to the entrance but remembered I had left my lunch box on the desk. I rushed back, scooped it up and headed out of the corridor. At the very moment I'd switched off the corridor light the doorman looked up and left, switching on the alarms and locking the doors, leaving me locked in. Total time from corridor light switch off to his departure, 12 seconds. He said next day that coincidentally it was the quickest exit he had ever done. I can still see him now leaving the car park – I was hoping and praying he would look back and see me there. I had to ring the other doorman to tell him what had happened, and in turn the procedure meant that he had to inform the Director, who was not a happy bunny. By this time of course the sensors had picked up that someone was moving about inside the building and activated all the alarms. The police arrived just as the Director turned up, accompanied by the two dogs he had been out walking, and Brian the doorman who had been called in to assist Himself. I apologised profusely and I have to say the Director was reasonable about it all. Brian had a good laugh, especially when my girlfriend Diana (more about her later) turned up and bought us all some fish and chips to eat while the alarms were being re-set. Brian still reminds me of the incident every time I see him. Mind you, I did owe the Director. He'd given me a good bollocking for not letting in a Councillor who didn't have any ID, the old "Don't you know who I am" scenario. Health and Safety were not having any of it and hauled him over the coals, but it was good to have my own revenge.

Another mini re-structuring meant that I was only part-time in reception and the rest of the time was spent inputting complaints and reports onto the computer. I hated it. Everyone had said I was good at the customer service side, and I enjoyed it too, but heaven forbid someone should enjoy their job. As my old pappy used to say, "If it ain't broke don't fix it." After some lobbying, I was given the mailroom to manage which was quite good fun. It was a large building of three and a half floors, typical early 70s glass and steel. I had the whole of Lawrence House to wander round and engage with all the staff, and I went home half an hour early if I had to take Environmental Notices to the Post Office to get them sent as recorded deliveries before 5.00pm. Which happened a lot.

Lawrence House was a great experience, made me a lot of friends – it wasn't a 10/10 like the Eastcroft days. I would say 8/10, but I thank all the colleagues and management for putting up with me and helping me out during some difficult times – and of course for allowing me all that time off to do TV work.

8

How-zat!

1993 to 1996

In the spring of 1993, I had a phone call from someone I hadn't heard from in eight years. I recognised the voice straight away: it was Barbara Plant from Central Television Casting.

"Hello Howard," she said. "I'm just checking your availability for a part. Could you do August and September?"

"I'm free, Barbara," I said.

"Don't you want to know what it is?"

"From you, Barbara, everything is good!"

"Flatterer! You haven't changed much," she said, with a smile in her voice. "Will you go to the Central Television studios next week for an interview, and can you play cricket?"

"No problem, Barbara, thanks," I lied, and she gave me the details.

The next week I met up with Nick Hurran, the director and Paula Burdon the producer, of *Outside Edge*, based on the Richard Harris play, about a Sunday League Cricket Team run by two couples from very different worlds. It starred Robert Daws as Roger, Brenda Blethyn as Miriam, Timothy Spall as Kevin, and Josie Lawrence as Maggie. It was a quick, fifteen minute interview in which we talked about what I had done before and when I would be available. I think Barbara must have put in a good word for me, since they didn't ask many searching questions, just looked me over and told me that it was a speaking part on the cricket team, playing a nerdy bloke lacking in social skills.

Nick told me they were to start filming in a couple of months' time.

"Well, we'll let you know if you have the part by the end of next week," said Nick. "Oh, by the way, you can play cricket, can't you?"

"Yes, of course," I lied.

On the way home I decided I would join the Lawrence House cricket team and learn how to play that way. They got to practice in the nets at Rushcliffe Leisure Centre.

When, for a part, you have to play snooker, ride a horse, be a ballet dancer, draw a gun as in a western, sword fight, you can get tuition and practice, practice on your own, but NOT CRICKET! We played football rather than cricket at school and it never interested me.

No idea. Nothing. Zilch! After three sessions in the nets, I still had great trouble hitting the ball, let alone throwing it. I decided to leave myself to the fates and thought that I probably wouldn't have passed the interview anyway. Then there was a call from Barbara, I'D GOT IT! The character was to be called Arnold. "Arnold is where I'm from Barbara!"

"Well Howard," she said. "Kismet I think they call it don't they?"

I went to my section leader at Lawrence House, Norman Charlton, and asked if I could use all my annual leave and add some unpaid so that I could be off work for two months. He was unsure about this and asked me to give him some time to speak with the service manager. I hadn't spoken with the service manager previously and I was not exactly high profile on the Lawrence House team. I didn't expect them to grant the leave and moped about that afternoon while they deliberated. They said "YES!" Terms to be discussed. So it came to pass, the start of one of my most enjoyable experiences in the acting game. It had taken twenty years to get to this stage and it was well worth the wait. Now I know how Michael Caine felt!

The first day's filming was out at Thrumpton, a village seven and a half miles south of Nottingham. All I had to do was walk for half an hour from my house to Central Television studios at Lenton Lane, where we would be bussed to the location. No risk of traffic jams or the car breaking down, no pressure here!

It was just like the first day of school. All the actors and crew were introduced to each other and the writer, Richard Harris. Nick Hurran and Paula Burdon gave us all a jovially informal pep talk. We formed ranks and had photographs taken. This felt good, really good. On day two, they realised I was a useless cricketer and sent me off to get some practice out at Linby Village. A fellow Midlander, Samih, from Birmingham and a great laugh, was also sent for cricket lessons, so at least I had company. However, in the sweatbox that was Linby, it was hell for both of us. It was a long, airless building annexed to the bungalow for cricket practice belonging to one of the crew who was a skilled cricketer. I must have lost half a stone that afternoon, trying to hit the ball, let alone bowl it. Sammy was the same. Each day that went by without improvement, we were expecting a heavy hand on the shoulder. 'Arnold' was only a small part, the odd line every episode, but I had to be seen interacting and playing on the cricket pitch, as part of Captain Roger Dervish's team. Sammy managed to get the hang of batting, but I never did, and we both avoided bowling on screen as best we could.

I don't know why they kept me on. Maybe there's always one dumbo in every cricket team! After filming at Thrumpton, on to Clumber Park cricket club for a week which was to double for Cromer Cricket Club in Norfolk, then we had another week's filming in Wollaton Village. Cricket apart, I was in my element here. Everybody was as one. No villains, no egos, just 40-odd people wanting to get the job done properly and successfully.

Whenever I could I took the opportunity to talk with the crew who had moved up to Nottingham when Elstree had closed down. I wanted to know about their life and the work they had undertaken. Occasionally they became quite emotional as the studios were in their blood and quite often their relatives' and parents' too. I felt so sorry for them having all that upheaval, especially as I loved those studios and the area, even though I never managed to work there!

From experience, I knew not to be too forward with the principles, however, even though they were pleasant when we were together. Brenda Blethyn and I found out we had someone in common: Janine Duvitski was a good friend of hers and she had been in my first year at drama school.

The filming of *Outside Edge* was Monday to Friday but on one occasion we had to film a funeral one Saturday. I didn't want to miss out on my Friday Indie night at the Kool Kat club and let down my friend Peter the Physicist (Peter Fitzgerald), so I figured that just for once I could leave at 1am instead of 2am, which would give me a comfortable six hours' sleep to get through Saturday's filming. At the club, we encountered Katy and Vanessa who by now had formed an indie band called 'The Melons' with records out on the Heaven and Sunday labels, and we had a fine old night of it. Then they all wanted to come back to my place to carry on the festivities. AAARGH! I was already exhausted after being on set all day and was faced with an 8am start to walk to the location next day.

Still, I didn't want to let them down. I had a few coffees and opened a bottle of wine for them, played some music, we chatted for a couple of hours. When we were ready to call it a night it was about 2am, so I drove all three home, Vanessa lived out at Giltbrook, near Eastwood, Katie in Sneinton and Peter at Dunkirk. I hit the sack at 3am. Three hours' sleep and then up next day to sober up by walking across Trent Bridge to the location at Wilford Hill Cemetery. One of the guest actors was Roy Holder who passed away in 2021. A true Brummie who had done lots of work in major films. We got on very well, as if we had known each other for years. Sadly, he only did a week of filming on *Outside Edge,* then his character Fred died of a heart attack. We were at the cemetery for Fred's funeral. I felt ready for a coffin by the time we had finished. No going out that Saturday night – I went straight home to bed.

Just as the end of filming series one was in view, I was also asked to be available for the last Friday in September. A taxi would pick up myself and Murray McGrath, a fellow actor, and get us to Cromer in Norfolk by early afternoon. The principles and other supporting actors were also transported there for filming at the regally gothic Hotel

De Paris opposite Cromer Pier. We arrived early afternoon and were put to work straight away for sequences around the hotel ending up in the bar. Real food and beer, makes a change. We wound up at about 8pm in quite a relaxed state. While we had been tucked away in the hotel for four hours a storm had blown in which gave a dramatic ending to our filming and our last supper. I left a card I'd prepared earlier thanking the caterers for all the excellent cuisine they had given us over the last seven weeks. They were the best – from up-market aperitifs down to fab bubble and squeak. We were ferried to the hotel we were lodged in, about six miles up the coast, to the soundtrack of howling winds and the waves crashing in.

As we arrived, we were taken into a room full of food and drink, a dance floor, for an end-of-shoot party. What a great surprise this was. Jacksy was in his element. A highly professional shoot, real alcohol for the filming, high quality location cuisine, a farewell party, and a taxi back next day. What more could you ask for? Next morning, I arrived back in Nottingham on Saturday exhilarated but wiped out. Hauling myself upstairs, I discovered that Mum, out of the blue, had laid a new carpet in my bedroom. I never knew she had those skills, but she was a very capable woman. I certainly didn't take after her with practical skills. I went to bed for three hours and was out round the town carousing that night. The perfect weekend.

In 1993 Lenton Lane Studios, the last link with ATV ended. Central Television was taken over by Carlton Television. *Outside Edge* was on ITV for eight weeks from March 1994. Ratings and the audience reaction was excellent. Barbara rang to make sure I would be free for filming a second series in August. Nottingham City Council were good to me again and gave me clearance for another eight weeks of absence. Ironically the unit vans were in Wollaton at the back of The Admiral Rodney pub with The Barn theatre adjacent to this, both old haunts of mine from the Wollaton Drama Group days. Round the corner is The Village Cricket Club, where we filmed the cricketing scenes. Perfect for me. Martin lived locally so we could meet up occasionally after a day's filming. However, my cricket skills had not improved. On set, Nick Hurran gave up on trying to film me batting. When I was due to bat on camera they would announce "Warning! Wild ball!" and put up a protective screen in front of the camera. Despite many hours of practice, I also had a lot of difficultly catching the ball. Yet again, I began to fear being told not to bother turning up next week. Towards the end of Series Two, 'Arnold' had to be bowled out. Quite easy in my case: "HOWZAT!" The scene was on Friday the last day of filming. What was required from me was a reaction shot upon seeing a huge, burly bowler from the opposing team, filmed in the morning.

"Alright Howard, show me fear," said Nick Hurren.

No problem, except I had to imagine him being there; he had left at lunch time. I was nervous about getting it right. The first take was not right at all.

"Okay, let's go again – take two," said Nick.

I had to get this right. Messing up as a would-be cricketer is one thing, blowing a poor reaction shot as an actor is another.

In my mind I said, "C'mon Jack L Warner, help me out here, I need you so much for this shot." I was shaking, but that was not helping me give a visual reaction. The actor who played the bowler was a big bloke. I thought of what I would do if he loomed out of the darkness at me when I was walking home from a club in the early hours.

"Action!" and then –

"Cut!"

Nick looked at the monitor. "That's fine. Well done, Howard. It's a wrap. See you in Corfu."

Phew, that was a huge relief – Nick was happy. I was happy too, and it was confirmed – a Christmas special: twelve days in Corfu in October. The supporting actors had formed our own group by this time: 'The Geronimo Ten'. Myself, John Sheriston, Roy Richards, Murray McGrath, and Bupinder, along with our 'wives/girlfriends' on screen, none of us believed we would be allowed to join the filming in Corfu. John's wife on screen was played by his real wife, Joan Sheriston. They were avid cricket fans, touring all over the country to play matches, or to watch as spectators. John was well known at Trent Bridge and Nottinghamshire County Cricket Club, and Nick frequently sought his advice about the technical points of cricket and its protocols. We thought the bubble would burst and that we would end up filming our Christmas scenes in the UK. We used 'Geronimo' as the code word for any snippets that we heard about filming in Corfu, feeling that we might tempt fate if too much was made of this. Filming the Wollaton Village Cricket Club episodes was idyllic though.

John Sheriston, Roy Richards,
Howard Jacks and Denis Lill

Corfu was once occupied by the British, and on St George's Day in 1823 the Royal Navy and the British Garrison played a cricket match there. On mainland Greece they have four cricket teams, but the small island of Corfu has an impressive eleven. After the Second World War, the popularity of cricket was on the decline but the vice consul for Corfu, John Forte, was determined it should start up again and put out an appeal for equipment in the press. It gained an impressive response with 380 balls and 60 bats sent to the island. We met there and were ferried by minibus to Manchester Airport for a late morning flight. Once we arrived at baggage collection in Corfu Airport, we went straight into filming a few scenes, alongside the principles. During a break in the filming, the unit manager came over to me and said:

"There's someone here who wants to meet you. She's not interested in any of the leads apparently, she just wants to talk to you. Can I bring her round?"

I thought this was odd. What a shock, and then I saw her – it was Lorna Bradgate, a friend from indie gigs and clubs.

I had forgotten that she was a tour guide representative based in Corfu. The word had spread that we were there for the filming, and she had come to the airport to see me. We were both too busy to meet up while we were there, but I will be forever in her debt, giving me cred. Shunning the principals, she only had eyes for me!

After the arrival shots at the airport, we were driven to our respective hotels. Supporting actors and crew in one, principles in another. Ours was a little seedy, gothic, and had seen better days, but it was comfortable in an old-fashioned way. I loved it. However, while we were waiting for them to fill the swimming pool, we discovered that the crew had complained that it was too far out of town. Two days later we were moved into the same hotel as the principles. This was better by far.

Most of the guests seemed to be German and a lively crowd they were too. They even ran a Sally Bowles Cabaret type show in the concert room, which I thought was hilarious. The hotel itself – wow! What a contrast, a five-star hotel without a doubt; we all had brick semi-circular chalets, very cosy. From the hotel there was a great view overlooking the bay to Albania. I used to get up early, have breakfast and watch MTV which was still a novelty for me.

The next day we were taken to the cricket ground, which was a large open space just off the town centre. During a lull in the filming, I wandered round to the far side where I had noticed another shoot going on, of six gorgeous models. I chatted briefly to a couple of them and found out it was a French fashion magazine taking photographs against the historic backdrop of Corfu. Then I wandered back. Typical Jacks' scenario. Why didn't I suggest to the photographer that I could be used in some of the shots, as a novelty, in full cricket gear taking position alongside these extremely attractive models. By the time I'd thought of it, the opportunity was lost.

One day's filming involved lying on the beach and a comedy cricket game. In the storyline, the wives challenge the husbands to a game, using children's mini cricket bats, plastic stumps, and a rubber ball. Luckily, I was not called upon to bat. The focal point of the scene was when team Captain Roger Dervish hits the ball out to sea. However, there was a gremlin around that afternoon because no matter how hard he tried, Robert Daws couldn't hit that ball, to the extent that he was counted down out loud by the crew each time he missed. Nick said, "Keep the camera turning!" and I knew he was saving this for the out-takes video for cast and crew. Eventually Robert managed to make contact, all to a round of applause by all concerned. I knew too well how he felt, so on the way back, walking up the hill for tea, I caught up with Robert and expressed empathy. "Harrumph!" he growled and stormed off. Well, I was only trying to help!

Our opposing team on the screen were the Corflot Players. Residents of Corfu, they had developed their own slang terms for cricket and nicknamed it 'Fernaro Kai Issia', which in English translates as 'Block And Wallop'. Out on the pitch one day, I was chatting with the Corflot Players and saw Robert, Timothy Spall and Michael Jason walking towards us. I whispered to The Corflots, "Pretend to understand whatever I said, as if it was in Greek." They fell in with it right away. Once the principles were in earshot, I came out with some improvised gibberish. It was a fine joke, the principles thought I was fluent, although Michael Jayston seemed to cotton on when I accidentally dropped in a couple of Spanish words. The Corflots laughed and responded patting me heartily on the back. I was accepted!

My teammate, Roy Richards, is an excellent, professional soul singer. That evening, he came to me and asked if I would accompany him to a meeting he had arranged with the manager of the hotel, in the hope of getting a season there. "Yes, or course," I said thinking he wanted me as moral support. As we neared the manager's office he said, "I was really impressed that you could speak Greek, that's going to help me a lot."

"Er um Roy," I said, "I can't, it was a joke to wind up the principles."

His face fell. By now we were walking into the manager's office. "Kalispera," I said, knowing that this meant 'good evening'. I had nothing more to offer. The manager smiled. "Good evening," he said, in English, "please take a seat." We were both hugely relieved and they agreed dates. Roy was in an excellent mood after this and invited me for drinks at the bar.

I realise that I am not seen that much throughout *Outside Edge*, however, I did enjoy watching the footage of series two, which we saw on the final night there, just before our end of shoot party. Not only was it very entertaining, but for me something magical happened. When it came to my batting up against the big, burly bowler and my reaction shot, I got a round of applause from the crew. It felt great to get that kind of reaction from colleagues – crew as well as actors. Thanks a lot Jack L Warner, very much appreciated. Our flight the next day was at 6pm. I had a few shots of the local brandy called Metaxa, the 'Elixir of Life' with the Corflot Players waving us off and slept happily all the way on the flight back to Manchester. It was a return to reality at the council the following Monday!

Later on in the year, a third series was being planned and Nottingham City Council again granted me time off. How lucky was I? This time, they built the club house specially, on a farmer's field in South Nottinghamshire. Close up, you could tell it wasn't a cricket pitch, but it looked good on the screen. For one episode we had the famed cricketer Godfrey Evans to lend a bit of gravitas to the proceedings. Of course, John and Joan Sheriston were delighted to meet him. Their ship had come in and they spent lots of time bonding over cricket anecdotes, which was lovely to see. I excelled myself on this third series by annoying wardrobe. First, I spilled coffee on my cricket whites. Taboo to take coffee and tea into wardrobe. Then I carried a reel of cable off the pitch to help the electricians, only to find it had unwound with black marks all over my whites. Wardrobe had to do extra washes in double quick time for the next scene.

Despite my efforts, the filming went through smoothly and we had a fab end of shoot celebration in Scruffy Murphy's on Derby Road in Nottingham. Paul Watson, the sound engineer, was in a band and they were the entertainment playing hits of the 60's and lots of cracking indie pop. *Outside Edge* proceeded to win nominations and awards in The Best Comedy Awards category 1995:

Top TV Comedy Drama (winner)

Best TV Comedy Actor – Robert Daws (Nominee)

Best TV Comedy Actress – Josie Lawrence (Nominee)

Best TV Comedy Actress – Brenda Blethyn (Winner 1994)

Writers Guild of Great Britain Award – Richard Harris (Winner 1994)

I wish I had spent more time with Richard Harris. I have since discovered that he's had an amazing career, working a lot for ATV/ITC. His credits included some of my favourite TV series: *The Saint, Man In A Suitcase, The Avengers, Sherlock Holmes* (1968), *Danger Man, The Sweeney* and many, many more. He was a frequent visitor on set. How I wish I'd gone over to him to chat about how he constructs a screenplay, and just generally about all the work he had done, especially at ATV.

I kept in touch with the others as we waited eagerly the call for a fourth series. Carlton TV were originally a 'publisher broadcaster' with their London franchise, commissioning projects rather than producing. When the IBA gave them the 16-acre Nottingham site they became a production company overnight. Trial and error are the words that spring to mind. When the application for a fourth series was put forward, we were all stunned when they said an emphatic "No!" We were shocked and saddened by this news. It made no sense at all. That was it – 22 episodes, and I was in 21 of them. Everybody wanted to do another series, producers, director, cast and crew, to no avail. The ratings were still good. That was it, end of, finito, nada, nothing, zilch. If they rang now to say they were getting everyone back together, I would do it for free, er, well, as long as the expenses were paid!

I did odd bits of work for Carlton TV after that: nothing worth mentioning, but it kept me in the grapevine.

I started to hear gossip about poor decision-making and money being wasted on projects. Rumours began about winding down the production studio at Lenton Lane with a view to a merger of some kind. Then in 2003, the closure was announced. Despite opposition from the 200-strong workforce the National Union of Journalists and 27 local MPs, it closed in the spring of 2005. In total, 350 jobs were axed. I understand that the chief executive, Michael Green, had a £15 million pay-off.

9

S.P.A.M! (60s Soul, Psychedelic, Alternative, Motown & Mod!)

1989 to 2018

The Garage Indie Club in Nottingham closed in October 1988 at which point one of the managers, Ian Gardiner, took over the venue and re-launched it as The Kool Kat late 1989, with a logo similar to a red-wrapped chocolate wafer bar for when you have a break. I went to the opening and found 'the beat goes on' – many of the bar staff and door security were the same and Pete Beckett was still DJ-ing there. From 1994, he also did Friday nights at a new club, The Beatroot, also in The Lace Market area. We rolled around them all, having a fine time. In 1996, I hired The Beatroot for my 50th birthday party. I cunningly made it May Day Sunday, thinking that with it being a short bank holiday, few people would go away for the weekend so I may well have a captive audience. My girlfriend Diana helped me to create some flyers. I picked up an illustrated book of old cartoons for inspiration and the pages fell open to reveal 'Happy Jacks Annual!' I superimposed myself and Popeye at the helm of the cartoon boat, and we sent them off to everyone I had ever known plus their friends. About 200 people turned up. I knew half of them – the other half were friends of – but they were all FAB people. The way some of the Indie girls dressed reminded me of 1966 all over again! Diana had worked with some friends and created pictures of my past that she plastered all over the venue.

I asked the head doorman Jeff at The Beatroot to do the door security. An ex-miner and all-round cracking guy, we had a few things in common. Very few in in the club scene had mining in their background. When I said, "Pete's a cracking DJ isn't he? He keeps 'em dancing," I can still hear him saying good naturedly "He's a pillock!" Sorry Pete. He loved you really. Honest. Made me laugh.

Jeff ran a fitness centre and gym called *Formula One* in Nottingham, still going and highly recommended. We did The May Day parties again in 1997 and 1998. The next time would be in the year 2001, when another adventure was to open up for me.

I had first met Diana Barber in the summer of 1994 at friend Maggie's house in Beeston, where she was the lodger. She tried to read my personality by how I responded to questions such as my favourite animal, the room where I felt the safest, the type of water I liked the most – stormy sea or a puddle, etc. I said to myself, "We've got a right one 'ere!" She was very attractive in an eccentric sort of way, strongly resembling a young Diana Rigg. She also rolled her own cigarettes with liquorish papers, as I did.

In those days, the Hockley Snooker Centre on Heathcote Street was open until the early hours and that's where I met her again. It was a great place with seven full sized tables scattered around on the first floor of what was originally a Victorian lace making factory. It had loads of atmosphere and was dark and seedy – suited me right down to the ground. It attracted a varied, cosmopolitan and diverse crowd, who I suspect went there to hide away from the critical eyes of family and work colleagues. There were rockers, mods, people of Chinese, Asian, West Indian and

Caribbean origin. It was also very quiet. No 'yawping' as in other establishments. Diana working in Loughborough on developing community arts across the East Midlands and spent a lot of time out on the road visiting community organisations, helping them with funding and staffing. She also went to some very weird performances of 'Live Arts'.

When we started going out together on a regular basis I would go along and witnessed everything from tabletop football games made from milk cartons to the fabulous and very professionally run Leicester Carnival. It was not my field of the arts at all, but I found it interesting, met a lot of students and attended some cracking end of year shows. Diana and I had friends in common and started to see each other at clubs and pubs in Nottingham. There weren't as many bars around compared to today and you could usually guarantee meeting someone in the Old Angel, Jacey's, Lord Robert's in the Hockley area or the Peacock and Poacher on Mansfield Road and, of course, the excellent News House on St James' Street. This pub was guaranteed to suit everyone.

The left hand side was alternative, appealing to mods, punks, and rockers, with a fab jukebox to match. The right-hand side was more like a country pub with MOR background music and brasses on the wall. Many were tempted to stroke the landlord's cute Jack Russell that sat on its own stool by the bar, but you only ever did it once.

One Valentine's Day night 1995, four of us were in Jacey's and decided to go on to Rock City. As we stepped out, me and the lads shared a spliff. Resin was good for me because it didn't make me feel as sleepy as weed. Alongside us, a council bin lorry pulled up, "Eyup Howard, how ya doin'?" said the driver.

I told him we were on the way to Rock City.

"Gerrin youth, I'll tek you all round."

We all squeezed into the vehicle and off we chauffeured round to the venue. Now how is that for style, clambering out of a bin lorry in front of trendy Rock City?! As we queued to go in, me and the lads finished off the spliff. Heck it was strong, but in a nice way. Then I noticed one of the door staff waving at me to come over. It was Jane, a FAB goth lady who I'd fancied for a quite a while, we'd always got on. She was an anomaly for Rock City security, as they were usually blokes and often bikers.

"Bring your three friends over and just walk straight in."

"Jane you are a star and you've just finished my night off in style, thank you. A drink coming your way as soon as I get served"

Now how's that for cred? A 53-year-old man jumps the queue of 20- somethings!

By the time we entered Rick, Wai and I were well and truly gone! Diana wandered off for a dance. Meanwhile, I entertained them with the story of going to Mum and Dad's for tea that Thursday straight from work.

"So, there I am dressed smartly, collar and tie with my work bag over my shoulder. Nobody around, walking for the bus, tumbleweeds blowing through Arnold main street. I'm so glad I live in town now. On the bus going back into town everybody was half my age and dressed for a night out looking at me in a weird way."

"They probably thought you were collecting the fares," said Wai.

That did it. All three of us went into hysterics, we couldn't stop, on and on. It lasted for at least fifteen minutes, until

Diana returned from the dance floor. She looked at us as we collapsed into hysterics again and again and, annoyed, she charged off home. The moral of this story is, save the spliffs for when you're at home. It wasn't something I made a habit of anyway, it always made me feel so tired.

Diana had her own unique style at this time. On our first date we were leaving a party in St. Ann's and while waiting for the bus, she leaned nonchalantly against the bus shelter glass frame. Unfortunately, there wasn't any glass! I helped her off the ground.

"Are you alright? I thought there was glass in there too!"

"Yes, I'm fine, thanks anyway," she growled.

Two weeks later, on New Year's Eve 1994, on the way to the Peacock she walked into a tree – and we were sober! Diana caught me out when one day in the early evening she came round dressed up to the nines, armed with a bottle of champagne and some erotic lingerie. But, you see, I'd had a very busy day in fifth gear at work, talking non-stop for eight hours in reception. All I wanted to do was go home and have an early night. When she knocked at the door, I was in bed nearly asleep. I ignored her persistent knocking; she would think I'd gone out. The next day Diana rang me to say that she knew I was in because she could see the key in the lock, which I had not thought of. Things went a bit cool for a while, but by February 1996 she had moved in and was helping me pay my mortgage!

The Bonzo Dog Doo Dah Band were created by a group of students in the early 60s. They combined elements of music hall, trad jazz, humour, and psychedelic pop. The lead singer was Viv Stanshall. In 1963 he and his wife Ki decided to buy an abandoned cargo ship left rusting away in Sunderland Docks. It costs £15,000. After a total refurbishment they set sail to Bristol where it remains to this day.

After trying it out as a theatre, they converted it to a venue for bands and called it The Thekla, where local bands and indie labels such as Sarah Records and Heaven held their gigs. Sarah Records were themselves based in Bristol. Set up in 1987 they issued their 100th single in August 1995 whereupon, as they'd always intended, the label closed down. The farewell party was held at The Thekla. Courtesy of Anton, Lynda, and Mark, I had an invite to the party, to dance the night away to Wedding Present, Heavenly, The Orchids, Blueboy, Secret Shine, Brighter and Boy Racer.

As we wandered back to the boarding house in the early hours, behind us fell the end of the Indie Pop scene and ahead loomed Brit-Pop, the war between Blur and Oasis, and many changes on the dance floor. As a parallel, The Word TV show ran 104 episodes on Channel 4 from August 1990 to March 1995. It was a thrill to watch at the time and notable for giving Nirvana their first international TV appearance. I recorded The Chart Show on Saturday mornings, and I would edit the best bits with the aid of two videos onto a master tape. When it moved to a late-night slot at 11pm on a Saturday night, guests began to show us a new style of outrageous party to watch. I would usually record it and edit for my master tape on Sunday mornings.

Diana and I are both totally 'humbug' about Christmas. In 1997, we decided to escape the annual furore by going to Malaga City in Andalucia. We arrived late on Christmas Eve and went into town straight away, looking for adventure. It was 11 o'clock at night and deserted. Not a sound except for the sound through open windows of happy families clanking cutlery and eating. We were bitterly disappointed and about to go back to the hotel when Diana noticed a small bar open down an alleyway, so we decided to have one for the road. There were only two people in there, from the States, talking loudly about "The good graaass in Morocco." I had heard much the same monologue in bars nearly thirty years before in Gibraltar.

We agreed that it probably wouldn't be a good idea to do Christmas again in Malaga and started to leave just as the midnight mass bells started to chime. Then, as if a curtain had been raised, all hell let loose. One by one, the bar shutters went up, the lights went on, and the streets filled up with people – it seemed like thousands of them! Down a street full of broken masonry, called Callé Beates, and among the numerous clubs we found a rock bar called Abyssinia and another playing Spanish pop with a bit of 60s called Milo.

We spent many happy hours in these clubs and bars that Christmas and many others after. On a nearby street, as the years went by, we found a club playing 60s and indie music called 'Village Green', where later Diana and I carted my records over from UK so I could do a DJ slot. At the airport Iberia check-in senoritas were 'maravillosa' about me bringing in old style vinyl for just one gig and a 20-minute slot at a small radio station halfway up a mountain. The suitcases weighed a ton, but they did not charge us any surplus, for which I will be forever grateful.

Diana was already fairly fluent in French and had picked up Spanish a damned sight quicker that yours truly (although neither of us can roll the Spanish 'rrr's' even after all those visits!). We were older than the crowd and there were no other Brits around at night in those days. They really did make a fuss of us, and whenever they could, would ask us questions about what we were doing there, and did I want some resin?

They thought we were Dutch because we did liquorice flavoured roll ups. It was so much fun: we were like kids in a sweetshop and continued to visit Almeria and Malaga at Christmas a further ten times, as well as various cities at other times of the year. I have Diana to thank for helping re-kindle my love affair with the Spanish and I will be eternally grateful to them both.

Once we went down by bus to Gibraltar on Boxing Day and spent a couple of nights there. It wasn't the same as it was in the 60's, with most of the armed forces having moved out. It had lost its magic and had a run-down feel to it, like a lot of UK seaside resorts.

The old TOC H commune was closed and run down, really overgrown, but when I knocked on the door, out came the TOC H manager, who was English, with his Gibraltarian wife. He vaguely remembered me and gave us a cup of tea and some cake. However, I could tell he didn't want to get nostalgic, so after half an hour we said our goodbyes. He wore an Arran sweater just like the manager of our hostel and just like my dad wore at Christmas. When we arrived back in Nottingham on 4th January 1997, the rushing about was over. All was still and quiet. No more season of goodwill either. Everybody was thinking of how to pay off all the bills they had acquired! That made us vow to do it again, which we did. The Spanish version of Christmas is fifty percent less frantic than UK's manic activity. We visited a number of other cities – Almeria, Santander, Madrid, Córdoba, Jerez, Cádiz, Alicante, doing our best to get to know the Spanish people and language.

Madrid was great fun, especially the year Real Madrid won the UEFA Champions League in Paris and Steve McManaman was on their team (¡Campeones!), but we usually visited Malaga and Almeria.

Tabernas on the outskirts of Almeria provided our most recent hitchhiking experience. Tabernas is the western town they used for all those 'spaghetti westerns' and Clint Eastwood's Dollar Films. We'd been to see a staged show there with shoot-outs, stunt work, horses etc. but when it was over and the sun was setting, we realised with horror that we had lost track of time and missed the last bus. There we were in the middle of nowhere up in the desert mountains at sunset. This was 1997 before either of us had mobiles.

"We'll have to walk back to the nearest town," said Diana.

"Not on these roads, it'll be dangerous when the sun sets. We'll hitchhike," I said.

"Hitchhike! You must be joking!" she said. She wanted to walk quietly along the road until we came to somewhere we could stay.

"Don't worry somebody will feel sorry for us. Trust me on this one!"

A half hour went by and zilch! Nada! Nothing! Nowt! By this time, it was practically dark.

"You and your big ideas, sunshine!" Diana said.

It was cold by now and we were not dressed for it. Then a car stopped. A Citroën 2CV with a Dutch couple in it.

"Yes, we are going to Almeria, please get in."

They were a great couple, about our age and we got on very well. They even dropped us off right outside our hostel. We asked if they would park up and go for a few drinks, but they declined as they had to get to Marbella. Phew! That was lucky alright. Even I started to have doubts about my luck with hitchhiking.

During one holiday in 2006, while we were in Almeria, we came across a back street night club called *Tormenta y Tormento*, which translates as Storm And Torment.

"Interesting name, let's give it a try," said Diana.

Well, that was definitely the right decision to make because it turned out to be one of the best times in a Spanish nightclub we'd ever had. Not only were they playing my kind of 60s music but also a lot of obscure Pirate Radio material that I hadn't heard for forty odd years—and it was all on vinyl. We had certainly come home to roost there. We were a bit self-conscious about having a bop, Brits Abroad and all that, especially as we seemed to be the only Brits there and were old enough to be their parents, but it was dark and after a few beers we went for it. It wasn't a large place, only holding about 50 people in total. Fortunately, it wasn't there in 1972 or I would have spent all my money quickly and had to get home a great deal earlier. Now, every time I play *Living Above Your Head* by Jay and The Americans and *It's Too Late* by Bobby Goldsboro, my mind immediately flashes back to Almeria 2006.

Two couples came over to us and asked why we had come there, were we working on a film?!

"If only," I said. "We just love the music, the vinyl and especially the Spanish, what more could we ask for?"

That seemed to go down well, and it became a classic session and no mistake. It was still there a year later.

We didn't hitchhike again in Spain, but Diana had the bug and we tried it out a few times in the UK, always with great success.

Our final visit to Spain was Easter 2019 for Semana Santa – Holy Week. Thousands gather from all over Spain to watch 42 churches and cathedrals process many times through the streets. Each one has its own wooden sculpture depicting the Passion of the Christ or images of the Virgin Mary. They are placed on huge 'thrones' which are carried by a hundred and twenty bearers accompanied by their own band. Diana found us a hotel room with a balcony overlooking the procession, although we didn't spend long indoors. We followed our favourite thrones until the dawn. People of all ages were out and about, and I was hugely impressed at the lack of shoving or shouting. Yet again, we were pleased to be two of the few Brits around. There is a footnote to all of this: a few weeks later on the tube at home in London, about 15 Spanish 20-somethings got off the tube to leave. When the doors started to close, I popped my head out shouting, "Felice Año Nuevo," (Happy New Year). They all turned, saw me and cheered giving me a nice round of applause. Well, you know how it is – me and Spain. ¡Viva Espana!

In the summer of 2000, I was up in the loft sorting out my archive of Films & Filming magazines, and Photoplay, and the like. I found my old newspaper clippings and studio photographs on old TV series and in particular the Warner Brothers series. They produced about fourteen series on primetime TV in the USA from 1955 to 1965. Their budget was about half of the other network shows. Studio boss Jack L Warner and his son-in-law Executive Producer William T. Orr arranged it so that everything was filmed on the Burbank studios backlot. Thus saving lots of loot by avoiding going on location, right through to 1962.

Originally on ITV from September 1957, *Sugarfoot*, starring Will Hutchins as Tom Brewster, was off the air in 1959/60 then re-appeared on the BBC as *Tenderfoot*, until it was axed in June 1961. The ending of other great series like *Cheyenne*, *Maverick* and *77 Sunset Strip* followed a year later. I was really into Tom Brewster as a youngster. He came over as a bumbling character, but like another favourite, *Columbo*, there was a lot of thinking going on behind his apparent ineptitude. He was less macho than the other leads in many TV western series, and he didn't carry a gun. The phrase Michael Caine uses referring to Harry Palmer is 'a winner who comes on like a loser', and this seems to apply too. I'm sure Will would agree with me.

I came down from the attic and on a whim rang the 'Screen Actors Guild' in Hollywood for information. The woman who answered the phone told me he was living in Glen Head, New York. Taking a deep breath, I asked if I could have his phone number.

"Sure, have you got a pen?"

Perhaps it was my telephone manner that swayed her. All those years on reception had paid off. I rang the number and Will Hutchins himself answered. The forty years since *Sugarfoot* had finished dissolved and melted away; his voice was just the same:

"Will, you sound just the same as you did in *Sugarfoot!*"

"Heck! That's kinda a compliment I s'pose! Who is this?"

I introduced myself and told him why I had been in touch, then we chatted for ten minutes about the TV and film business and cowboy shows.

We have kept in touch ever since. Will, his wife, Babs and I are all Taureans, born in May: down to earth, reliable, creatures of habit and routine. At the time I was in a desert regarding old TV shows, so I asked Will if I could purchase any old *Sugarfoot* episodes he may have.

He put me onto Boyd Magers who lives in Albuquerque, New Mexico and through him I purchased six videos, which kept me going until all 69 episodes were released on DVD a few years later. Contacting Boyd Magers opened up a whole new chapter for me. He is an aficionado of western films and TV series, particularly from the 1930s to the 1970s. He has written many excellent books on the subject and runs a monthly on-line magazine with his 'Western Clippings' website: westernclippings.com. If you should ever want to know anything about classic western films and TV series, this is the man to contact, on vidwest@comcast.net. For the last twenty years, Will has had a monthly column in this magazine where you can read all about life as an actor at Warner Brothers, working with Clint Eastwood on *Magnum Force* as a stakeout cop and with Elvis Presley on two films. There are very few actors who get asked to appear in Elvis films twice.

Will was in *Spinout* in 1966 and *Clambake* in 1967. He speaks well of Elvis; they had been friends before the films, and he emphasises that there was no ego there. We seem to have a lot in common, especially our sense of humour, but during 2019 my two worlds collided quite by accident. Diana and I were eating out at a café in Crystal Palace. We had chosen this one because there was a large poster of Michael Caine as Harry Palmer outside. When I asked the owner why, he said, "That scene *in The Italian Job* – 'You're only s'posed to blow the bloody doors off!' was filmed in the nearby park."

Ha! We took a photo of Mr Caine and used it for a giant birthday card that we sent to Will. Two weeks later Will contacted me to say he had put it out in pride of place on the gatepost outside his house. Ain't life wonderful?!

When Ian Gardiner finished running the Kool Kat in 1996, he started up Dubble Bubble and K9, on Nottingham's Greyhound Street (get it?!). Ian was a star and knew exactly how to pitch it towards the Indie and Dance scene.

I will always be grateful, not only as a punter, but because it was Ian who gave me my first job as a DJ. He originally asked if I knew anyone who could do a 60s night in the bar downstairs at K9. I asked him to let me have a crack at it and offered to put together a demo-tape. "The ball's in your court then Howard, I'll leave it with you," he said. For the next three weeks I went through my 60s records – singles and LP's – checking out all the best tracks and then putting them down onto a C90 cassette. That's how we did things in those days, folks. I dropped it through his letterbox one morning on the way to work and waited for the phone call, flicking hopefully through my singles and LPs for more material.

Ian rang and gave me a date for one Saturday starting at 9:00pm and finishing at 2:00am. In the meantime, I thought I ought to find out how to work the equipment! I knew two DJs who were on the decks at Trent University student's bar in the basement. They agreed to give me a bit of a tutorial, so I went along nice and early to watch and learn as Jane and Sheila pushed out the sounds. A fine job they did too, and I really appreciated their patience and help because I don't pick things up quickly. Ian rang the next day and asked what I was going to call myself for the night.

"SPAM," I said.

"SPAM? Is it going to be a Monty Python night?"

"Oh no, it'll be 60s as arranged, Ian. SPAM! stands for either Soul Psychedelia Atlantic and Mod or Sixties Pop Alternative and Motown."

"Like it, Howard, I think we can run with that."

I turned up at K9 an hour before I was going to play, to meet the manager, Martin Goddard and his partner, Hazel. Not to be confused with my best friend, also called Martin Goddard, K9 Martin looked very much like Paul Weller when he was in The Jam but in nature similar to marketing Martin in that both had the ability to be enthusiastic and inspire you – getting you into fifth gear instantly. That is a rare gift especially as I am usually in second! K9 Martin was great, I couldn't have wished for a better boss – thoughtful and deeply knowledgeable himself about 60s artists and tunes, particularly on the Mod side. On that first night, he placed me on the bar where the serving hatch was, *Only Fools and Horses* style.

It was a little awkward having to stand back whilst a member of staff clambered underneath to either collect empty glasses or bring in supplies, but I became used to it. K9 was a long, narrow bar and crowded if forty people were in. But Martin, Hazel and the punters were into alternative Indie and 60s music and playing there was a dream.

I made so many friends from that gig, all on the same wavelength. Martin had a rare gift of being able to enthuse everyone, with that necessary charisma that gets people in the party spirit. There was also a small stage at the end where various artists and bands would perform on other nights. A whole new social scene opened up for us. I had compiled video cassettes of 60s artists which Martin would play on the TV screens above the bar, visuals only of course. Whenever people could dance in that cramped bar they did. Which is what the 60s is all about for me.

My toons are all three minutes long and you can dance to every one.

After a year there was one weird weekend when it all went very, very strange. About midnight, Frank, the K9 doorman, suddenly moved into the doorway where he blocked a couple of policemen. Parking them outside, he came to me and said:

"Howard, the police are outside. They want to have a word with you."

Frank was in his fifties and always a star. He is a professional carpenter/joiner and always a good laugh when I saw him in Nottingham. He obviously thought I might need to get away quickly, but I could see that Diana was with the police. She should have been at home entertaining her mum and dad who were visiting. It turned out that my dad had been taken to hospital. Mum had called for the ambulance but when she arrived at the hospital with my dad, being in a state she couldn't remember my telephone number so called the police and asked them to go to my house. Martin took over on the decks and off we sped lights flashing through the centre of Nottingham, full of punters having a great time while I was panicking about my dad. In a way, it was lucky that there were no beds available that night on the ward. It meant Dad had a private room – the sluice room, with big sinks along one side and crowded with laundry bins and hospital trolleys. They had sedated him with a view to starting some tests later that morning. There was one spooky moment when Dad woke up. Diana and mum had gone to get a drink and I was on my own in the darkened sluice room.

"There's a woman over there standing in the corner!"

I turned but couldn't see anyone.

"Where, Dad? I can't see her."

"Over there, in that corner behind you."

I said, "Of course, you're right" and with that he fell asleep. We all thought we were going to lose him, he looked so pale and drawn.

At dawn, Diana went to Cliff Road, and I went to Mum's where we had a rest, then went back to visit Dad in the afternoon. He had perked up and they were talking about sending him into a care home for some respite care. We were elated. Dad dozed off quite happily and Mum and I went to Arnold. Diana brought her parents over and we took my mum out for a break to Arnold Working Men's Club (CIU Affiliated). After all those years of going to Basford Miners Welfare Sunday lunch time sessions, but only winning the odd line at bingo, that night I won £120 on a full house. This didn't make me very popular with the regulars. I wondered if Dad had passed away and this was his parting shot farewell gift. When I got home, I rang the hospital straight away, but they reassured me, saying, "No, your father is doing well and remaining stable." Unfortunately, after many tests, it turned out to be stomach cancer, probably a throwback to being a prisoner of war all those years ago.

The respite home was great with him, but he and Mum really wanted him at home and to be honest it might have been better to have passed away then. I wish it had been like in the films – you know, passing away in the sluice room with me, Diana and Mum, sitting around him, holding his hands, closing credits.

But it was in a respite home surrounded by others with the subsequent lack of dignity attached, which was such a shame. For your continuing patience and support through some very difficult times, and for introducing me to social skills, the cinema, age three, thanks a whole bunch dad. ¡Vaya Con Dios!

The gigs at K9 on a Saturday night were thoroughly enjoyable and great fun. On a Thursday night I would call in and after everyone had left around midnight, we had our own private party. There were usually just half a dozen of us: me, Martin, Pish, bass player in The Sound Carriers, and Martin Hansen (Hanny), who did my website.

Putting the world to rights with a few drinks and... getting stoned. Sometimes using the Ouija board, and yes, we definitely had someone speaking to us. K9 was in an old building. Every time I went down to the loo somebody was whistling, but by the time I had surfaced to the bar I had forgotten to ask who was doing the whistling. Until that last Thursday before Dubble Bubble and K9 closed for good. This time I remembered when I stumbled back into the bar.

"Something I've been meaning to ask you. Which one of you whistles every time I go downstairs to the loo?"

They looked at me. Nobody had whistled and thinking about it they weren't really the types to whistle. It's a shame that I was too far gone on drink to appreciate that moment. Left alone down there with a ghost didn't bother me at all; I think it was a friendly spirit who enjoyed the tunes as much as we did.

Once a month for 18 months I honed my craft on the turntables. With vinyl you don't have time to get bored, especially if you are flitting from LP's to singles and back again, and particularly if you forget to change the speed! That last night was incredibly sad, but we finished it off in style. Hazel, Martin, Diana and I went back to drop off the records at Cliff Road, had a few snacks and drinks, ordered a taxi up to Bestwood Country Park and watched the dawn come up, sharing a couple of spliffs. Martin and Hazel were excellent company over the years – they always managed to make things happen in an exciting way. The supreme host and hostess, whether in their home, in their narrow boat or in the pub. I would never have guessed that spinning some vinyl would be the catalyst to meeting so many interesting and fun-loving people. Ahoy Hazel and Martin – I salute you and all who sail with you.

At the beginning of 2002 I did some DJ work at The Wheatsheaf on Ilkeston Road.

Every Thursday for six months I would turn up and play for three hours in the lounge to only a handful of people, all the customers were in the bar. We roamed the streets around Radford regularly, putting advertising flyers through letterboxes to no avail. I consoled myself by thinking that at least they could hear me in the bar. Plus I was honing my craft, practice makes perfect etc.

Eventually, not surprisingly the landlord thought it would be better if we called it a day. But it was good fun while it lasted.

After this experience we coined the phrase – "Nothing can be as bad as The Wheatsheaf!"

Local Nottingham boy made good, Mr George Akins, came from humble beginnings. Starting as a barrow boy and then moving on to betting shops in 1960 and, I reckon, I was the only regular punter at Rescue Rooms who can even remember George Akins Oyster Bar. Why am I writing about this man? The Heart of the Midlands was an up-market variety club similar to the well-known Batley Variety club. Artists from all over the world appeared there. I saw Dave Allen the comedian, who did three hours instead of the arranged two. He sat on a high stool next to a table, lit a cigarette and said:

"Well, I'm having such a good time here, will somebody top up my glass and I'll do another hour – if that's alright with everybody?"

Of course it was, he was brilliant, it was a magical night.

The Beatles manager, Brian Epstein, also had The Fourmost in his stable. I didn't know in 1964 that their hit *Baby I Need Your Loving* was actually a cover of The Four Tops Motown hit but it was fab. They came to the Heart of the Midlands in 1976, which involved me picking up Mum and Dad from Arnold, driving them back to Nottingham, and staying sober in order to drive them back four hours later. Why I didn't get them a taxi I'll never know! I was worn out. These were 'chicken in a basket' nights.

However, on 11th December 1980 George Akins Snr took over The Heart of the Midlands which he re-vamped as Rock City and, astonishingly, put new bands Orange Juice and The Undertones on the programme on the first night. The Undertones had only had their hit *Teenage Kicks* two years before. My own first visit to Rock City was to see Sweet in 1981. It wasn't quite the original line-up but a driving fast-paced rock set. In 1994, George Akins Jnr took over the running of Rock City at the age of 19, right at the height of Indie rock. I saw so many bands there throughout the 90s it started to be my second home – that is until Rescue Rooms.

Situated round the back side of Rock City, Rescue Rooms opened on 22 February 2003. Anton Lockwood was the man who put the bands on, he of the Old Vic, who with Lynda Bowen had built up a serious reputation as DJs and promoters as *The Night With No Name*, promoting many Indie bands around the Nottingham area. Anton went on to promote The White Stripes and The Strokes at the Bodega in Nottingham, which I think is where he drew the attention of George Akins Jnr. On the Rescue Rooms opening night it came up about having a 60s night, whilst we were knocking the pints back. Okay, Anton may have been gone on drink but when I said I could do it he said I could give it a whirl, although his 'sleech was somewhat spurred'! I do hope he never regretted it. From April 2003 to August 2017, I played in the Red Room and then the main bar most months with the occasional extra guest slots. Diana helped me with the marketing and was a roadie, helping me cart heavy trolleys of vinyl across Nottingham. We had more than just a laptop to carry. Every tune was on vinyl.

We would arrive early to get the feel of the place, hauling two trolleys of vinyl up the stairs to the Red Room. Down came the lights to be replaced by flashing, psychedelic style effects and my own 60s compilation videos, made on a couple of Hitachi video recorders which had a very useful handset that you could use to toggle between them. Originally, these were on a large TV screen, and later Diana rigged up a screen for a projector. At 10pm the punters poured in. Rescue Rooms appealed to a mainly 18- to 30-year-old age group, which suited me no end. This crowd were very open to all types of sounds and didn't usually have a particular kind of 60s music they liked, so I could play around with a variety of tunes – making sure they were danceable of course. We were frequently packed out, and at 2am the crowd often had to be shepherded into the main room downstairs which was open until 3am. Later I was playing until 3am. I could have carried on until dawn. The nights just flew by. I never, ever drank while playing, it spoils your judgement and slows you down.

A year later a sister club opened up next door called Stealth which we feared would take our punters, but it kind of added to it. Stealth was more up to date with its music scene of dance, grime and electronic music all pumped out with Funktion-One sound system. The punters tended to take their enjoyment more seriously – whereas I went for the fun aspect and the same with the main room DJ, Martin Nesbitt (The Reverend), who has been a DJ since the late 80s and was 'The Face' at The Garage. He played across the board pop music from the 80s onwards. The crowd were now able to roam from the Red Room to Stealth and the Main Room and back again, so we had a continual turnover of customers.

The girls were particularly funny, outgoing, and outrageous. They were very good dancers, really getting into the 60s vibe with a kind of raunchy, cheerleader, Go-Go girls cavorting.

Being a DJ at Rescue Rooms certainly gave me cred for getting other gigs. For two years I worked once a month at two pubs, The Ropewalk and Junction Seven, on Canning Circus. They both had large bars with a small dance floor, although not quite the larger get up and groove space I'd been accustomed to. The Junction was a pleasant surprise in that it was a punk and garage pub. That said, I expressed concern to Adey the manager about my playing 60s tunes there, even though these were on the alternative side.

"Don't you worry about that Howard; they'll need to unwind after all that frantic punk and heavy rock!"

And he was right. It was the more the commercial sixties that went down well like *Build Me Up Buttercup,* and Motown of all things.

As time went on at Rescue Rooms, the punters' habits started to change. They of course realised that they may as well get sloshed in their pads and turn up at midnight out of their heads at half the price, so it tended to be quieter up to midnight. I had an extension up to 3am so we could keep the beat going. Five solid hours? Well, to be honest I never noticed the extra hour, it went by so quickly – a strong bladder helps! In about 2014 I asked if we could play in the large bar downstairs. This would take the pressure off having to fill the dance floor, the bar was busy all the time and there was a dance area too.

With the opening of The Student's Union Bar and Club, nearby on Shakespeare Street, it was decided in August 2017 that having DJs in the bars was not an option anymore and I was told that was it. But what a FAB fourteen years it had been. So much fun and I was paid handsomely for it. There was no big fanfare or party. I would have been hugely embarrassed. We just packed up and went out as usual by the back door. I still miss it. Trundling home just as dawn was coming up and sleeping in til midday. I miss all the students and friends I made there.

Right from when we started I always expected to be told that this would be the last gig, , but fortunately they kept me on. If it weren't for Diana though I wouldn't have sustained that level of popularity, she was definitely the other half of VinylJacks DJ, from compiling the website to promotions and moral support, plus learning how to use the sound levels and pass that knowledge onto me. She was very active in doing the promotions.

One Saturday evening, en-route to Rescue Rooms we passed through Slab Square. Diana said, "I'll put a couple of posters on the lamp post and the bus shelter right here. Lots of people will see them that way."

Famous last words! Two weeks later I was summoned into the Public Health Office. It turns out that Nottingham City Council had brought in a new rule about flyposting and doing so on public property came with a £50 fine. Oops! The Public Health Office was in the Lawrence House building where I worked. I had to have an interview and sign a form. Diana was distraught and offered to come in with me to explain, but they only wanted to see me. They had a CCTV footage of Diana doing the deed while I looked on. Okay, it was a fair cop – guilty as charged. A woman by the name of Christine Walker literally interrogated me. Sergeant Major Walker barked at me, "To be honest I think you were a bloody fool, and it could be a sacking offence." It really annoyed her that I didn't give a damn, for two reasons:

1) I was intending to take early retirement in a couple of months anyway; and

2) If disciplined I would have to mention that when she was in the Highways Section the men had been watching pornography on City Council computers, which was well known, but they were not disciplined or sacked.

However, I was embarrassed for Anton, because I knew he was on some kind of Council liaison committee about managing venues and student nights as well as fly posting in the city. Sod's Law again, but I was lucky enough not to be told to go by either establishment, and the beat went on.

From 2003 to 2017 I think I must have been the oldest person in Rescue Rooms, be it punters or management. The funny thing about it is that in those fourteen and a half years, not one of the crowd ever mentioned or suggested, "Aren't you too old for this sort of scene?"

Thank you so much George Jnr and Anton for fourteen and a half years of DJ heaven, much appreciated. HAPPY DAZE.

10

The Season Of The Witch

2001 to the present

Hazel from K9 called me to ask if Steve and I would be interested in doing some role-play work at the Law School. She needed actors for their Bar Vocational Course Exam and thought we would be well suited. We passed the interview and a month later our brief came through the post. Part scripted, part improv, we had to play a part being asked questions by the students, one at a time as part of their examinations. My script was playing a policeman, who with a colleague gave chase to some youths who had stolen a car and there were drugs involved. For this we were in the actual Guildhall Courts, where we spent half an hour in the dock grilled by the prosecution. You could tell straightaway the ones that had the necessary element of performance which would enable them to get on in the legal system, although it was all taken seriously.

The tutors were experienced lawyers who were very demanding. There were humorous moments, for example for some reason they often forgot to bring the 'drug bag' prop to use as an exhibit. One of the tutors, Rob Manning, used to milk the drug scenario to the hilt. The students would go into a scrum to find out who was responsible for the exhibits, then one of them would break away and run off to the office to scoop them up. On another occasion, someone else was playing the judge and we would have to 'mime' the drugs bags. Personally, I always came out of those sessions on a high and we were paid very well for the privilege. The interview sessions were somewhat different. We were based in the Taylor building in what was once an old Victorian house on Chaucer Street, nicely tucked away from the modern steel and glass of the main college building.

Depending on the scenario, I could be playing a military type in the throes of a custody hearing, a yob who had smashed up a pub, a guy who assaulted his ex-girlfriend's partner or an elder person who was burgled by his helper. Each interview lasted fifteen minutes and we did eight per day. It was not an easy job to keep up the pace, to make sure it was fresh for every student, but I enjoyed it immensely. I was never bored doing the same thing time after time, and relish lengthy rehearsal schedules.

After about ten years things began to change. Cutbacks came into play and half the actors were dropped, although luckily, Steve and I were kept on. We lost the lovely Taylor Building with its great atmosphere, to be transferred to the main glass and steel building on Goldsmith Street. I have to confess my last days there were not particularly brilliant. A new head tutor Amanda had been drafted in and she was not keen on the informal atmosphere that tutors like Rob had engendered. (In the films she would be played by Lotte Lenya as Rosa Klebb.) Whatever I did was wrong, but I wasn't about to be rattled. I put on my best 'Columbo' act – all smiles and polite courtesy.

They were in a tough situation, and I made sure to play it the same informal way in their exams. The last day was a really hot one and after lunch Amanda became even more irritable, so I increased my solicitude. Just before each interview started, I would shut the windows to block out the noise of the university gardeners mowing outside, opening them for fresh air in between students, and then often popped out and bought her a strong coffee. Despite this, she wouldn't discuss or engage in conversation between students. After all, one does not indulge minions does one? The only question she ever asked was:

"I gather you are a DJ?" I felt as if I was on the stand!

I gave her brief details of what I played and where.

"Hmm, The Rescue Rooms. I suppose you get a lot of students there? Any from the Law School?"

"I wouldn't know, I'm too busy concentrating on the vinyl. Being a vinyl DJ, you don't have much time to chat. It's all go from 10:00pm to 3:00am! You know, in the 14 years I've been at Rescue Rooms, not one student has come up to me at The Law School and said, "You're a DJ aren't you?"

Then came the fatal day when a girl said at the end of her interview, "Well, that was fun – can we do it again?"

The head tutor's face was a picture, if looks could kill, etc. Under her auspices, they were not meant to enjoy the situation. Perhaps I had been too friendly, too welcoming. It didn't help matters when I replied amiably, "Well, yes, alright then."

That was my last day with the Law School. I didn't get another booking.

During the years 2004 to 2012 Nottingham Law School were in the top five throughout the country. In my own small way, I like to think we helped to contribute towards that.

In the early part of 2010, I was asked to take part in a series of record review programmes at Radio Nottingham.

It was about contemporary artists who had decided to put their latest releases onto vinyl. Being Vinyl Jacks DJ attracted all sorts of people. Luckily, up to now, no one has thought I was involved with tiling! However if you go on the internet you'll find 'Vinyl Jacks – Flooring Specialist'. Just my luck to be confused with a tile person.

You couldn't make it up.

While waiting in reception at Radio Nottingham I became intrigued by the woman who was behind the desk:

"You have a very clear, resonant voice," I said. "Have you worked in the theatre?"

"Not at all, it's because I talk a lot and host a lot of seminars."

I'm very nosy in more ways than one. I asked, "What sort of things do you cover?"

"Oh just one," she said. "The Craft of Paganism. I'm a witch."

I then had to go upstairs to the studios, but when I came back down after the broadcast we continued our conversation. Two weeks later, I returned to the studios for another programme, and she presented me with a couple of crystals for my 'spiritual wellbeing'. Caroline James was her name. (In the films she would be played by Fenella Fielding.)

I went round to her place in Netherfield for more chats about the craft. The 'spiritual coincidences' started just prior to that first visit.

I decided to walk there and when I was at Colwick level crossing, I had to wait for a train to cross. In my usual early afternoon daze, I had kind of switched off, but I was soon jolted awake. The level crossing steel pole came down literally a foot in front of me. It could have been a really nasty case of concussion. Shaken, but not stirred, I had recovered by the time I arrived at Caroline's. She had a magnificent Victorian terraced house with lots of Pagan symbolism, and five cats. One cat turned out to be called Howie, which is what my friends call me sometimes and the other was called Jack! We had two or three meetings where Caroline informed me about the craft and did some Tarot card readings. However, unlike me, Caroline is a solo pagan and very rarely went into town, especially at night, so I couldn't get her to come out and meet Diana and my friends.

The Tarot readings were a first for me and told a lot of truths. When we were looking at her laptop screen, Howie the cat leapt up and walked over the laptop. This annoyed Caroline but made me laugh a lot. Howie by name, Howie by nature!

She gave me a Pagan exercise book to work through, which was really useful for a complete beginner like me. One exercise I did was imagining going down a hole in a forest, Alice in Wonderland style. You went under the roots of the trees and wound your way down to the bottom. There was a desk, a cane, a notepad and pen. You signed the book and banged on the table three times with the cane and from the back came a hooded woman dressed in a big purple garment. She had long black hair and her face was shadowed over. I had to imagine this and ask her, "What is your name?" As clear as anything a voice came out in my darkened bedroom. "Rowena," it said. This lady had been designated to watch over me. The bizarre thing about it was that Rowena was Caroline's middle name. Up until then I hadn't realised! Fascinating. I started down this path hoping to be eventually romping naked in the churchyard in the early hours of the morning with a group of nubiles à la Dennis Wheatley (ha!), but it turns out that's Satanism, a deviation from Christianity. Shame really!

Eventually, Caroline came round to our house a couple of times after work. I only lived a five-minute walk from BBC Nottingham. However, she then kind of disappeared and no longer responded to texts or phone calls so I was out on a limb. I'm not the type to try something alone, I need others around me. I found a couple of pagan groups in Nottingham. One held meetings once a month at the Theosophical Hall, next to the Salutation Inn on Maid Marian Way. All aspects of Paganism were covered by some excellent speakers, frequently tongue in cheek, which appealed to me greatly.

I was learning a lot, and not just about Paganism. The very best speakers were Daniel Bran Griffith, David Knight, Cayt Hewitt, Ian Overton, (who was great, and I learned much about how to be natural in front of an audience from him, funny too), and Ashley Mortimer, an advocate of the greatly eccentric and fascinating Gerald Gardner, The Wicca Man. (In the films he would be played by William Shatner.)

However, while they were excellent, the truly fabulous speaker was Moira Hodgkinson. Her talk on how she found her way into Paganism was hilarious. I was hooked well and truly. It's not surprising that she has three books published – highly recommended. At 10pm we would finish by going next door to the Salutation Inn for a few drinks. Ten minutes staggering distance from my house, perfect.

The monthly Wednesday night sessions were called 'Moots'. They were held at The Poacher Pub on Mansfield Road and were more on the social side with an occasional speaker. Twenty people squashed in a small annexe made it quite interesting. As time went on and I started to get to know people, I found that several had one thing in common: they were all rubbish at getting a round in. Time after time I would be at the bar and 'Got 'em in' but it was never reciprocated. Conversely, they would be at the bar as I arrived but didn't offer. For me, this is a cardinal sin, even though Paganism doesn't have sinning as such. Easily resolved this one, I just bought my own from then on regardless of the guilty feeling. I found it hard work getting to know them; eye contact was frequently poor. It was through the monthly meetings at the Theosophical Hall group that I got to find like-minded souls, especially Howard Davies (who, in the films, would be played by James Hayter).

If it was not for my purple crew neck sweater my friendship with him might never have taken off. At the interval during one meeting, he came over with his daughter, Maddie, and said, with a deadpan straight face, "Have you been sent here undercover to report back to the Vatican?"

"I'm sorry!?"

"We've noticed you're wearing your Vatican Purple crew neck!"

Then he smiled, Maddie smiled and that was where it took off, 'Blessed Be'. Afterwards we went to the Sal. and it was an excellent bonding session which has carried on till fairly recently. He's a very knowledgeable man and can talk on many subjects, drama, films, TV, pop music (although he is a 70s man, but each to their own). Howard would have fitted in nicely with Martin and Steve, then we would have most certainly been *The Four Just Men*. (An excellent TV series, made by Lew Grade's ITC in 1959. Jack Hawkins and Dan Dailey were my favourites.)

Howard asked if I would like to join him and a few others on some Pagan oriented walks. He had been made redundant with his job at EON and was free during the week. This suited me fine. Weekends were always sacrosanct with the DJ work and time to spend with Di.

My first Pagan walk was on one bleak morning at the top of Broxtowe visiting 'The Catstone at Strelley'. This is a Bronze Age collection of large rocks. Originally there were seven of them, but one was moved, no one knows how, or where it went. After a good walk around, we settled into a pub for drinks and decided on a name for ourselves: 'The Catstone Ramblers'. That was the start of many excellent adventures around Derbyshire and Nottinghamshire.

The list of 'spiritual coincidences' accelerated: Howard saw figures when he pressed himself onto a rock; the weather holding out until we finished a walk; buses stopping for us just when we needed them, between stops in the middle of nowhere.

The most dramatic occurred when we were on the way to do a ritual. A ritual basically consists of someone standing at each point of the compass, with a small fire as an altar in the middle, usually something like a small burning log or a lit incense stick. East is air, south is fire, west is water and north is earth. Incense is usually burned. During the ritual you thank the relevant God/Goddess and the elements, offer best wishes to all present and for the future, then close the circle, followed by a drink of Mead and a nibble of cake. On the way, we stopped to eat the snacks we had brought, in a small rocky hollow somewhere in Derbyshire. I clambered up to the top of a high rock, about forty foot high. I stretched out my arms and shouted to Howard and Paul Clipsham, "Do you know the intro to Arthur Brown's *Fire!*? 'I am the God of hell fire, and I bring you – FIRE!'" I bellowed.

Howard and Paul did their best to ignore me, being sensible men who take their rituals seriously as I do usually. We continued our walk to the pine forest where we were going to conduct the ritual. As we started the sky opened up on us: light showers had been forecast, but this was no light rain; it was a monsoon. The trees blew wildly about and were absolutely no protection from this gale-force deluge. It reminded me of a similar scene in the 1957 film *Night Of The Demon.* We had to abandon the ritual and run out of the pine forest trying to find shelter. As we came out of the forest the rain and wind drizzled to a halt. That was me told. I will never be disrespectful at a ritual again!

It is the Goddesses I call upon whenever I need help, protection or guidance. I have a collective name for them SWAG which stands for Spirits, Witches, Angels and Goddesses. Don't laugh, but they made it very plain they didn't like WAGS for obvious reasons! They take many forms. I often get a feather, especially a black one stuck upright where it couldn't have fallen naturally, to let me know 'they' are looking out for me, or a cat will appear in the most unusual places, such as walking into Epsom Hospital Reception when I was waiting there for an operation. After a ritual at The Nine Ladies stone circle on Stanton Moor,

I took a photograph of one of the stones. The next day I looked at the picture and enlarged it. What I saw was amazing, unusual imagery. Alsatian type dogs, rabbits, silhouettes of a few figures. Even Di, who is very much an atheist, admitted she could see the shapes of animals in the stone. The stone is only about four foot high. It doesn't seem feasible that someone from a few centuries ago, had a finely sharpened tool to create this imagery does it?

During a 2016 Spring ritual at the Robin Hood Statue in the castle grounds I felt something like a piece of thin wire in my sleeve. When I arrived home I investigated. Picking away at the threads I gently pulled out a large black crow feather.

On the train up to Nottingham in 2017, I had a nap. When I awoke I checked what time it was and found the watch had turned itself inside out with the back where the face should be. I couldn't understand it. I'm not in the habit of twisting my phone around. It hadn't happened before. It was a warning. When I met up with the group a newcomer had joined us. And he was a grade one manipulative sociopath, a 10/10 villain. I jest not. I was so uncomfortable with this guy and tried to keep as much distance from him as possible. As my 'Ol Pappy used to say, "Never trust a guy who doesn't look you in the eye." It happened again at the end of 2021. We had new neighbours, three lads in their early twenties… and before I had got to know them my watch turned inside out. Eventually I started to feel very uncomfortable with one in particular so I kept well clear. SWAG was absolutely right yet again! Hasn't happened since though.

The pub is now called The Lost Society, but at the time they had a great way to take a photograph of a 'lost angel'.

During 2016 to 2017, I did half a dozen DJ gigs in London, usually replacing someone who was on holiday. However I did manage to get a Thursday night residency during 2018 at a trendy pub called The Lost Angel in Battersea. The crowd were interested in the tunes, and the bar staff, who were mostly from Brazil, even more so. We had a fine time and they particularly liked Santana. Tom, the boss was great. He was into my Surf-Garage tunes and very knowledgeable about the genre. But something weird kept happening. I would be playing the vinyl when for no reason at all the stylus just slid over the record. It only lasted for a minute or so and then things went back to normal for an hour, then it happened again and there was nothing wrong with the records. Diana bought me some heavy middles and learnt how to set up the arm-weights. I tried the old penny on the stylus, not good for the record but I was desperate. I moved the turntables around and bought new mats for them. All to no avail. It made no sense at all, totally illogical. I liked Tom and his team, and the crowd, and I didn't want to let them down. After a few sessions of this I was starting to feel like a complete amateur. Then one night I saw the lights on the cooler cabinet behind the bar blink and kick in at the same moment that the stylus skidded across the record. Lightbulb moment. Turns out that the DJ console was on the same power source as the cooler cabinet and when the power supply changed it affected the turntables. You couldn't make it up!

I love corvids – crows, blackbirds and ravens. When I was at Cliff Road there used to be a blackbird on next door's chimney pot that whistled the introduction to Laurel and Hardy films. I would regularly leave bread out for the blackbirds on my lawn, and just once they left the crumbs in the shape of a heart to show their appreciation. It's true, I have that picture on my phone front screen. Plus, for one autumn, there was a symmetrical pile of leaves 5ft square at the side of my house for a whole month.

During the Great 2020/21 Covid Lockdown, Diana and I discovered a magical pond at Putney and Wimbledon Common woods. It gives us a good long walk for the exercise and there's hardly anyone around in the early hours just as dawn is breaking. We meet lots of very nice people and their funny dogs. We still visit regularly feeding about 30 crows, 10 coots and 6 moorhens, giving pellets and worms. I don't feed the ducks and the swans though, no empathy. For some weird reason Diana gets pooped on regularly by the crows. I'm saying nothing about that.

Recently we were shouted at by the crow group (I'd rather not call them a murder, the official term), for apparently no reason. Round they flew squawking and refusing to come down to eat. We followed where they led and found a young crow in the water who looked injured. I don't think crows have the right feathers for water; they avoid going into ponds even when some tasty nibbles fall in there. Between us, Diana and I pulled out logs and planks to try and give the crow a bridge onto land, but it wouldn't move. Diana managed to get it onto a flat bit of wood and bring it up to dry land where it was facing the sun to dry. To my mind, the crows made a fuss because they knew we would help.

Recently, going up the access stairs to our flat in London, I noticed that on the depth of the step was a paint splash of a crow..

Of course, it would be perfectly natural, dear reader, if you thought I was losing the plot, but this is 'My' Paganism. You don't have to do a ritual or worship in any other way than to take the joy in and respect nature's mysterious side. Don't forget what Arthur Seaton said in *Saturday Night and Sunday Morning*:

"You think you've got me weighed up? Let me tell you summat, I ain't got mesen weighed up yet!"

London is my oyster now – gigs, plays and up to Covid the odd bit of DJ work.

Remember how in my early days I had this fear of the capital? Hitchhiking and driving around it to avoid the centre? All my fears were pushed to one side once I lived here. Initially I kept my house in Nottingham until Mum passed away in November 2016. From then onwards the next eighteen months were spent winding things down and selling the house. After being in Cliff Road for thirty years, it was a heck of a wrench, but it was something I wanted to do.

You know people talk about how unfriendly and stand-offish Londoners are? Well that's a myth! London is its own separate country, very cosmopolitan. I'm more relaxed here, which goes against all the brainwashing we've been conditioned into. That is not to say people don't rush around like maniacs in London, they do, but when it's backs against the wall everybody does their best to help.

I saw that during the height of Covid. Clapham Junction has become our playground, having easy access to the

Greater London area and the countryside at points – south, south-east and west. There's nothing better than sitting on a bus on the front seats.

I'm still fond of Elstree and Boreham Wood where my heritage, ATV and Warner Bros were based. These days, if you go to Watford train station, you'll see the Warner Brothers shield all over the platforms. It's one of the few places in the UK where largescale film productions are made, the largest and most state of the art, secure film making facilities in the world. In 2012 they opened The Harry Potter Studio Tour, and we were there at the end of the first week of opening. I'm not too good with museums, after about an hour and a half I start to flag, and my mind begins to wander. This was not the case at The Warner Brothers Studio. We were there for five hours, and we could have stayed longer, and I'm not even into Harry Potter – never read the books or seen any of the films. The care and detail they showed at the studio about the production of those films is remarkable. Outside, over the fence, are the hangers where current films are in production. No doubt about it, Jack L would have been proud of those.

Cats are very shrewd and perceptive aren't they? One followed my mum's coffin right up to the graveside. The staff said they always followed the procession of someone who loved cats.

Two cats appeared on the meadow below our flat in May 2016. One was a ginger tom and the other a very small tabby kitten. They seemed to be feral, never appearing to go home anywhere. They kept looking over at us and we did them, so I did the tapping of the bowl business as you do. Shrewd felines! That's all they were waiting for, permission to come over. We began to feed them daily, although we couldn't get near enough to stroke them.

Eventually, Diana found out from neighbours that the ginger tom had a home with an elderly lady nearby, but no none knew who was taking care of the kitten. After about a fortnight, the ginger disappeared, and it was only the little tabby that was in the meadow day and night.

I think Ginger had us clocked and was checking us out for being able to take care of his offspring. We only ever saw him once again, a couple of years later, when he popped in to inspect matters. The kitten had a squashed-in nose, so we called him Billy, after Just William. Initially I could pick up Billy for about fifteen seconds, but as the weeks went by, it became less and less as he became more uncomfortable with it. Then he suddenly seemed to put on weight when he was about four months old and yes, you've guessed it – Billie was a girl! The trouble was we couldn't get hold of her to keep her indoors. It was very upsetting, but after about three weeks or so she suddenly appeared without the bulge – apparently, she had lost the litter and became very subdued, lacking her previous liveliness.

It was very sad seeing her so down. We bought a cat bed and with the aid of a big towel trapped her and took poor stressed-out Billie in a carrier during the morning rush hour by train to the vets in Barnes and have her neutered and vaccinated.

She was kept in overnight and had to sleep indoors for a couple of days. Throughout the whole of this experience she had been very brave, as if she knew that it was for her own good. She was quiet on the journey to the vet, let him pick her up without struggling and was quiet on the journey back. Very, very impressive.

She wouldn't come back inside again though. She has a basket outside our door and a variety of places to go away from us, depending on what the weather is – on the meadow, under the hedges or in the maintenance men's Aladdin's Cave storage area. They like her because she is good for catching mice and rats. We give her breakfast and then off she goes for the day and knows when it's 5 o'clock to come for her tea. There are many facets to Billie's personality – day cat, night cat (when her eyes turn black), pre-food friendliness, post-food aloofness... We're the only ones who can stroke her, bless her. She's so cute, a real lady.

> ♫"Our flat is a very, very, very fine flat, ♫
> With one cat in the yard,
> Life used to be so hard,
> Now everything is easy...." ♫

In the summer of 2019 a film was released which was absolutely me. *Once Upon A Time In Hollywood* directed by Quentin Tarantino. What a guy.

It was the film I would have written and directed. It zoomed straight into my top ten ever. And even though he's seventeen years younger than me, his knowledge of the 60s is really good. The pop music and references to T V series was so right on. I've seen it twice and I guess I'll be seeing it again.

I often think of how difficult life must have been for Uncle Arthur in East Kent – 'Hellfire Corner' – especially working the night shift in winter with the blackout and waiting for the bus to take him to Betteshanger Colliery.

In my top twenty films is Michael Powell's *A Canterbury Tale*. It was filmed during the hot summer of 1943 during those difficult times halfway through the war. I've watched it many times now over the last forty years and it's impossible for me to keep a dry eye during the last fifteen minutes or so when the travellers finally arrive at Canterbury.

We never went to Canterbury on our seaside holidays to Kent, so the first time I entered the cathedral was in the spring of 1994. We were staying with a few others in a friend's flat in the centre, but on the Sunday before returning, I walked around with an American girl. I was in awe of the place and could see what Michael Powell was aiming for, but I couldn't find where the organ loft was in that crucial last scene.

I was lucky enough to catch a rector going up the steps and asked him the whereabouts of where the organ would have been during the war, and guess what? When I returned home, I checked out the scene and sure enough it was those step where he picks up the dropped sheet music.

I had a small glow of satisfaction with my find. However, 'art imitates life' and I turned out to be oh so wrong! It was not Canterbury Cathedral in *A Canterbury Tale* at all, it was a duplicated mock-up at Stage 4, Denham Studios, because the church authorities wouldn't allow the unit to film inside the Cathedral due to the war. The main organ had been taken away for restoration in any case, the stained glass windows of the Nave had been removed and the frames boarded up. It would have been a difficult and gloomy place to light. However, they were allowed in the precincts, so lots and lots of photographs were taken as well as filming with secret cinecameras, then it was all mocked up at Denham Studios. The singing of the choir was recorded in the studio but the bells you can hear striking eleven are the actual Canterbury ones. The finished results amazed the experts who really couldn't see the join, "I say, I thought we refused permission for those chaps to film here!"

Background shots blown up, matte shots etc, this film really is quite brilliant. It would be a great epilogue to my life if I were able to persuade the cathedral organist to play Bach's *Tocatta and Fugue in D Minor* at my funeral, as in the film with the congregation and the troops leaving for the front line.

¡ Vaya Con Las Diosas!

Epilogue

My mother Edna was born in 1920 in the village of Boughton, twenty miles north of Nottingham. As the youngest of four sisters and two brothers, she was the one to fetch water from a well in the field at the back. Leaving school age 14 to work as a scullery maid at Thoresby Hall, she moved to the Darley Dale Dental Practice to help the nanny, then found a job with her sister Gladys at the Meridian hosiery factory in Sherwood. Going out on the town with the factory crowd, she met my dad's sisters, Mary and Joan Wheatley, and through them my dad, George, at a dance in 1938. He was born and bred in Arnold, one of two brothers and three sisters in the Wheatley family. His father worked down the pit at Gedling Colliery, but George and his brother Lawrence vowed never to earn a living that way. Dad worked at the local brewery, Home Ales, and 'Lol' took up the cobbling trade.

The Wheatleys were a lively bunch, often going out to the pub and the Working Men's Club. My mother's family, the Scotherns were quieter. "I like you Auntie Edna," my niece Rachel once told her, "because you're posh." Edna and George were married in 1940, just a few weeks away from dad being shipped out to North Africa as a gunner in the Royal Artillery to fight the Nazis and the Italian fascists at Tobruk. Edna went to work at the Royal Ordinance Factory making weapons. Shortly after dad went abroad, she had a little girl but unfortunately my older sister only survived a few months. As did the twins she had a couple of years after I was born.

Early 1941, Dad was captured in Tobruk, North Africa, by the Italian fascists and transferred to a prison camp in Italy. He escaped with two others, and all three of them found refuge with an Italian farmer and his family. On the fourth day, the Nazi occupiers found them there and recaptured them, as well as shooting the whole family. Branded a troublemaker, he was transferred to Germany, where he was almost shot himself when he tried to stop a Nazi guard rifle-butting a Jewish prisoner. He only survived because his fellow prisoners held him back and dragged him away before they could hear the abuse he was shouting.

However, he made it home in 1945, to our rented terraced house in Arnold, which had grown from a rural village into a suburb of Nottingham, near to the pits in Gedling, Calverton and Bestwood, with textile factories springing up, adding to the job opportunities at companies like Boots, Players and Raleigh. The house had a nice big coal fire in the living room and another in the bedroom (which faced East and could be very cold). At that time, it had a coal fired range and a stone boiler in the kitchen to heat the water for washing, and an outside toilet, where a paraffin lamp was placed in winter to stop it freezing over. Dad passed away in 2001. My mother lived in that house all her life until she moved into the Manor Nursing Home opposite in 2014. She passed away two years later. The Redhill Cemetery cat followed the procession to her graveside. The cemetery staff said the cat always followed someone who had loved cats. I like to think the ghosts of ginger Ollie and black and white Ollie, had been waiting there until she came, and joined the procession.

Thus far, an ordinary tale of working-class folk. Dad taught me that if I was a hard worker, I could play hard, but not otherwise. From my mother, I learnt the importance of being considerate to others and to have an interest in the arts. They both expected me to enjoy life and make sure I always got my round in, as well as "This above all else to thine own self be true".

Edna & George's Golden
Wedding Anniversary, 1999

The trouble was my escapism started early. My parents loved dancing, films and music, and spoilt me rotten as their only surviving child, sitting me aged four on a tipped-up seat at the cinema. I was lucky enough to be around for the first boom in US colour comics in the UK and the new TV westerns, and to have a childhood of *Just William* games in the woods. I really did walk to school with a hot Hovis bun. Then came teachers who, while they never actually told us we were factory fodder, made it clear that we were destined for either the pit or the factory – and all the girls had was homemaker, wife, mother. To keep us quiet meanwhile, we were allowed to play with paints and listen to classical music. "You'll have to liven up your ideas, lad, if you want to get on in life," they said. So I did. Entranced by comics, films and TV, I didn't really have a goal, what I did know was that I wanted out.

Trying to draw my favourite cartoon characters, like Popeye, Superman and Marvelman. I decided I would be a graphic artist. Whatever that was. The only thing I could imagine was an apprenticeship in printing. I thought it would lead to drawing the fantastic characters I loved, to meeting the stars on the posters, so I pursued it doggedly despite it being far from what my dad thought was a proper job. Then it didn't quite go to plan.

I got distracted by the sounds of rock and roll, and the music of pirate radio. I cleared off to Gibraltar and read a load of TV magazines and autobiographies of directors then actors. I came back and fell into TV acting. I rolled along with those who were much younger than me into the indie music scene, then started DJing age 60. I'm not famous. My life has been one amazingly enjoyable event followed by one disaster after another. I live with she who prefers not to be named in a tiny studio flat in Wandsworth. It has all been a blast.

Well, things didn't work out quite as I expected when I started, but as someone once said, It's more about the journey than the destination!"

To have been acting most of the time would have been a ten.

But I've been really lucky most of the time and for that I'll give it a nine.

So, nine outa ten on the journey isn't bad at all is it?
"THATS ALL FOLKS!"

"I JUST WASN'T MADE FOR THESE TIMES" 1966

♫ I keep looking for a place to fit in,
Where I can speak my mind,
And I've been trying hard to find the people,
That I won't leave behind,
They say I got brains, but they ain't doing me no good,
I wish they could.

Each time thing start to happen again,
I think I got something good goin' for myself,
But what goes wrong?

Sometimes I feel very sad (¿cuándo seré?)
Sometimes I feel very sad (un día seré)
(Ain't found the right thing I can put my heart and soul
into)
Sometimes I feel very sad (oh, ¿cuándo seré?)
(Ain't found the right thing I can put my heart and soul
into)
I guess I just wasn't made for these times. ♫

WRITTEN AND SUNG BY BRIAN WILSON AND THE
BEACH BOYS FROM THE ALBUM 'PET SOUNDS'

'GOIN' BACK' – 1966

♫ I think I'm goin' back
To the things I learned so well in my youth,
I think I'm returning to
Those days when I was young enough to know the truth,
Now there are no games,
To only pass the time,
No more electric trains,
No more trees to climb,
But thinking young and growing older is no sin,
And I can play the game of life to win.

I can recall a time,
When I wasn't ashamed to reach out to a friend,
Now I think I've got,
A lot more than just my toys to lend,
Now there's more to do,
Than watch my sailboat glide,
But every day can be my magic carpet ride,
A little bit of courage,
Is all we lack,
So catch me if you can I'm going back. ♫

WRITTEN BY GERRY GOFFIN AND CAROLE KING
RECORDED BY DUSTY SPRINGFIELD AND THE BYRDS

Printed in Great Britain
by Amazon

43259809R00185